John Kroes

S0-AYS-300

BLOOD ON THE MOON

DR. VALENTINE T. MC GILLYCUDDY

BLOOD ON THE MOON

Valentine McGillycuddy
and the Sioux

By
JULIA B. McGILLYCUDDY

Introduction by James C. Olson

University of Nebraska Press
Lincoln and London

Copyright 1941 by the Board of Trustees of the Leland Stanford Junior
University
Copyright renewal © 1969 by Valentine McGillycuddy Gianturco
Introduction copyright © 1990 by the University of Nebraska Press
All rights reserved
Manufactured in the United States of America

First Bison Book Printing: 1990
Most recent printing indicated by the last digit below:
10   9   8   7   6   5   4   3   2   1

Library of Congress Cataloging-in-Publication Data
McGillycuddy, Julia G. (Julia Blanchard)
[McGillycuddy, agent]
Blood on the moon: Valentine McGillycuddy and the Sioux / by
Julia B. McGillycuddy: introduction by James C. Olson.
p. cm.
Reprint, with new introd. Originally published: McGillycuddy,
agent. Stanford University, Calif.: Stanford University Press,
1941.
ISBN 0-8032-8170-6
1. McGillycuddy, Valentine, 1849–1939. 2. Indian agents—South
Dakota—Biography. 3. Oglala Indians—Reservations. 4. Pine Ridge
Indian Reservation (S.D.)
E99.O3M355   1990
978.3′66—dc20   90-35176
                                                                CIP

Reprinted by arrangement with Adriana Gianturco, Delio E. Gianturco,
and Manuela Gianturco Banerjee

TO

MY DAUGHTER

Valentine

INTRODUCTION

BY JAMES C. OLSON

Dr. Valentine T. McGillycuddy had a long and productive career in the American West—as a contract surgeon with the army, as a banker, as an educator, as a public health physician (in which role he performed heroically during the influenza epidemic of 1918), and, most importantly for his place in the history of the West, as the controversial agent at the Red Cloud Reservation from 1879 to 1886.

The reservations were both symbols and instruments of United States policy for dealing with the Indian tribes that stood athwart expansion into the plains and mountains of the West after the Civil War—a policy that called for removing the tribes from the principal transportation routes and areas of potential agricultural settlement by locating them on reservations outside the mainstream of western travel and settlement. The Indians were lured onto the reservations with promises of food, clothing, guns, land in severalty, agricultural implements, teachers, and schools. They also were given the right to leave the reservations periodically to go on hunting expeditions, although it was assumed that as the buffalo and other wild game disappeared this right would be exercised with decreasing frequency. Ultimately, it was hoped, the Indians would forsake their old life for the "White Man's Road," becoming industrious farmers and good Christians. As this occurred, the need for a strong military force in the West would decrease and the costly, frequently unsuccessful, and increasingly unpopular military efforts would no longer be necessary.

The "Peace Policy," as it was called, bogged down in failure from the beginning. The old chiefs who signed the treaties were not really certain as to what they meant. To be sure, they were tired of fighting, and some of the more far-sighted among them saw that ultimately the whites would overrun their land. During a visit to Washington in 1870 Red Cloud put it eloquently when he told the Secretary of the Interior: "The white children have surrounded me and left me nothing but an island. When we first had this land we were strong, now we are melting like snow on the hillside while you are growing like spring grass."[1] But his people did not want to give up their old ways, and they surely had no interest in becoming farmers. Moreover, they were both fearful and envious of the hostiles, led by such men as Crazy Horse and Sitting Bull, who refused to come in and who loomed on the horizon as a constant threat to the peace and safety of the entire western country. Under the circumstances, successful management of the reservations and their unruly wards would have tested the mettle of the most competent and upright agent. Unfortunately, few of the Indian agents were both competent and upright, and many were neither. The reservations became centers of graft and corruption, an embarrassment to the government and to the well-intentioned friends of the Indians in the churches, philanthropic societies, and Congress who had brought about the Peace Policy as an alternative to the rule of force applied by the Army in its management of the tribes.

Of all the chiefs, none gave the government more difficulty in its efforts to administer the Peace Policy than Red Cloud, head man of the Oglalas. He had been the principal signatory to the Fort Laramie Treaty of 1868 by which the Indians agreed to accept reservation status. Whether he understood the terms of the treaty or not, he spent most of the rest of his long life arguing about what the treaty meant, and he objected to almost every attempt by the Bureau of Indian Affairs to implement it. He enjoyed widespread fame as a warrior, and he had refused even to talk to the emissaries of the Great White Father at Fort Laramie until the army abandoned its posts along the Powder River, built to protect travel to the gold fields of Montana. Because of his reputation and the belief—erroneous, as it turned out—that he had great influence over the hostiles, the government was particularly solicitous to keep him in a reasonably good humor.

So it developed that when Red Cloud refused to locate his reservation other than on the Platte River, saying that he wanted to receive his goods near Fort Laramie, the government, instead of using force, tried cajolery. Numerous emissaries went to Fort Laramie to try to persuade the chief to change his mind and move north to Dakota Territory outside the mainstream of overland travel and beyond the borders of the newly created state of Nebraska. Red Cloud made two trips to Washington to visit the Great White Father. Finally, in 1874, after six years of negotiation, during which he continued to collect his annuities at the old agency on the Platte, Red Cloud agreed to move to the White River.

Any hope, however, that this would quiet things in the Indian country was doomed to failure. As Red Cloud was moving his people to the new reservation on the White River, Lt. Col. George A. Custer was leading the Seventh Cavalry on a much-publicized expedition to the Black Hills, an expedition which confirmed rumors there was gold in an area that the Indians believed had been set aside forever for their exclusive use. Although the Indians had not interfered with Custer in 1874, they were terribly agitated at the prospect of whites moving into the Black Hills, and two years later Custer, in an effort to put down the tribes once and for all, would lose his life and that of every man under his command.

Although Red Cloud continued to protest his friendship for the whites, conditions at White River were unsettled from the beginning, and the new agent, Dr. J. J. Saville, a physician nominated for the post by the Episcopal Church, repeatedly called for military protection against real or perceived threats of violence. There was a steady movement of hostiles from the north in and out of the agency, putting heavy demands on the agent's limited supplies and creating trouble generally. Moreover, Saville was poorly prepared for the heavy responsibilities placed upon him.

Red Cloud disliked him from the beginning, and before long was charging the agent with fraud, a charge that was supported by a number of army officers and several prominent civilians, including Professor O. C. Marsh, the noted paleontologist. Saville was not a crook—he might be characterized as an inept victim rather than the perpetrator of fraud. Nevertheless, he was forced to resign.

There followed a succession of agents, interspersed with a period of military control—during which General George Crook "deposed" Red Cloud as chief of the Oglalas, replacing him with Spotted Tail—characterized by the fruitless wrangling over a permanent home for the Indians that had been the hallmark of the Indian Bureau's administration. Both the Army and the Indian Bureau had come to the conclusion that the best place for the Sioux was on the Missouri River where they could be supplied much more cheaply than farther west. Red Cloud and Spotted Tail were adamantly opposed to locating on the Missouri. Red Cloud told President Hayes, "The Missouri River is the whiskey road, and if I went there I would not do good; I would come to nothing at all."[2] Finally both chiefs were persuaded to spend the winter of 1877–78 there with the understanding that they could then select their own agencies in the western part of the reservation, away from the Missouri River.

Even after the promises had been made, the government dragged its feet, and it was not until the fall of 1878 that removal was finally effected, with Red Cloud going to White Clay Creek—the agency being designated "Pine Ridge" to reduce its identification with the chief—and Spotted Tail to Wounded Knee Creek.

Red Cloud was quite happy with the agent who supervised the removal, J. W. Irwin, a holdover from the Grant Administration, but Irwin did not get along with Ezra Hayt, the new Commissioner of Indian Affairs, and on January 1, 1879, he resigned. Hayt lost no time in accepting Irwin's resignation and appointing as his successor Dr. Valentine T. McGillycuddy, a contract surgeon with the army at Fort Robinson. Dr. McGillycuddy was very familiar with the Sioux, and had made a favorable impression upon Hayt and Secretary of the Interior Carl Schurz during a prolonged visit to Washington. The appointment was rushed through while McGillycuddy remained in Washington. Stern, fearless, and incorruptible, he seemed just the sort of man to break the will of Red Cloud and the other recalcitrant old Oglalas and drive them along the white man's road.

It proved to be a frustrating task, and for his entire term as agent McGillycuddy was engaged in a never-ending struggle with Red Cloud, who for the most part refused to recognize the authority of the agent and who devoted himself almost full-time to effecting his removal. McGillycuddy was both hot-tempered and bull-headed and at times his struggle with the chief assumed comic-opera characteristics. He was convinced, however, that if the Indians were ever to move along the path toward work and self-reliance, the power of the old chiefs would have to be broken. But McGillycuddy was frequently motivated by personal and sometimes petty differences with his principal antagonist as he sought to get control of the agency. He ruled the agency with an iron hand and his stern discipline was felt by all who ventured within its borders. As a result he was unpopular not only with the Indians and their friends—some of whom were well-placed in eastern philanthropic and journalistic circles—but also with many whites who did business with the agency and much preferred the slipshod ways of previous administrations to the strict accounting of the McGillycuddy regime.

Red Cloud's oft-repeated demands for the removal of his agent fell on numerous receptive ears. Despite the pressure, however, McGillycuddy remained secure during the Garfield and Arthur administrations. He was controversial, but in many ways he was effective, and, in the final analysis he was furthering the policy of the Republican reformers in the Indian Bureau. Just before leaving office President Arthur reappointed him to a second six-year term. The Democrats, anxious to get rid of the troublesome agent, found themselves in a dilemma. Repeated investigations revealed nothing of substance on which to base removal, and it wouldn't do for a president who had been elected as a strong supporter of the Civil Service to remove an appointee solely on political grounds. The administration, however, found a way to achieve its goal by indirection. As George Hyde put it, "The Democrats gave up and resorted to Red Cloud tactics. Make McGillycuddy angry and let him hang himself."[3] The tactic was almost too simple to be credible. The Indian Bureau asked McGillycuddy to remove his chief clerk. He refused to comply and was relieved of his post.

McGillycuddy was only thirty-seven when he left the agency; he lived to be ninety, and as I have indicated, his life was productive as well as long. His business ventures flourished; he and Fanny, the wife of his youth who had shared his adventures at Fort Robinson and Pine Ridge, lived comfortably in a large house that they had built in Rapid City, South Dakota. After a long illness, Fanny died in 1897 and some years later McGillycuddy married Julia Blanchard, the daughter of George Blanchard, a trader at Pine Ridge who, unlike many others, had sided with McGillycuddy during his troubles with Red Cloud. She gave him a daughter, and two years after his death published *McGillycuddy, Agent.*

Although the book was published by the Stanford University Press, it received relatively little scholarly attention when it came out. The *New York Times* published its review among "Books for Younger Readers,"[4] though the review itself, by W. J. Ghent, well-known western historian, is a serious and highly critical piece, pointing to a number of factual errors. George E. Hyde deals extensively with both McGillycuddy and the book in *A Sioux Chronicle.*[5] Hyde is fairly objective in his treatment of McGillycuddy but harsh in his criticism of the book, calling its author "partisan" and "far from reliable."[6] I used the book in my study of Red Cloud and also found it to be partisan and somewhat error-ridden, although my strictures were not as severe as those expressed by Hyde.[7]

Yet, despite its shortcomings, *McGillycuddy, Agent* may be, as Addison E. Sheldon, longtime superintendent of the Nebraska State Historical Society, wrote, "the most important contribution that . . . will ever be made toward a history of the early transition period for the Oglala Sioux."

McGillycuddy's years at Pine Ridge were indeed years of transition for the Oglalas as they were being forced to give up their old life as hunters and warriors for that of the farmer and rancher. The transition had begun before McGillycuddy arrived and it was not complete when he departed, but no one had brought the issue home to the Oglalas with greater force and no one drove them harder toward a new way of life. In many respects McGillycuddy was the quintessential exemplar of the Peace Policy—stern, upright, conscientious, and utterly convinced that the only route to salvation for the Oglalas was along the white man's road.

The book reflects attitudes as much as it describes events, and it is from this that much of its importance derives. Indeed, the book is more autobiography than biography, with the author functioning primarily as a devoted amanuensis. *McGillycuddy, Agent*, retitled *Blood on the Moon: Valentine McGillycuddy and the Sioux* for this Bison Book edition, is a primary source for the history of the Oglalas at Pine Ridge, and the University of Nebraska Press does a service to all who are interested in the history of the Indians and the American West by making it available.

Moreover, it is an entertaining story, replete with adventure, danger and hardship, peopled with warlike Indians, soldiers, lawmen, traders, and assorted frontier desperadoes who come to life in a well-written, fast-paced narrative.

Enjoy!

NOTES

1. Quoted in James C. Olson, *Red Cloud and the Sioux Problem* (Lincoln: University of Nebraska Press, 1965), p. 105.

2. Olson, p. 249.

3. George E. Hyde, *A Sioux Chronicle* (Norman: University of Oklahoma Press, 1956), p. 105.

4. *New York Times Book Review,* February 1, 1942, p. 10.

5. Hyde, especially pp. 26–28, 31–36, 84–106.

6. *Ibid.,* pp. 88–89.

7. Olson, pp. 264–325, is devoted to Red Cloud's struggle with McGilly-cuddy. The errors in Julia McGillycuddy's account are relatively minor and some of them may derive from her obvious interest in telling a good story as well as from her partisan point of view. For example, in discussing a meeting between Red Cloud and McGillycuddy on August 19, 1882, during which McGilly-cuddy "deposed" Red Cloud as chief, she writes, "With a cry of rage, the old chieftain sprang toward the Agent, a knife brandished in his hand" (p. 196.) This is supported by no other account, including McGillycuddy's own contem-porary report. Again, her account of McGillycuddy's trip to Omaha in August 1882 to meet six women hired to teach in the Agency's boarding school (pp. 197–204) is confused and unreliable. To cite another example, the date of T. A. Bland's visit to the reservation is given as 1881 rather than 1884 (p. 221).

PREFACE

As the second wife of Dr. Valentine T. McGillycuddy—whose first wife I asked, before I was old enough to know better, if she thought the Doctor would marry me when she died—I have listened to his stories since my earliest childhood. After our marriage he jestingly parried requests that his reminiscences be taken down by dictograph or in shorthand for publication.

But when I read aloud to him a fictionized story of his life which I had attempted, in disgust he protested that if I wrote of his experiences I must not deviate from facts; his life was history, he said, and must be exact. He then began relating the story of his life. Daily I intrigued my husband into a continuance of the story, including his altercations with government officials, with the press, and with men on the frontier, both white and red.

I am deeply indebted to Marie Sandoz and Mrs. Julia Cooley Altrocchi for information and advice; to General Robert E. Wyllie for assistance in obtaining data from the War Department; and to the Nebraska State Historical Society for data and for encouragement in my sincere effort to make this book historically correct.

If anyone living—either some victim of McGillycuddy's maledictions or a descendant of one—feels resentment at the Doctor's estimate of him, he may rest assured that his judgment at least was sincere and that the responsibility rests with him who has gone "over the divide" and not with his biographer.

J. B. McG.

Houston, Texas
January 10, 1940

CONTENTS

Part 1. THE ROVING DOCTOR

LIST OF ILLUSTRATIONS

PART
I

THE ROVING
DOCTOR

Chapter I

A NEW VENTURE

ONE DAY in March 1879 a slab-sided army ambulance jittered over the Great Plains, a sea of snow unmarred by wagon track or hoof print, drawn by four mules inured to hardship plodding stubbornly over the invisible trail, their long ears sagging except when a jack rabbit scurried from some snow-laden brush across their path. Night had fallen, a night so black that even the white-coverleted earth afforded no moderation. Fifty miles of whitened plains, frozen streams, and snowdrifts had been covered since the gray dawn which seemed to have concentrated in it all the bitterness of winter to wreak vengeance upon anyone who ventured into its solitude. Snow was falling, and the wind moaned through every crack in the shambling ambulance.

Inside the dreary vehicle a lean young man, Valentine T. McGillycuddy, and his fair-skinned wife, Fanny, spoke sparsely from the depths of buffalo-robe swathings. Their voices, though muffled, were confident. Only the soft Southern drawl of the mulatto girl, Louise, picked up at Fort Robinson as maid for the home of the new Indian agent, suggested uneasiness as she peered from a pile of buffalo robes in the corner and asked through an emergence of freezing breath, how far it was to Pine Ridge Agency, their destination.

"Not many miles more," the slim man answered, his breath frosting the aperture through which he spoke, guessing the distance with the keen sense won by four years' service on the plains.

All was silence again, silence enveloped in night.

At last the odor of dying campfires marked their approach to

Indian villages. The mules, their heavy ears thick laden with snow, now pointed upward as they swung into a longer stride. Their hoofs clanked a different note as they crossed the White Clay Creek bridge, resonant with the void between it and the frozen stream. Dim lights struggled through the nigger blackness; the mules champed their bits as the lights grew brighter. The snow crunched under their hoofs as they broke into a gallop and passed through the gates of the wire fence which enclosed the buildings of Pine Ridge Agency and set it apart from the vast area of four thousand square miles of territory, the apportioned land of the Oglala Sioux. It was midnight.

McGillycuddy, his wife, and the Mulatto girl uncoiled the wrappings from their stiffened legs and stumbled up the steps of the unfinished house which was to be their home. Except for the kitchen, in which J. R. O'Bierne, constructor of buildings, had installed a stove, and the dining room which enticed a share of the heat through its open door, the home which welcomed McGillycuddy and his wife was as cold as the out of doors. The wind lashed furiously against the frost-patterned, uncurtained windows and rocked the light frame house, in which crates and boxes, shipped ahead, were piled in corners. But the kitchen fire glowed; steam poured from the kettle; and while O'Bierne made coffee the newcomers thawed out beside the stove.

Fanny refused to admit that she was tired, even though a drive from Sidney, Nebraska, the railroad terminal, in a stagecoach bucking its way across ninety miles of snow-covered, freight-wagon-guttered road to Fort Robinson, the four-horse teams having been changed regularly at stations sixteen miles apart, had immediately preceded the ambulance journey to Pine Ridge. The young wife fell easily into sleep when, made comfortable by the coffee and some venison sandwiches, she and her husband lay down in a bed set up in the dining room, while Louise betook herself to a mattress on the kitchen floor.

Pine Ridge Agency, situated on a plateau in what in 1879 was the Territory of Dakota, escaped few of the snowstorms or sand-laden winds which swept the Great Plains. It rested beneath the sky unsheltered by tree or bush. The section enclosing the Agency buildings required to carry on the official business of the Indians was a diminutive portion of the vast territory covering almost the entire area, between the Missouri River on the east and the White River on the west, which comprised the great Sioux Reservation. It was approximately a quarter of a mile in length, and somewhat less in width. It lay not far to the north of Nebraska, though at this time there was only a general idea along the frontier as to just where the vast plains ceased to be Nebraska and became Dakota. When, many years previous to the establishment of the Pine Ridge Agency, the survey determining the boundary line between the state and the territory had been made, there was not a citizen living within perhaps a hundred miles of that locality. In the long years intervening the boundary posts and other markings had disappeared entirely.

The valleys of the White Clay, Wounded Knee, and other streams flowing through the reservation were fertile. Low, rolling hills lay placidly to the north of the Agency, while toward the south, in what supposedly was Nebraska, rose a lonely ridge—spiked, desolate—where in previous years the Sioux had sought shelter from other warring bands. On it driving gusts of wind and sleet whistled through pine trees standing sheer against the sky. Snow covered the crags in winter and slithered in muddy streams down the gorges when thawed by sun in spring. In summer eagles soared above the peaks and rattlesnakes slid among rocks almost bare of vegetation.

At this time there was probably no more autocratic position under the United States government than that of an Indian agent at a remote agency. The governor of the territory had no jurisdiction over the Pine Ridge agent. Though the Sioux Reservation was in Dakota, it was not properly a part of it. According to the treaty made with the Sioux in 1868, ownership of this region had not been relinquished by them. There was therefore no authority intermediate between the agent and the President of the United

States together with that part of his official family which dealt with Indian affairs—the Department of the Interior. The agent was thus in his dealings with the Indians the representative of the Great Father, the connecting link between him and the bands of which he was solely in charge. Approximately fifteen hundred miles from Washington, one hundred and fifty miles from the railroad, and fourteen miles from the nearest army post, Fort Sheridan, the Pine Ridge agent ruled four thousand square miles populated by about eight thousand Indians, some of whom were fresh from their triumphs in the Sitting Bull campaign.

With this vast territory to utilize, the Oglala Sioux, the wildest of the tribe, congenitally lazy, were living huddled in lodges within a radius of five miles of the Agency. Not a house and scarcely a wagon was owned by an Indian at Pine Ridge, no school existed on the reservation, and every Indian was blanketed.

McGillycuddy was fond of the red men and felt convinced that he understood their needs. His sympathies were with them. And he was well aware of the events which had produced the present situation at Pine Ridge, where the rightful chieftain, Tasunka Kokepa (Young Man Afraid), and the usurper-dictator, Mahkpia-luta (Red Cloud), occupied separate camps with the line between them as sharp as a razor blade. For the chieftain, known as Young Man of Whose Horses They Are Afraid, was a progressive; he would uphold any civilizing innovation. But Red Cloud, McGilly-cuddy felt certain, would oppose his every move.

The young agent was aware of the nearly four centuries of disaster following upon disaster as the red men had been driven from haunt to favorite haunt pursued by white men who had come in winged ships from where the sun got up. He knew that their numbers had increased, their demands had multiplied. The Indians had danced war dances and chanted war songs, relating their woes as well as their triumphs—the coups they had counted, the scalps they had cut from enemy heads, battling ever to preserve their integrity, while being continually driven westward like sagebrush before high winds.

For a time they had maintained a wisp of faith in the treaties made with them. For a time as they had settled in new territory with the promise that it was to be theirs forever, they had believed the white man. But almost as quickly as it had come to birth their faith had been destroyed by the broken word.

At last, instead of a continent, the natives, by treaty, were assured possession of thirty-two thousand square miles of territory—the Great Plains of the Middle West, a vast land trodden by enormous herds of bison making the earth tremble and by fleet-footed deer and curious antelope, a land covered with velvety buffalo grass dotted with brilliant-hued flowers or blanketed with snow, a land channeled with great rivers and rippling streams in which gleamed schools of fish. Here towering mountains and black-cloaked hills offered hiding places in tribal warfare. And the Indians had been free and happy for a time. Nature was lavish in her gifts. Their needs were supplied by Wakantanka the good God. He gave them buffalo meat and venison, fish, and fruits. Buffalo skins furnished them clothing and lodges. There was no call to labor; hunting and fishing were sport.

But the Indians' hunting ground had lured the white man, and the treaty which had determined that this territory should belong to the Indians for all time had been broken like many former treaties. The whites had spattered over the border lines; traders had stolen in and bartered with the Indians; settlements had been established; and the heralding of gold in California in '49 had sent emigrants and freighters trailing across the plains, sometimes in continuous, twenty-mile-long stretches.

The Indians had resented this. At length they had attacked parties moving westward, but from general animosity rather than with definite purpose and with savagery rather than strategy; their enmity had been racial and but blindly reasoned. They had called upon the Great Father in Washington to heed his promises. They had demanded that the white man should not come into their country, should not kill or drive off the game which furnished their subsistence, and should not dispossess them of their lands.

But no heed had been given to their pleas or demands. Soldiers had been stationed here and there at some lonely, windswept post and sometimes they had descended upon friendly and peaceable bands and killed them by hundreds.

Of all the tribes on the plains the Sioux were the greatest warriors. They more than any other protested against the invasion of the whites. Their chieftain, Man of Whose Horses They Are Afraid, was a fearless fighter. As long as the Oglala Sioux could remember, their chieftain had been a member of the Man Afraid family. By acclamation the mantle of chieftainship had fallen in turn on the shoulders of the son of each preceding ruler.

But by the troublous times of the 'sixties Man Afraid was growing old. The snows of many winters had bent his shoulders and furrowed his face, and the wounds of many battles had scarred his body. His hope for victory in future wars lay, not in his son, who was too young to become a war leader, but in a young warrior, Mahkpia-luta (Red Cloud), more daring than any of his followers, who had fought by his side in many battles. Gradually the chief had advanced this promising subaltern from soldier to head soldier and finally to war chief and at the same time had relinquished the chieftainship to his son. The retiring chief now became known as Old Man Afraid and his son, the nominal chieftain, Young Man Afraid.

Soon after this change had been accomplished the Sioux engaged in a war with the Crows. Young Man Afraid lacked experience to lead in warfare and, according to the Indian custom, in cases where the head chief was less skilled than some member of the tribe, martial law was declared and Red Cloud—who had won his name when, in a previous battle his scarlet-blanketed young warriors had covered the hillsides like a red cloud—was appointed dictator for the period of the war.

Now drunk with power after his conquest of the Crows, Red Cloud had refused to relinquish the leadership and, with the ever increasing need of a war leader as the whites pressed closer upon the Indians, neither the old chief nor his son had protested.

New troubles had come upon the red men. A telegraph line had been set up across their lands. With awe they had listened to the wind sighing over the wires, which they were told carried messages to great distances. The buffalo had welcomed the excellent scratching posts in the treeless area; but the Indians had sensed only disaster in the innovation.

Still worse was the determination of the government to open a road to Montana by way of the Powder River, a road which necessarily would pass through the hunting grounds of the Sioux. If ever they were glad of a war leader it was now; and Red Cloud had proved himself worthy when he had denounced the treaties and had threatened to kill all whites who ventured into the Indians' country. He not only threatened but, when Fort Phil Kearney was established to guard the trail, he had planned and executed the massacre of December 21, 1866, in which a detachment of ninety-one men had been wiped out.

But it had availed them little, and the Indians had watched wrathfully as scrapers sank into the soil which had never known a plow, iron rails were dumped from flat cars, sledges fell, and shining rails crept westward across the Great Plains. The Indians saw only the spoliation of their lands, their herds, and their freedom as shrieking engines had mocked the silence of the prairies and proclaimed an echoing triumph in the mountain sanctuaries.

To add to their woes, hordes of buffalo hunters, sent out by Texas ranchmen to rid the northern plains of the native herds in order that they might serve solely as cattle ranges, had invaded the country and slaughtered the animals by thousands. The scheme had been aided by the railroad, eager to have the subsistence of the Indians destroyed. General G. M. Dodge, in charge of the construction of the Union Pacific Railroad, had declared, after an attack made upon the party, "We've got to clean the damn Indians out or give up the job." The government also had contributed hunters to assist in the slaughter for the purpose of starving the red men into submission.

The Indians' wrath was unbounded when they saw great areas

covered with the bodies of the slain beasts, their hides torn off clean by means of horses tied to the four corners and driven from the animal after the skin had been split up the belly. The stench of the decaying bodies heralded one's approach to the slaughter grounds from miles away; wild animals glutted their appetites on the rotting flesh, and vultures swept the sky and slithered to the feast.

In desperation over their fast-diminishing lands and herds, the Indians had appealed to the Great Father to protect them from further invasion. In response to the appeal a commission had been sent from Washington to meet the chiefs in council at the Whetstone Agency in Dakota. In this council a treaty had been made in which the Indians (with the exception of Red Cloud) had agreed to a reservation including the land north of the Big Horn Mountains to the Missouri River—a reservation shrunk now to half the size agreed upon in a former treaty. Red Cloud had refused to sign the agreement until, in November 1868, four months later, his demand for the removal of three army posts on the reservation had been acceded to.

But even this agreement had failed to keep the Indians' land free from white invasion. Rumors of great wealth stored in the Black Hills, the treasure spot of the reservation, had soon increased the number of invaders. With respect to these various events McGillycuddy had already played a part which had led him to his present post. In it, beside the opposition he anticipated from Red Cloud, the usurper, he knew he would be condemned and opposed by the "Indian Ring." That Ring had originated with the establishment of the Indian Bureau, which had charge of purchasing supplies for the nation's wards. Contractors for these supplies had seen vast opportunities to increase their wealth by overcharges, by shortages in deliveries, and by conniving with Indian agents to withhold goods bought by the government for the Indians and to dispose of them to private parties at an enormous profit. Exploitation of this sort became epidemic; the fact was generally recognized by the public. The temptation to filch from the red men seemed irresistible, and greed-poisoned Congressmen and high officials of the Department of the Interior and the Indian Bureau who were controlled by the Ring either acquiesced in the frauds perpetrated on the government or by their official positions actively aided the Ring. The magnitude and power of the organization had prevented its destruction. From the pollution of the gilded halls of Congress the virus had spread to Indian agencies, where squawmen, half-breeds, interpreters, and teamsters had joined in the orgy of theft. At some agencies it controlled steamboats, post offices, United States deputies, a missionary or two, and nearly all those connected with the work.

The first blow had been dealt the Ring with the election of President Rutherford B. Hayes, the reformer, in 1876. But in spite of his activity it was far from annihilated. It had survived even the merciless inspection of General J. B. Hammond, appointed inspector of agencies in 1878. By keen ferreting, Hammond had discovered that supplies delivered at agencies and signed for by agents as having been issued to the Indians had been turned over instead to scheming members of the Ring for them to dispose of at will. Day after day he had discovered goods—axes, handsaws, hatchets, and butcher knives by the hundreds in original packages; scarlet and blue cloth; shawls and blankets by the bale; calicoes and ducking by the bolt—stored in preparation of private sale. Cattle had been stolen by hundreds and even fed at government expense.

It had proved but a slight handicap to dishonest agents that several head men of the bands were required to witness the issue of annuities and to attest the receipts in the presence of the interpreter, since not an Indian and but few interpreters could read or write, and more than likely the interpreter was a member of the Ring.

Pine Ridge Agency, the largest in the United States, naturally would be the objective of ambitious money seekers eager to accumulate the money they owed the red men for enormous areas of land. Every action of the new agent at Pine Ridge would be spied upon by the Ring, which would exert its utmost power to prevent an honest handling of government funds and supplies, thereby reducing its chance of spoils.

McGillycuddy, however, had already formulated plans for the development of these idle bands of Indians who had been placed in his charge: They must learn to work. They must have some incentive to effort. Huddled in lodges, swarming like bees in a hive, there was nothing to engage the thoughts of the warriors but dreams of the past. There was no thrill in agency life, no anticipation of the morrow—nothing but dull monotony and an ache in their hearts. A purpose in life was their only hope. McGillycuddy had conceived the idea of having the tribal system abolished and the bands scattered. He imagined farms and homes covering the valleys and schoolhouses filled with red-skinned children. He envisioned a home government with a native police force, and Indian teamsters transporting their own freight from the railroad.

McGillycuddy was an optimist and he felt no apprehension. He was young and full of courage. He was a clear thinker with a dynamic nature. He made decisions quickly and was unswerving in his purpose. His hope was to establish the Indians as citizens of the country which had been theirs before the white man brought disaster upon them. We shall review the events which metamorphosed the young doctor into an Indian agent.

Chapter 2

DOCTOR - ENGINEER

A volley of oaths accompanied the footsteps of a spare youth as he passed along the row of sailors lined against the wall in the Marine Hospital of Detroit in 1866 applying acid nitrate to their rotting sores. They could not withdraw from the glass-bristled brush McGillycuddy used. Though they swore tempestuously, the sailors respected the youth of seventeen, whose first-year studies in the Hospital had been interrupted when Dr. T. A. McGraw strongly recommended him as a substitute for its regular physician, a dipsomaniac.

The boy paid no heed to the patients' curses, though the droop of his left eyelid lent an expression of sympathy for their pain rather than scorn for their indiscretions. He was accustomed to curses, though previously they had been uttered in yelps and meows when from his early childhood he had ministered to ailing dogs and cats. Their broken legs he had set and bandaged and on their wounds he had poured healing lotions for which he had spent his entire small weekly allowance. He was prepared now for the howls of men.

Only one fear had entered the mind of the youth after his appointment to the Hospital—fear of the foul diseases prevalent among sailors. After each treatment he washed his hands with infinite caution in a strong disinfectant. Precisely he drew the towel from the tip of each tapered finger to its base, the fingers pointed upward, and with unhurried movement finished drying his hands, tender from continual use of the solution.

Though a tireless worker, the boy never seemed precipitate as he passed about the Hospital turning the doorknobs with his coat tails.

13

Drunken sailors raising hell in the wards usually crept into bed when McGillycuddy, summoned by a nurse, appeared in the doorway, an Irish sense of humor mingling with the natural sternness of his eye. He originated tricks which he substituted for his limited physical strength. When Captain Hunting of the Chicago–Cleveland Line fought all who tried to prevent his battle with the snakes which writhed on his bed and slithered over the walls, the boy threatened him with a "rock"; that sent the captain to his bed, where docilely he tried to shake the peacock out of his slipper, while the embryo surgeon concealed the wet sponge he had in his hand.

His nights were seldom unbroken. In addition to his work at the Hospital, Valentine, born February 14, 1849, was called at any hour to the houses of prostitution which dotted the waterfront. Boisterous men and women quieted when the serious-looking boy appeared to minister to their needs. In drunken paroxysms of remorse the women sobbed the tales of their downfall, swore in maudlin tones to change their lives, or wept more bitterly at the impossibility of doing so. At first the boy protested against the inevitability of their fate; but soon he learned that, once on the downward trail, one seldom turned back.

After six months at the Marine Hospital, McGillycuddy decided again to give his entire time to his studies. He graduated at the age of twenty, and began his service as interne. He promptly became a member of the faculty and delivered lectures on splints and bandages. He administered anesthetics daily and, to add to his experience, served with the city's police-ambulance corps. Not satisfied that he was carrying a sufficient burden, he assumed further duties as physician at the Wayne County Insane Asylum.

A year passed before he felt that work was telling on him. His discovery came a short time after he had noticed that the whisky bottle in the laboratory was being emptied unreasonably fast. He would be on the watch to see who was taking the liquor. The next time he passed hurriedly through the laboratory on his way to the operating room he picked up the bottle and took a swallow of the stimulant. He thought nothing of it: he was tired; his heart was slow. When he returned from the operating room he took another swallow of the whisky. Still he thought nothing of it: he was very tired; he could scarcely feel his pulse-beat. When he caught himself doing the same thing an hour later, it occurred to him that possibly he himself was reducing the contents of the bottle beyond expectancy. He did not know that Dr. McGraw was watching his paling face until the older doctor called him to his office and advised an examination by the faculty.

McGraw's fears for his favorite student were established: McGillycuddy's heart was weak. He must give up his practice for a year and live in the open. The doctor spoke regretfully. Could "Mac" find something to do that would keep him contented for that time? His place would be waiting for him when he came back. He expected the boy—McGraw still thought of him as a boy—to take his place eventually both in the college and in his practice. For a long time he had looked upon him as his own son. McGillycuddy hesitated for a moment before answering that he had taken a course in engineering at Michigan. Perhaps he could get a job with the Lake Survey. He must leave at once, the older doctor said, and repeated that his place would be waiting for him, as the two men shook hands at parting.

The lean, pale young man accordingly set out for Lake Michigan. His hands rested listlessly in his pockets as though accepting defeat. The customary whistle which accompanied his footsteps was silent. He went into the office of General Cyrus B. Comstock, superintending engineer of the geodetic survey of the Northern and Northwestern lakes. After a short talk with the engineer he was given a contract as assistant engineer and recorder for the expedition which was to set out the following week.

For the first time the young doctor now thought a trifle seriously of a girl as he walked back to his home. He had never had time to think of girls, but he had stopped sometimes on his way from the college when he saw Fanny Hoyt sitting on the porch of her home not far from his own. She was very pretty, he thought, with her fair skin and her eyes as blue as the lake water. He did not stop at her house; she was not on the porch, or probably he would have done so. He wished she were there: he would like to tell her of his changed plans; he would see her before he left. He wondered if she would feel sorry. He had never considered an interruption to his work as a possibility, even when he discovered that he was taking a little whisky to stimulate his heart—it beat somewhat faster as he thought of Fanny.

He passed on to his home, expecting an outburst of emotion from his temperamental Irish parents. He was not disappointed. His father covered his anxiety by spluttering, and his mother wept. She had noticed his paleness but had thought it merely the result of overwork, against which she had often cautioned him. He consoled her with assurances that the summer months on the Lakes would put him in perfect condition and that he would be able to see her occasionally during that time.

Life on the Great Lakes with the expedition was a new life. Previously there had been only short rows on Lake Michigan between calls to return to sickrooms. A new world opened before the eyes of the assistant engineer as the fresh air filled his lungs and rocked the boat in which he sat at the rudder, steering its course, directing and recording soundings. He immediately improved in health; his face grew bronzed with sun and wind. Friends frequently visited the lakeshore camps; and McGillycuddy felt pleased when, one warm evening, Fanny drove out with a group of young people.

The summer months passed rapidly, and fall came on. The days grew chilly and the Lakes mist-shrouded and squally. Shortly before the Survey party was to return to Detroit for the winter, one day, after an ominous sunset, clouds gathered, spread, and enveloped the lake. Lightning split the heavens amidst aerial cannonading, while torrents of rain beat uncompassionately on McGillycuddy's party of eight men out in a small, open boat not far from shore. The light craft had about as much chance in the breakers there as a feather in a tornado. McGillycuddy steered off shore, yelling to the men to row for their lives. Three miles out he turned to the north and battled against a northeaster. Mingled with the howl of the storm and the lash of the waves rose the prayers and curses of the French-Canadian oarsmen: "Holy Mother save us!" *"Sacré mille tonnerre!"* "Jesus, Son of Mary, hear us!" *"Sacré tort Dieu!"* In the darkness the compass could not be seen. There was nothing but intuition by which to steer the boat while the heavens and the waters below conspired against the mighty efforts of the oarsmen.

Unmeasured time passed while the small boat fought its way through the raging waters, until at last a pale light struggled through the murk. McGillycuddy shouted now to the oarsmen to pull toward the shore. The light grew brighter as they headed in, but again the breakers threatened. The boat was no match for the riotous waves; it leaped, bounded, and somersaulted, spilling the crew into the lake. Their lives were now the price of their endurance. Prayers and curses went unuttered as the men fought their way through the stormy waters toward the light, which grew ever brighter. At last hands stretched out from the shore and drew the exhausted men to land. Tears rolled down the face of old Julius Meyer, the chief engineer, as he put his arm around McGillycuddy's dripping shoulders and led him to the huge bonfire which had been built as a beacon.

"Mon Dieu, boy," the old man said, "I never expected to see you alive again."

The survey party returned to Detroit soon after the storm and settled down to the work of drawing maps of the summer's work. Dr. McGraw was delighted with the result of outdoor life on his former student and advised him to return to practice. But the young doctor had not had his fill of fresh air; even the map-drawing was less confining than medical practice, since the hours were shorter; and he was unwilling to relinquish his position with the Survey.

For the first time he found himself free to enjoy some social life. He visited frequently at Fanny's home; he attended a few dances, though he danced badly—he had had but little practice. The theater attracted both him and Fanny, and he bought tickets for every performance played in the city. The hours spent with Fanny were the happiest he had ever known.

Despite the attractions of the city, McGillycuddy set out again in the spring with the Survey party, this time to act as surgeon as well as assistant engineer. Toward the close of the Survey season, in October 1871, when fire had destroyed the city of Chicago, McGillycuddy was detailed to make a re-survey of the district.

Three summers were thus passed in the survey of the Great Lakes, Dr. McGraw more surprised each year that McGillycuddy did not return to medical practice. But his surprise was raised to incredulity when he learned that his protégé had accepted an offer from Major W. J. Twining of the United States Engineering Corps to join the expedition of the International Survey of the boundary line between the United States and British America as topographer and surgeon.

McGillycuddy had seen Fanny often during the winter, but felt his life too uncertain to ask any promise of her. He found it difficult to keep his resolution as they sat together on the porch in the warm spring evening—the evening before he was to leave for the West. She looked very lovely in her white muslin dress, with a blue-ribbon sash matching the color of her eyes. She seemed to him all that was finest in womanhood. Yet he spoke not a word of love when he bade her good-bye. He only asked her to write to him.

Chapter 3

THE BOUNDARY SURVEY

W<small>AKENED</small> one summer morning in 1874 by the early light Mc-Gillycuddy lay peacefully outside his tent on the unfathomable Great Plains near the Marias River in Montana, stretching his lean length beneath the moon paling with the dawn. No sound disturbed the sergeant, the orderly, and the ten men of his detachment, separated from the main command on the Forty-ninth Parallel; they still lay asleep, unconscious of the play of color preceding the appearance of the sun's huge red disk above the horizon. Only then did the horses rise from the thick buffalo-grassed earth, and the men stir on the padded ground.

Suddenly in the distance something moved. It grew in size as it approached, dividing into units—horses, eagle feathers, bright metal flashing in the sun. The thirteen men now leaped to their feet, buckled on their cartridge belts, and seized their guns.

"Hun-hun-he, Akicita," the Indians yelled as they surrounded the little group of white men. *"How kola,"* the chief said, *"Mea Ta-ton-ka-i-yo-ton-ka."*

There was no one on the plains who had not heard that name, for Sitting Bull, chief of the Hunkpapas, was known to everyone at least by reputation. There was a note of pride untinctured by animosity in his voice as he gave it.

The sergeant, one of Marcus Reno's Seventh Cavalry command, which had joined the expedition as escort at Fort Buford, understood a few Indian words: The red men were out in search of buffalo. Sitting Bull asked if any had passed that way. The sergeant gave information that a great herd had rocked the earth as they had lumbered past the Survey party the previous day journeying westward. Sacks of tobacco were now given to the Indians;

19

and, after much handshaking and friendly grunts of *"How kola,"* Sitting Bull's hunting party rode off.

McGillycuddy's detachment, after completing the survey of the prescribed section, returned to the main camp, which included both the British and the American contingents. When all the divisions were assembled, the expedition moved toward the west, assignments being made to parties for the survey of different sections.

Days had been swallowed by weeks and weeks by months, twenty miles of a strip two miles wide being the customary daily survey, the tangent and astronomical parties preceding the topographical party. At times the astronomers were delayed for days by the trembling of the earth which was felt hours before an enormous herd of buffalo hove in sight, jarring their instruments and preventing accuracy.

In the late summer, when McGillycuddy with his division had been separated from the main party for a fortnight, he determined to finish his assigned section that day. All were still at work when the slanting rays of the sun cast lengthening shadows. Theodolites towered into steeples and cactus bushes stretched into trees. Rodmen strained their eyes, watching the topographer's motions as he directed the location of the stakes. When the work at length was finished the detail moved toward camp, riding along the foothills, the plateau stretching endlessly before them. A stream rippled ahead following a shallow basin.

The men sagged in their saddles. Coyotes bayed remonstrance to a pale half-moon in the domed sky. Only an occasional remark passed from man to man. After the hard day's work the ride seemed long. Mile after mile they rode, unthinking, until suddenly their attention was attracted by fantastic shapes strewn on the floor of the basin, casting weird shadows in the moonlight. The men dismounted and, leaving a few to hold the horses, climbed down into the basin to investigate.

Skeletons strewed the hollow. Strips of dried flesh still clung to whitened bones. Not a head retained a scalp, and only patches of eyebrows topped eyeless sockets, which leered vacantly. Here and there a shred of red calico, like a bloodstain, was gummed to a bony frame. McGillycuddy took out his belt-knife and, kneeling beside the least mutilated of the skeletons, deftly disjointed the head. It would be a good specimen for the Detroit museum, he said, as he rolled it in a gunny sack and strapped it to his saddle.

McGillycuddy's detachment soon joined the main party, and the expedition proceeded on its westward survey. They were well out one day from the preceding night's camp when the doctor discovered that he had left behind the precious Indian skull. He was determined not to abandon the prized possession and, re-marking casually to the nearest rider that he had forgotten some-thing, turned about to recover it. Reaching the campsite he found the gunny sack lying on the ground where he had placed it. He strapped it to the saddle and started off again.

The day stretched out while McGillycuddy rode alone. He had not realized the distance back to the camp; he expected momen-tarily to see the party ahead. Startled deer raced across the prairie, curious antelope gazed in surprise at the stranger and hastily darted off, and buffalo tramped their heavy way to the streams, as his horse followed the trail of the wagon wheels and the hoofs of the cavalry horses. Nimbly he picked his way over the prairie-dog holes pockmarking the plains, the little animals protesting violently the presence of the stranger in their domain. Sudden oscillations indicated his evasion of rattlesnakes.

Darkness fell, and the lone traveler no longer could see the trail of his party. Strange voices struggled through the night breeze; the air was full of smothered sounds. Birds mumbled in the bushes; frogs croaked along the streams; owls hooted reproach-fully; and the dry grass crackled. The darkness seemed limitless.

McGillycuddy's keen sense of direction failed: He must trust to his horse. He gave him the rein.

How long he rode before he felt a quickening of the animal's gait he did not know, but as he roused he saw in the distance the light of campfires, barely distinguishable in moonlight. It might be the camp of his party; it might be the camp of Indians. The horse traveled on. The rider's body lurched as the animal descended into a ghostly canyon, sank into soft mud, and then clanked on rocks as he crossed a stream. The lights were bright as he emerged from the cottonwood trees rustling in friendly fashion along the bank. And cavalry horses whinnied as the doctor rode into camp.

Major Twining had not heard of McGillycuddy's absence until the end of the day. He had been greatly troubled and was outspoken in his rebuke. "Damn it," he exclaimed, "haven't you any sense of danger?" The doctor said he had not thought they had gone so far when he turned back. Twining reminded him that if he had met any Indians, with that skull in his possession, he could have expected nothing less than capture, with dire results. He wished he would use more discretion in the future. There were plenty of skulls about but he was short on topographers, he said.

Over seemingly endless mountain ranges, through deep canyons, and across rippling streams the survey continued, the nights in the high altitudes growing colder as the season advanced. At last, towering above its neighbors in the northwestern part of Montana, rose the great Chief Mountain, twelve thousand five hundred feet high, with its spiked ridges resembling an armored tower as the high sun poured radiance upon it. Many miles of survey had to be accomplished before the foot of the mountain was reached, miles of climbing over jumbled, tree-covered neighboring mountains or skirting the heights. Shadows cast by the buttressed and indented flank of Chief Mountain darkened the canyons as the party reached its base and began the ascent, with the soft crunch of needles underfoot and the smell of fir in the air.

Now the howl of wolves and the dismal bark of coyotes broke the night's silence in the mountainside camp. Brown bears ventured near, in search of food when darkness came. On the north shoulder of the mountain the party encountered a mass of giant sprawling trees, a twisted labyrinth of trunks and roots, and tangled heaps of branches, the result of a terrific hurricane.

With Gargantuan efforts they overcame the difficulties and located the monument terminating the survey by the Northwestern Expedition in 1858 of the boundary line between the United States and British America. A comparatively short time was consumed in the return journey to Fort Benton, where the expedition was delayed while eight rough-hewn Mackinaw rowboats, twenty-five feet long, were built. Thence the expedition rowed toward Bismarck, Dakota. The shores were glamorous with forests of ash, birch, oak, cottonwood, and aspen. Elk, startled by the intruders when camp was made at night in the forests, whistled a note of protest. Great herds of buffalo, crossing to the south on their way to the Yellowstone country, seeking shelter from storms in the breaks and gulches, swam along unmindful of their fellow travelers. Sometimes it was necessary to prod them with the oars to secure a passage for the small boats.

The judgment of the herds in selecting a time for their crossing was not infallible. It happened occasionally that their journey was delayed until the river was frozen over. Sometimes the ice was not sufficiently thick to bear the weight of the lumbering creatures, and then they would fall through by thousands, to be sucked under the ice by the current and carried down the river to perish.

Several days out from Fort Benton the party overtook and hailed a lone boat carrying three passengers. For two days they rowed and camped together, the surveyors and the three occupants of the boat—Clubfoot Boyd, sheriff of the county; Yellowstone Kelly, a famous scout; and a murderer in irons whom they were taking to the county seat for trial. Then as the boats landed, while a white half-moon hung suspended in the sky and a fringe of pink streaked the horizon, the three men, all in the best of humor, "hit the trail" for the county seat.

Eighteen days after the expedition had left Fort Benton they reached the landing at Bismarck, where a celebration was held, everyone soon feeling gay from the large amount of liquor he had consumed. Even McGillycuddy walked happily down the street and invited Pocahontas, a wooden tobacco sign, to join him in his amble. The train which at length carried the survey party east bore also General George Armstrong Custer, on his way to Washington from Fort Lincoln, Dakota, to report on his findings as to gold in the Black Hills.

At the conclusion of the survey, headquarters for the Northern Boundary Exploration were transferred to Washington, D.C. McGillycuddy was detailed to convey the papers containing the full record to the capital. But before leaving Detroit he obtained Fanny Hoyt's promise to link her life with his when it offered a probability of becoming less nomadic.

Map drawing, now being meticulously done by McGillycuddy, was the fly in the ointment of his changed life. Always the outdoors called; always he saw the Great Plains velvet-green or brown-withered, rushing rivers, and towering mountains, and heard gay meadow larks singing in the wild-rose-scented bushes.

His pulse quickened one spring day when, summoned to the main office of the Boundary Expedition's headquarters, Major J. W. Powell, geologist and explorer of the Grand Canyon of the Colorado, asked if his services could be secured for the Black Hills exploration. It had been decided that the presence of gold in the Hills must be determined once for all. President Grant had appointed Powell to select four men, engineers and scientists, to go to the Hills and pass on the question. Three of the men had been chosen. Would McGillycuddy act as topographer for the expedition?

His quickened heart throb slackened as the doctor answered that he was still engaged in drawing maps of the Boundary survey, but gathered speed when Powell said that he had made arrangements for a substitute at the drawing-board if McGillycuddy accepted the offer. Not a moment was now lost in indecision: he would go to the Hills. The four men who were to decide on the question of gold in the Black Hills were to meet at Fort Laramie, Wyoming, in three weeks.

Chapter 4

CALAMITY JANE

IT WAS the evening of May 20, 1875. Over wine cups in the home of Colonel R. I. Dodge at Fort Laramie the four men—Walter P. Jenny, in charge of the expedition, and Henry Newton, both of the Columbia School of Mines; Horace P. Tuttle, of the Naval Observatory in Washington; and McGillycuddy—discussed with their host and other officers the coming exploration. On the judgment of four men, it seemed, rested the hope or despair of the red men: With little gold appearing in the Black Hills, the Indians' paradise might still remain to them; rich quartz there would prove a death-knell to the Sioux.

The expedition which would accompany the engineers to the Hills was in process of organization, the Colonel said. News of the proposed exploration, spread abroad, had brought the usual complement of scouts, prospectors, and hangers-on from all parts of the country to the post hoping to join the party. During a lull in the conversation, when plans had been thoroughly discussed, McGillycuddy remarked that he had noticed an unusual-looking girl on the parade grounds that day, one not over sixteen and wearing spurs, chaps, and a sombrero. The Colonel said that was Calamity Jane, regimental mascot in spite of her name. Many stories were told of her exploits. She had been living at the post when he had come to Fort Laramie. This was what he was told of her origin.

In 1860 a private of the Fourteenth Infantry named Dalton had married a girl named Jane living thereabout, and when a baby had been born to them they had named her for her mother. Dalton's term of enlistment had expired when the child was a year old, and he had decided to leave the Army, strike out into the valley of La Bonte, and build a home. In spite of warnings of attack by Indians the young couple, with the baby, had set out. They had made the entire journey without coming in contact with any redskins. Together they had built their home, a small cabin, and planted a garden. They had ceased to consider any trouble from the Indians, when late one afternoon, as Dalton was working in his vegetable bed, a war whoop had suddenly broken the silence of the plains.

Jane, startled, had flown to the window of the cabin and, peering cautiously through, had seen a band of young bucks riding toward the garden, shooting arrows at her husband, their steel points glistening in the sunlight. She had seen him fall; a chance shot had pierced the glass through which she peered and had sunk into her eye. She had torn out the barbed arrow and, without waiting to see if her husband was dead or if she was leaving him to a fate worse than death, had clasped little Jane in her arms and, slipping through the back door of the cabin, slid into the bushes.

She had lain motionless, silencing the child by the power of will, while she watched flames shoot from her cabin and listened to the shouts of the Indians as the beams crackled, the walls fell, and sparks blew near. They had huddled in the brush until night settled in the valley and a pale moon rose behind the cottonwood trees. War whoops no longer dinned in her ears; the painted figures which had danced about the flames of the cottage had ridden triumphantly away; and Jane stole from her hiding place. She did not return to see if her husband's body lay under the night; that was useless, and every moment was precious. One hundred miles lay ahead before she could reach the only place of safety of which she knew—Fort Laramie, the haven for her child.

Jane knew it would be comparatively safe to travel by night. She had often listened to stories of Indian superstitions told by the soldiers. They believed that ghosts wandered over the country in the small hours, and also that if they should be killed in the dark they would remain forever in darkness. Only when driven by dire necessity did the Indians leave their campfires by night.

Jane had headed southwest, making her path through the brush of unbroken country. During the day she had hid in the bushes, hushing the child's cries for food, if she had not been fortunate enough to find roots or berries along the way, with warnings of horrors worse than hunger. Sometimes hours had passed without their reaching a stream or a spring. Their throats had become parched and their lips swollen, and her wounded eye sightless and festering. Their clothes had caught on the bushes and been torn into shreds.

After seven nights of such travel, as the bugle sounded reveille, the woman with the child in her arms had staggered on the Fort Laramie parade-ground, scarcely a stitch clinging to her torn body. No one had at first recognized her as the girl who had left the post a year before. She had stammered her story and had begged the troopers to be kind to little Jane. Such had been her last words.

The child had promptly been taken into the home of Sergeant Bassett and informally adopted into the regiment. Because of her hard luck they had called her Calamity Jane. She had been petted and spoiled and, belonging to many, she had belonged to no one and had become her own mistress.*

Jane was now a queer combination, the Colonel said. He had known her to sit up night after night caring for sick soldiers. She mended their clothes and cooked for them. But as for morals, she didn't know the meaning of the word. And she was crazy for adventure. He would swear she was thinking that moment that she would give half her life to be setting out with the expedition to the Black Hills.

The party broke up soon after dinner, Tuttle giving the excuse that they must be up early in the morning making preparations for the journey which would begin the next day.

* This is the story as it was told to Dr. McGillycuddy in 1875 and as conclusively accepted by the regiment at Fort Laramie. Not only did he hear it then from members of the Fourteenth Infantry in which Bassett had served as sergeant and Dalton had served as private, but many years later when he talked it over in Portland, Oregon, with General D. W. Burke and Colonel Murphy, retired officers of the Fourteenth.

Whatever evidence has appeared to prove the story untrue, the Doctor said she was known to everyone in 1875 as Jane Dalton.

McGillycuddy had asked to have the horse assigned to him from the Quartermaster Department for the expedition ready before his tent at ten o'clock in the morning, so that he might try him out before the long journey began. The beautiful black horse stood quietly, the orderly holding the bridle, while McGillycuddy mounted and gathered up the reins, then trotted amiably out of the post. It was a warm morning. McGillycuddy confidently hung the bridle reins loosely over one arm and started to remove his coat. Just then the horse seized the bit and bolted. McGillycuddy bent low on the animal's neck, drew up the slackened reins, and sawed on the bit. He had not gone far when his hat sailed off his head. Even in the excitement the incident struck him as peculiar, since the hat fitted almost too tight for comfort. It seemed the horse had a mouth of steel as he sped on, the blood dripping from it as McGillycuddy pulled on the reins. At last the mad pace slackened, sweat pouring from the animal's flanks and bloody foam covering the bit.

McGillycuddy now turned the horse about to go in search of his hat. After riding some distance he saw it lying in the road ahead, and above the spot where it lay hung a loosened telegraph wire sagging just low enough to catch his hat as he had leaned over the neck of the flying horse straining on the bridle.

"God!" he exclaimed. "If I hadn't been bending over I'd have had my neck broken." He dismounted and picked up his hat. He stroked the sweaty flanks of the horse and wiped the foam from its bleeding jaws, while his voice quieted the wild tossing of the animal's head and the champing on the bit: "Damn it, old fellow, you almost did for me, but I nearly sawed your mouth in two. Let's call it square and be friends from now on." The horse seemed to understand, and quietly trotted back to the post.

McGillycuddy had been in his tent but a short time when it was darkened by a figure standing in the doorway—Calamity Jane, dressed as on the previous day, in chaps and sombrero. "How-do, Dr. 'Gillycuddy," she began her conversation. The doctor invited her to sit on a chair which he brought out from the tent; but she declined the chair and sat on the ground, he following her example.

She inquired about his horseback ride; but when he began to relate his experience said she had heard all about it from the sergeant, who had given him the worst horse in the Quartermaster Department, "jest because he thought you was a city guy who didn't know how to ride." The sergeant and a private had followed to see the fun. But they had not seen the slack telegraph wire. "They ain't so cussed as that," Calamity said in excuse for her friends. They had hid in the bushes near the dropped hat and waited for the doctor's return. "They heard y' swear and they seen y' pat the horse and talk friendly to him and they knows now y'ain't jest a city guy."

But the purpose of Calamity's visit had not yet been stated. She looped an arm around her crossed knees and beat an irregular tattoo on her boots with her quirt while she told the doctor she wanted to go with the expedition to the Black Hills. McGillycuddy said she would have to get permission to do so from Colonel Dodge—he had no authority whatever concerning the accompanying party; he was only the topographer for the expedition. Calamity said she had already asked the Colonel but he had refused. She urged McGillycuddy to speak a word for her; but when he told her that would be absolutely useless, she did not seem entirely discouraged. She bade him a cheerful good-bye and sauntered off toward the barracks.

Several of the officers lunched with the engineers in their camp an hour later. As they sat about the table, Captain Sam Munson remarked that an old scout, having heard of the proposed expedition, had come into the post hoping to get a job as guide but that Colonel Dodge was taking José Merrivale, the official guide and scout at Fort Laramie, instead. Mr. Jenny said he had been thinking of taking a special guide with the engineering department and asked how the old scout would do for the job. Munson said he couldn't get a better one anywhere, for "California Joe" seemed to have some psychic sense of location and direction. He was a queer sort, most of the time wandering about alone except for his dog—seldom rode—just tramped over the country, and rarely stayed long in one place.

McGillycuddy asked how he came by the name of "California Joe." Munson explained that the man had gone out to California in the gold rush of '49 and had scouted all over the West. He was not a young man. No one knew much about him; he never talked about himself. Many stories were told of him, a few of which Munson happened to know were true.

California Joe was in the Civil War, he said. He was a member of Berdan's sharpshooters in the Union Army. After the war he had drifted West and become known by reputation if not by sight in every hunting and mining region from British America to Mexico. He had served the Army as guide and escort over the West, and was considered one of the finest shots in the country.

A queer incident had occurred when he was scouting for Custer in his campaign against the Cheyennes. It was in the fall of 1868, a few days before the Battle of the Washita. Chief Black Kettles' followers had outnumbered Custer's troops four to one. Custer had had advance parties scouting over the country feeling for the hostiles. Joe had set out alone one day in December, mounted on a mule, to look for Black Kettles and his troublesome band. His hound had followed. A canteen filled with whisky had hung on his saddle. Joe had said not a word to anyone as to his intentions or his destination.

After dark that evening one of Custer's scouting parties, looking down a valley, had seen in the distance a flash of light and soon had heard a shot. They had surmised that both the light and the shot had come from Black Kettles' camp. Presently, through the darkness, had rung a series of war whoops, shrieks, and yells, the walls of the narrow valley redoubling them.

The scouting party had drawn themselves up in readiness to resist the attack of the oncoming foe, while they strained their eyes to catch the first glimpse of the enemy. As the war whoops drew nearer they had distinguished vaguely a lone figure astride a mule, followed by a baying hound. In one hand Joe had carried a rifle and in the other a hunting knife.

After emptying the canteen, Joe had begun seeing things—bands lurking in hidden places; painted, naked bodies crouching behind bush and tree. In a frenzy of bravery he had spurred his mule to an attack on the phantom enemies, brandishing his knife and whooping his defiance. At the height of his imaginary attack the mule had turned about and had now borne his rider into the scouts' camp, where by superiority of numbers the lone scout had been captured and disarmed.

Mr. Jenny said that was just the sort of guide he wanted. And Captain Munson sent his orderly to look for California Joe. In a few minutes he returned, followed by the old scout. Long red whiskers concealed the lower part of his face. His large scout hat overshadowed but did not hide his blue eyes, which had an extraordinary look. It was as if he saw through mountains, heard the running of water in distant places, and had secret communion with the winds.

Mr. Jenny told him he was looking for a special guide and that Captain Munson had recommended him. Would he like to go out with the expedition to the hills? The soft, blue eyes emphasized the answer: "That's why I come inter Fort Laramie."

The morning of May 25 was not far advanced when the expedition moved out. The journey across upland country, its heavy, sandy roads dotted with creamy, cone-like hills and knolls with flat summits, revealed fragments of the surface of the plains before the intervening hollows and gulches had been carved out by water. All these things McGillycuddy noted as he dashed from the column on his beautiful black horse and surveyed the country with a prismatic compass.

At the first night's camp on the purple-hued Rawhide Peak of coarse granite rising from the plains, pickets were thrown out on prominent points and a guard was assigned to watch the herds of hobbled horses, mules, and cattle upon which the success of the expedition depended whether the party rode or walked, whether or not they were properly provisioned, almost whether they lived or died in the country where Indian trails and signal fires indicated their presence.

But the night was undisturbed and, after coming down the steep decline, the party crossed green valleys dotted with clusters of pine trees, smooth, slippery rocks, and granite boulders. Here fresh tracks of an Indian pony raised the question: "Was the rider a courier carrying the news of the presence of troops to hostile natives in the Black Hills?"

The first four days of the march passed with but a minor mishap, one which should have shaken the cocksureness of the official guide, José Merrivale, who belonged to the breed of scouts who knew everything about the country—"jest ask him ennything and he'd tell'ye." And he laid out the third day's march, saying: "We'll cross the Cheyenne in the mornin', go up a goolch on the other side—quite a long ways, several miles—and then we'll be up on a flat ground where I hunted antelope last year. Then we'll cross that flat three, four miles north and come to a nize easy slope to the foothills."

Several hours were spent the following morning building a road up the gulch for the wagon train. The plateau was reached as José had promised, and the party found good traveling for several miles. At length Colonel Dodge asked if it wasn't about time they were reaching the easy slope to the foothills.

"Soon, soon, Colonel. Not more'n a mile further."

The expedition marched on—one mile, two miles, many miles —before they encountered, not an easy slope, but a precipice rising about five hundred feet. A worried look crossed José's face but remained only for a moment as he exclaimed: "Jese Christ, how this damn country he change since I was here last!"

The party now turned back and marched down the Cheyenne valley, looking for another way out. After a long trail they at last made camp in the foothills. Merrivale's prestige had waned somewhat, though he maintained his cocksureness.

Four days had passed since the expedition had left Fort Lara-

mie—days in which an unaccounted-for young private had remained undiscovered. Camp had been established according to
custom, with soldiers' quarters at one end of the line and officers'
quarters between them and the sutler's store at the other end. The
store on wheels was an important part of an army entourage.
Trappers, stray settlers, and vagabonds, hearing of the expedition,
drifted in to purchase supplies from the traveling van. The stock
comprised a queer assortment of ammunition, cigars, cigarettes,
patent medicines, groceries, and other useful as well as useless
articles.

The confidence of the unaccounted-for young private had increased as the days had passed until by the fourth evening all sense
of caution had disappeared. At last, tripping down the line past
the officers' quarters and heading for the sutler's store to purchase
cigars, Calamity Jane saw an officer approaching. Several young
officers, standing in front of their tents as she passed, recognized
her in spite of her disguise. They smiled and nudged each other,
though they had no intention of betraying her. But as Calamity
saw the officer of the day approaching they saw her pull her cap
over her eyes as she muttered: "My God, Von Leutwitz, the damn
little German!"

It was too late to turn back, and Calamity straightened her
shoulders and saluted with military precision. With equal precision the officer of the day acknowledged the salute. This aroused
the humor of the onlookers, who burst into laughter. "What in
hell's the matter with you?" Von Leutwitz roared, feeling that he
was the cause of their amusement.

"Don't you know the lady who saluted you?" asked Lieutenant
White. "It's Calamity Jane."

"I'll report this," Von Leutwitz shouted. "It's a damned outrage. No woman's allowed on an army expedition."

He went on to the commandant's tent, spluttering to himself,
and reported the presence of the hitherto unsuspected female in
camp. An investigation followed. It was true that Calamity was
among those present in soldiers' quarters. Through the aid of the

army tailor, who had fitted a soldier's uniform to her slim figure, Calamity Jane had been metamorphosed into a private in the United States Army.

The commanding officer was a kindly man, but to have an unassigned female on an exploration in the field in time of war could not be considered otherwise than subversive to good order and military discipline. Colonel Richard I. Dodge—the younger officers called him Richard the First—tried to look impressive as he rolled off the judicial speech; but a smile hovered about his lips. Calamity must go. But where? The nearest habitation was Fort Laramie, now sixty miles to the rear. The trackless West was a wilderness ahead. They were in the heart of the Indian country. Yet army discipline must be maintained.

As the expedition pulled out the next morning, Calamity, standing with her pony by the roadside, watched troop after troop of cavalry and company after company of infantry pass in review, while she frequently questioned: "Gee, fellers, where'm I goin' ter hang out ternight?" Yet there seemed no genuine anxiety in her manner.

"It's hell, girlie," the troopers answered, though none showed any special signs of uneasiness at leaving the girl alone on the prairies sixty miles from the nearest lodging with the probability of Indians lurking near. Calamity appealed to McGillycuddy as he dashed back to the line from a lookout. He was sorry, he said, but he could do nothing to help her.

As the wagon train and the train guard with some led horses passed at the rear of the line, Calamity Jane turned her pony in among the led horses and, making her choice of vehicles, slipped under the wagon bows and disappeared from sight. The commanding officer had complied with army regulations by ordering the girl out of camp, while she had fulfilled her desire by going on with the expedition. The ceremony was repeated daily, as she obeyed the order to leave camp, returned promptly, and joined the day's march. She helped about camp and was a valuable member of the wagon train.

CALAMITY JANE

CALIFORNIA JOE

As José Merrivale had lost the confidence of Colonel Dodge, California Joe had gained in his favor. He never volunteered information, never intruded his knowledge. Frequently he disappeared from the command, the hound his sole companion, while he took in the lay of the land. At irregular intervals he returned to camp, satisfied with his knowledge of the country ahead on the line of march.

Once, however, when he had not scouted ahead, Dodge asked him where they would camp that night. "Well, I've never bin exac'ly in this country," Joe answered, "but it looks"—pointing north to a group of small hills—"it looks as if we'd oughter find plenty water and a good campin' ground over thar." The Colonel asked him why he thought so, and Joe explained that knowing such things was his business; he couldn't just say how he knew.

They camped that night by the hills. The sky was heavy with clouds. Dodge asked him which way was north from the camp. The old scout stooped down and pulled a blade of grass, held it between his thumb and forefinger, studied it intently, then turned it over and examined it on the other side. "If you'll take your store compass, Colonel, you'll find north is out thar," he said. Joe's finger and the store compass pointed exactly in the same direction.

On the seventh day out from Fort Laramie the party had traveled ninety miles across a high divide, six miles in width, between the Niobrara River and Crazy Woman's Fork (Wakpala Wea Witkola). Down from this divide at Crystal Hill, they descended into the valley of Crazy Woman's Fork and continued a series of tiresome marches over stretches of sand, long corduroys, deep ditches, and precipitous breaks, passing the butte named after a crazy woman whose ghost the Indians believed haunted the place. At stated intervals she was said to appear and dance the scalp dance, singing with an unearthly voice a tale of horror. Sometimes a dog followed the old hag, howling an accompaniment to her wailings; it was disastrous for a warrior to see the dog.

Up toward Pumpkin Buttes, as the expedition neared the Black Hills, smoke could be seen rising from the Bad Lands. From time to time the vast elliptical dome-like mass of the Hills rose to view and then dreamily faded away, until in mid-June the entrance to the Indian Eden was reached. Fruit trees and flowers covered the hills and valleys. Gentle breezes blew from hidden recesses as the party made camp on the East Fork of Beaver Creek, velvety bottomed and overhung with box elder trees. At night the gentle breeze swelled to a great wind, formed from two blasts blowing out of opposite canyons through the mountains, which threatened to demolish every tent in the camp.

A stockade was erected here for the storing of supplies. Pickets were posted on the hills at two sides of the camp, commanding a view of the canyons from which an attack, if contemplated by the Indians, would be made.

On June 23, when a permanent camp was established on the East Fork of French Creek, word was received that Red Cloud, Spotted Tail, Iron Nation, and other chiefs had returned to their agencies from Washington, where they had attended a council concerning the sale of the Black Hills. The chiefs were reported as dissatisfied with the terms offered, causing Dodge to become more vigilant and to increase the number of videttes and pickets.

Tuttle, the astronomer, and McGillycuddy, inseparable in their work, with a party consisting of a sergeant and ten men, were surveying twenty-five miles from the main camp in the foothills at the mouth of Beaver Creek when they saw, riding toward them from the south, a large band of Indians. As they drew nearer squaws and children showed among them.

The Indians rode up in friendly fashion and greeted the surveyors. The squaws were laden with wild plums and berries, which they shared with the white men while they all sat about on the grass by the creek and conversed to the best of their ability. Little Big Man, the diminutive chief, spoke a few English words. The children waded in the stream, while the bucks smoked their long pipes filled with a mixture of kinnikinnick and tobacco, the latter presented by the white men. An hour later the Indians all rode to the north.

While surveying in this vicinity McGillycuddy came upon a cave in the bluffs in which were a pair of broken steel spectacles, a rusty spade, and some old camping utensils, obviously left by white men.*

When McGillycuddy's party returned to the main camp they were much entertained by the accounts in the papers, brought recently with mail from Fort Laramie, of the visit of United States Senator W. B. Allison, chairman of a commission appointed to barter further with the Indians for the Black Hills. A great council had been held on Chadron Creek in Nebraska in late September, with leading Sioux chiefs present. "Teddy" Egan's gray troop of the Second Cavalry from Fort Robinson had acted as escort for the commission. On the second day of the council a gray cloud of dust had been seen to the north, the direction in which lay the Standing Rock Agency, the home of Sitting Bull, who had refused to attend the council. As the cloud of dust had drawn nearer, three hundred warriors had emerged and charged into the grounds, the leader crying: "I am Little Big Man, sent down by the chiefs of the Northern Sioux, to say we will not sell the Black Hills and if the white men of this commission do not get out of the country at once, I and my warriors will kill them."

Consternation had prevailed in the council. Captain Egan had ordered his command, fifty in number, to mount and throw themselves between the Indians and the commissioners. Little Big Man's warriors had drawn up in battle-line formation with the butts of their carbines resting in Indian fashion on the pommels of their saddles or the necks of their ponies. The cavalry men's carbines had rested across their saddles.

It had seemed that but fifty soldiers stood between the white men and death when, mounting one thousand of his warriors, Young Man of Whose Horses They Are Afraid, chief of the Oglala Sioux, had wedged them in between Egan's troops and

* McGillycuddy learned years later from Little Big Man that in 1849 some travelers to California, attracted by the Hills, had branched off the main trail and made a camp in the cave while they inspected the country. There the Indians had discovered them: "They never left the camp," the little chief concluded.

Little Big Man's warriors crying: "We are not here to fight but to listen to the words of the men sent here by the Great Father. My brother from the North"—he addressed Little Big Man—"if you have come here to fight this commission you will have to fight my warriors also. The white men on the council grounds of the Southern Sioux are under my protection."

For a moment there had been stifling silence. Then a cry had risen from Little Big Man, an order from the diminutive chief to his warriors; and like a flash they had whirled their horses to the north and departed as rapidly as they had come.

The conference had ended in failure on September 29. The newspaper stated that thereafter at the mention of the name of Little Big Man Senator Allison had turned pale.

Tuttle and McGillycuddy congratulated themselves that their encounter with the warriors had been on a more friendly basis. The squaws and children doubtless had been left on the trail to the council grounds and picked up on their return.

As the survey progressed, miners panning out gold from the gravel in the streams were gathered up as invaders operating in violation of the treaty with the Indians and were sent with the supply trains, escorted by guards, to Fort Laramie. The miners were finding but small quantities of gold, the pans, holding about ten quarts of earth as the miners used them, averaging from "nothing to fifteen cents a pan."

Calamity Jane flitted from camp to camp, frequently striding into the hills with her rifle and bringing back a deer or an antelope. It was useless to order her out of any one camp, since she easily slipped into another. She was not quarrelsome. She cared for sick soldiers, mended their clothes, and continued to be a valuable though unauthorized addition to the expedition.

After weeks spent in the survey of the Beaver Creek district, with work frequently delayed by heavy rainfall, the party pushed on to the northeast. Elk and deer roamed over the hills in large herds. The bison of the Black Hills were smaller and more active than the plains buffalo, owing to their strenuous climbing.

The main camp was established on French Creek, and Tuttle and McGillycuddy set out to explore Harney's Peak, accompanied by a troop of cavalry and wagons carrying supplies. Before the ascent of the mountain was begun, McGillycuddy made arrangements for the wagons to trail down the valley, appointing a night camp where he and Tuttle would join them. Near the summit of the granite peak the climbers seemed to have reached an impasse. The steep and rugged bluffs soared overhead; ten feet of perpendicular, creviced wall confronted them.

At last McGillycuddy hit upon a plan of ascent. A tall tree was felled, its fall directed into one of the crevices. Up the tree the lithe topographer climbed and, working his way up the rocks, was the first white man to stand on the top of the lofty mountain, 7,500 feet high.

On the return journey to Washington, following the completion of this survey, McGillycuddy made a detour to Detroit, where he and Fanny Hoyt were married.

Exaggerated accounts of the report of the wealth stored in the rugged hills standing sentry over the possessions of the red men sped like wildfire to all parts of the country. Settlers living in cabins bordering the Hills gazed on specimens filched from the earth and listened, breathless, to tales of fabulous wealth waiting only to be poured into their coffers. Trains vomited forth a motley horde at all stations adjacent to the Hills, and mobs poured in ignoring rights and treaties.

Added to the lost hope of maintaining their lands was the suffering at frontier agencies, inaccessible for the transportation of supplies agreed upon by treaty in exchange for the vast territory already relinquished by the Sioux. In a starving condition many of them fled from the agencies hoping to find game. The patience of the red men had by this time become exhausted, and Sitting Bull set about organizing a war party. Bitter cold, frozen rivers, and snow-covered plains alone delayed action.

Chapter 5

SITTING BULL AND CUSTER

PERCHED on a high stool before a drawing board, McGillycuddy found difficulty in concentrating his attention on the maps of the Black Hills Exploration. His gaze turned often toward the window, through which the Washington May sun awakened memories of life on the Great Plains—jumbled mountains, squally lakes, venison steaming over campfires, and the wail of coyotes in black mountains. His pen loitered on meticulous, pencil-drawn maps as his mind strayed to thoughts of the troops already in the field against Sitting Bull, many of them his friends.

There had been and still was deep feeling in diplomatic and army circles over the offense of General George Armstrong Custer against President Grant in openly criticizing one of his official family—W. Belknap, Secretary of War, in whose department post and army tradership appointments were made. The traderships were considered sinecures, and it had happened that sometimes a hitherto unsuccessful aspirant received the appointment after widows of former officials, acting as lobbyists, had been in attendance on the wife of the War Secretary. One of the traders supposedly so appointed was located at Fort Lincoln, and Custer's comments on the affair had lacked diplomacy. Custer was a soldier; he was not a politician. For these comments and for his testimony in the impeachment which followed, the President had relieved Custer of the command of his regiment, the Fighting Seventh, then preparing for its campaign against the Sioux.

This was probably the bitterest pill the fearless Custer ever had been forced to swallow. His pleading by letter—the President refused him audience—that he be allowed to fight with his regiment, even though deprived of his command, had been acceded to finally only through the influence of Generals Townsend and Sheridan.

In the circles frequented by McGillycuddy little but the Indian campaign was discussed. General Alfred Terry commanding the Department of Dakota and General George Crook commanding the Department of the Platte were by this time in the field in the vicinity of the Little Big Horn Mountains in Wyoming. Their operations as well as those of the Sioux were continually speculated upon. And always McGillycuddy's blood stirred at the thought of the open plains.

It was with difficulty that he spurred his pen to quicker action; and as it was responding to discipline, a copy of a telegram was brought to his office. His eye fell first on the name of the sender: it was Crook. It read: "Can McGillycuddy's service be secured for the field. Stop. If so send him at once." His brain whirled. Fanny, Great Plains, drawing board, Indians, fighting, the open road! At the War Department he learned that again a substitute would complete his map-drawing, and he asked for time in which to consult his wife before accepting the proposal.

Fanny was enjoying life in Washington, but she made no demur when told of Crook's message. She remarked only that she hoped nothing would happen to "the Doctor." She always spoke of McGillycuddy as "the Doctor" and addressed him by his title. They decided it would be best for her to return to Detroit and remain there during his absence. She asked when they would leave, and McGillycuddy told her that Crook had asked that he come at once—he would like to get off on the evening train—he would inquire what time it left. He hurried to the War Office, and his contract was drawn up.

Fanny's trunk was packed when the Doctor returned. She was sorting out the articles which were to go into his trunk and his bags. She consulted him as to his need of one thing and another, and made no protest when he shifted some of the things she had designed for his bags to the pile intended for the trunk. He would need but little in the field, he said. It doubtless would be very hot on the plains. He knew that country in summer. Of course there was no telling how long the campaign would last. Fanny uttered no complaint. No tears were shed when the Doctor kissed her good-bye at the Chicago station where she changed trains for Detroit. Fanny was made of soldier stuff.

The nickel-plated revolver which fitted neatly into McGillycuddy's pocket needed polish—it had lain idle since autumn. It was midafternoon, and no train left Cheyenne, Wyoming, for the West until morning. Hours to spend before he could be off to the field—he'd shine up his gun. His room in the Interocean Hotel was gloomy. He liked seeing men move about the lobby. He enjoyed catching bits of conversation about the Indian campaign. Where was Sitting Bull? No one knew.

The Doctor sat down at a desk and took his gun from his pocket. Carefully he rubbed the butt until he could see his face—distorted, broadened—in the shining metal. He liked that gun—it was neat—not the clumsy kind soldiers and cowboys carried. But he was not a fighting man; he was a doctor, an engineer. A small gun was all he needed, and he was not quite certain that he needed any. But every man on the frontier carried a gun; it was companionable and one never could tell—he might want to use it.

There was a low chuckle behind his chair. McGillycuddy glanced up and saw a picturesque-looking man in black frock coat, white shirt and turned-down collar, and plaid bow tie, who stood gazing with an amused smile at his gun. A broad-brimmed hat sat above his long hair, and a black mustache covered his lips.

"Say, young man," the stranger said, "if you was to shoot me with that thing and I was to find it out I'd be right vexed. Where y' going and what're y' going to do with it?"

McGillycuddy was no greenhorn, though his pale, office, map-drawing face and his lean young body looked inexperienced. He laughed. "I'm going out to join Crook," he said, "as surgeon in the field."

"You don't say," Bill Hickok ejaculated; "you must meet my friend." He beckoned a slim, handsome man with long chin whiskers, dressed in scouting costume. "Come here, Bill," he called. "This young feller's on his way out to join Crook. This is my friend William Cody—Buffalo Bill, he's called. He's going out as scout with the Fifth Cavalry."

McGillycuddy introduced himself. When the two men heard of his plan to go out alone to the field they protested against his foolhardiness. The three talked long and dined together; and in the evening the two men took the Doctor to call on General W. Merritt, with whose command, now organizing, Bill Cody was to act as scout. The general strongly advised McGillycuddy to wait until his command was ready to set out; but the Doctor said he had been ordered to join Crook as soon as possible and he would just push on and take his chances on getting to him.

The chill of early morning hours lay on the plains when the train pulled out from the station. The train moved across great spaces, serene in spring newness. The sun was high when he got out at the desolate little station of Medicine Bow, less than one hundred miles from Cheyenne. There was no one in sight. The station agent looked up when McGillycuddy approached him, surprise on his face at the sight of a city man with business in the tiny village. McGillycuddy asked the agent if he could suggest any way for him to get to Fort Fetterman. The agent said the mail-driver would be leaving that afternoon; perhaps he could get a ride with him.

The mail-driver was glad to have company on the two-hundred-mile journey. "Lonely trip all by yerself," he said. "Never know when the damn Injuns'll begin shooting. Heven't hed no trouble so fer."

For some time after the two men set out across the long stretch of plains they talked intermittently of conditions on the frontier, speculating on their chances of encountering war bands; but as the afternoon waned, silence prevailed between them. The Medicine Bow River which they were following ran happily with spring waters, its bank green-shaded. Water dripped gently over stones in small streams, crickets chirped, and only occasionally a wolf's bark was heard afar.

The buckboard joggled along the prairie trail. At widely separated stations the horses were changed and driver and passenger seized a few hours of sleep.

Day followed day, until they reached Fort Fetterman, without a sign, except signal fires on the hills, to indicate that thousands of warriors were assembling to guard their lands from further invasion.

A wagon train with supplies for Crook's command was preparing to set out shortly from the post. With it went McGillycuddy on horseback, one hundred and ninety miles across sage-covered plains, silvered in the moonlight, to Crook's camp in the Rosebud Valley.

After a warm greeting and an assignment to the Second Cavalry, McGillycuddy went to the hospital supply tent to investigate the equipment. Among the supplies was a stretcher which he decided would make an excellent bed. An orderly carried it to his tent. During the afternoon every officer in camp stopped at his quarters and commented on the luxury of McGillycuddy's bed. He felt guilty on seeing the rolls of blankets spread on the ground in the other tents, and wondered if he had better suggest that the general use the stretcher but he feared that might seem presumptuous. McGillycuddy could endure hardship, but saw no reason to evade comfort if it was at hand. After the camp supper the officers sat about telling stories and speculating upon the possibility of an early engagement with the Sioux. As the light of the campfires dimmed, each one sought his sleeping quarters.

The fires burned out; there was no sound on the prairies but the quiet munching of cavalry horses and the hourly call of the sentry. Then suddenly shots were fired into the camp. McGillycuddy started; sat up. Had he been asleep? A bullet had pierced the side of his tent, and he slid off the stretcher and lay belly to the ground while the firing continued. He knew he would never again sleep on a stretcher in an enemy country—one was much safer flat on the ground. He would send the stretcher back to the hospital tent in the morning if he were still alive.

"Sleep well?" was the greeting which met him on all sides at breakfast. The Doctor grinned.

Shooting into the camp at night was one of Sitting Bull's favorite pastimes, Crook explained. The bullets were pretty well spent by the time they reached the camp.

"Good joke," McGillycuddy said, sheepishly.

Crook's expedition consisted of eleven hundred officers and men of the Second and Third Cavalry and the Ninth and Fourteenth Infantry, together with fifty Shoshone and Crow scouts, whose bands at that time were friendly to the whites while they hated the very name of Sioux. They were as eager as the troops for the capture of Sitting Bull and his followers.

On the morning after McGillycuddy's arrival the march to the northwest was continued. Regular camp was established only at night. At hourly periods during the day a halt of ten minutes was ordered, when saddle girths were loosened and bridles were removed to allow the horses to graze. Officers gathered around the wagons and passed the bottle around. Whatever had been salvaged from the morning meal was carried in saddlebags and eaten at midday.

At ten o'clock on the morning of June 17, with the Third Cavalry half a mile ahead, the Second halted for the usual ten-minute rest. Saddles lay ungirthed and bridles unbuckled, while officers and men lay stretched on the ground. The laughter and chatter of the groups was suddenly broken by the sound of shots ahead. "The Third must have found game," someone remarked. But in a moment six Crow scouts, sent in advance, darted back, clapping their hands and shouting wildly, "Sioux, Sioux!" Instantly the bugle sounded "Boots and saddles!" Girths were at once tightened and bridles adjusted, and, responding to the order, "Forward, trot, gallop," the Second dashed across the prairies, over sagebrush and tumbleweeds clinging to slim stems, over undulating hills gashed with shallow ravines, guided by the sound of the now,rapid firing.

As support for the troops approached, the Sioux ahead forced an engagement favorable to Indian tactics, that of skirmish-line formation. Above the screech of rifles and the war whoops of savages rose the screams of wounded animals. On the surrounding hills signals were being given by waving blankets and flashing mirrors.

Crazy Horse, the slim young warrior, directed the Sioux charge, his strategy unequaled by any of the white leaders. In high, strident tones his voice rose above the tumult: *"Okici ze anpetu waste; anpetu el tapi waste. Cante wasaka, cante chitika tokahepi; cante hunkesni me cante wankapi hena lazata iya yapi!"* The great leader, crying that it was a good day to fight, a good day to die, called the strong hearts and the brave hearts to the front and warned the weak hearts and the cowards to fall back.

Bands of warriors appeared on one flank and, suddenly disappearing, emerged from the bushes on the opposite side or from the rear, following no practice of civilized warfare. At the end of a four-hour engagement, with the advantage on the side of the Sioux, the Indians made a feint at the troops and dashed down the canyon.

Troop K of the Third was ordered in pursuit. The Crow scouts shouted to Crook that it was a feint to lure the soldiers into an ambuscade. Recall was sounded, and the troop turned about. Two horses became unmanageable, broke column, and charged among the Sioux, where the soldiers were quickly dragged from their horses and cut to pieces. The Crows listened to no orders but dashed among the Sioux and, dismounting two of the warriors, dealt with them likewise. When the Sioux withdrew there was no means of ascertaining the number of their losses, since, according to Indian custom, they had carried off their dead and their wounded.

The doctors with the stretcher-bearers now passed over the battlefield gathering up the casualties. The valley, bordered with cream-colored bluffs outlined with pink, purple, and black, was dust-dimmed by the surging hoofs of cavalry horses and Indian ponies. Quaking ash and willow trees whined in the breeze. A man staggered about blindly, blood pouring down his face. McGillycuddy set him up against a tree, while a soldier remarked, "That poor guy's done for."

"Not by a damn sight," Captain G. V. Henry shouted.

After giving him first aid, McGillycuddy passed on to a soldier kneeling beside a log, his gun aimed. The doctor spoke to him: "Put down your gun; the battle's over." There was no response. He touched him on the shoulder. The body was rigid. A bullet had pierced his left eye and passed through his brain, causing instant paralysis and death.

A groaning in the bushes attracted the attention of the Crow scouts. A wounded Sioux had been overlooked by his band. With a wild yell they placed a lariat around his waist, and mounting his horse one of the Crows tore across the valley dragging the wounded man until his body was lifeless pulp.

After gathering up their women and children at Deadman's Lodge Creek the Sioux struck northwest and joined Sitting Bull's forces in a naturally fortified camp in the valley of the Little Big Horn. Three thousand of the best fighting men of the Sioux nation under Sitting Bull the prophet, Gall, a greater leader, and Crazy Horse, the brilliant young warrior, were now entrenched in a valley protected on the sides by precipitous walls, while at either end was a narrow opening.

Crook fell back and went into camp on the forks of Goose Creek to repair damages, while his scouts roamed the country in search of Terry but got no word of his whereabouts.

Days later Louis Richard returned from a scouting trip with word of the Custer disaster; but details were meager. It was on June 25, he said, that the battle had occurred, but how many had been killed he did not know. The hostiles were reported to have moved back toward the Rosebud Mountains, and Terry was trying to locate them. It was impossible to get in touch with him.

Crook continued on Goose Creek hoping to get word of Terry before moving on to the Tongue River, twenty miles northeast, where General Merritt had been ordered to join him. Setting out for the Tongue River some days later, Crook resorted to pack-mule transportation in order to hasten his movements. Crook's pack-mule train, under the splendid supervision of Tom Moore, who had a quarter of a century's experience behind him, was exceptional. The mules followed the bell and were as hard as nails. Each man was outfitted with one suit of clothes, an overcoat, a blanket, and an India-rubber poncho. There were rations for fifteen days and two hundred and fifty rounds of ammunition to a person.

At the Tongue River they were joined by Merritt, whose command included a body of scouts under Buffalo Bill calling themselves the "Montana Volunteers." Among them was "Ute John," reported to have killed his grandmother and drunk her blood. He boasted proudly that he was a "Klishun [Christian]," having been "heap washed" by the "Mo'mons" three times in one year.

The march continued along the Tongue River over a tableland elevated, undulating, and covered with thick buffalo grass. Small streams flowed down the hillsides and spilled their contribution into the river, bound for the Yellowstone. Small timber, cottonwood, and willow dotted the banks, while the scent of roses filled the air. Blue butterflies hung over blue phlox; birds twittered among the trees; rattlesnakes slithered through the grass, standing their ground if necessary but preferring a hiding place from the hundreds of feet that stomped across the plateau.

As the column marched on, everyone was thinking: "Where is Terry?" At each curve of land which opened a new view the country was scanned with the hope that his troops would be discovered; but the march continued without a glimpse of human form until, on August 11, scouts brought in word that a line of Indians was coming up the valley. Indian scouts sent out to investigate returned soon with a report that a long column of white canvas-covered wagons was behind the approaching red men.

The news spread along the line: "Terry's coming up! Terry's coming up!" and the shouts of Crook's men through the valley were buffeted from hilltop to hilltop and echoed from crag to crag: "Terry's coming up!" The answering salutations doubled the clangor, expressing on each side the joy that the oncoming columns were friends instead of foes. Buffalo Bill, waving his hat and shouting vociferously, dashed down the valley and returned by the side of Major Reno, who led Terry's advance guard.

After the first outburst of enthusiasm over the meeting, the subject uppermost in the minds of all—the Custer disaster—became the main subject of conversation. In the face of the tragic outcome it was with hesitation that the survivors of the Seventh Cavalry, as they sat about the campfires in the evening, referred to the fact that Custer had taken it upon himself to map out a plan of campaign after receiving orders from Terry to scout ahead with his regiment and feel for the hostiles. If he located them, he was to wait for the main command to come up. They were slow to mention that Terry had offered him a battalion of the Second Cavalry, which Custer had declined, though all knew he had done so because of his unwillingness to share the honor—if honor there were to be—in the adventure.

Though Sitting Bull was keeping watch over the troops, they said, Custer succeeded in slipping away in the dark and, traveling by night, came near the Little Big Horn. On Sunday morning, June 25, while crossing a plateau, these Indians were sighted by one of Terry's scouts on detached duty, who, recognizing the party, rode down and reported to Custer that the hostiles were encamped in the valley of the Little Big Horn, about ten miles northwest. Custer asked how many Indians there were in the camp. The scout replied that he couldn't say how many but, "judgin' from appearances I should think damn near the whole Sioux nation."

"They must be the nontreaty Indians, then," Custer remarked.

He saw no reason to await Terry's arrival. The Sioux were trapped in the valley, and he had a simple and feasible plan:

He divided his command into three battalions and ordered Reno with one hundred and five men to go down Sun Dance Creek to the junction with the Little Big Horn and there attack and stampede the hostiles. Benteen's battalion of about one hundred men was to pass beyond Reno and go down the west side of the valley. And Custer himself, with four hundred men, would follow along the bluffs on the east side, paralleling Benteen. When Reno had stampeded the Indians, the other two battalions would charge into the valley and bottle them up. Custer's plan, on its face, seemed a brilliant one.

Now Marcus Reno, a personal friend of McGillycuddy's since the survey of the Forty-ninth Parallel, told him in detail the part his battalion had taken in the engagement. In addition to his assignment of troops he had in his division a band of Arickaree scouts, a formidable-looking lot in warpaint and eagle feathers. These he deployed on the skirmish line to fill in the gap between the left flank and the foot of the bluffs in order to prevent the escape of the Sioux up the valley or from outflanking the battalion.

After marching down the valley and turning a bend, he said that as far as one could see there stretched thousands of Indian lodges. Though he felt certain of the hopelessness of the situation, he obeyed orders, opened fire, and attacked. But, contrary to Custer's expectations, the Sioux did not stampede but charged back on them like hornets and returned their fire.

The banks of the Little Big Horn were heavily timbered with cottonwood and willows. Reno gave orders to dismount, push through the underbrush, and ford the stream. The Indians, quickly seeking ambush, continued the attack, some of them getting possession of the ford and forcing the soldiers to seek another crossing, which they succeeded in doing after half an hour or more of fighting. When they reached the bluffs on the other side they dug themselves in to secure a defendable position. By that time Reno had lost approximately one-third of his men.

Benteen also explained to McGillycuddy his inability to get down into the valley according to orders on account of the precip-

SITTING BULL

"WILD BILL" HICKOK　　　　"BUFFALO BILL" CODY

itous walls and the irregular ground and that, hearing the rapid firing of the Reno engagement, he decided to fall back and join forces with Reno. This he did, and Captain McDougal with his troop of sixty men who had been left to guard the supply and ammunition pack train also succeeded in joining Reno.

Lieutenant Charles A. Varnum, but four years out of West Point, further informed McGillycuddy that Custer ordered him to scout around with a band of Rees and Crows, but that he came in contact with no Indians and returned to ask the general what he should do next. Custer answered laughingly, "Do anything you like; scout around and get any information you can."

Lieutenant G. D. Wallace, a close friend of Varnum, was near the general, who had shown a special fondness for the two young officers.

"Come on with me, Wallace," Varnum called, as he started off again; "don't stick around with those old coffee-coolers."

Custer lifted his hat in mock salute. "It was the last time I saw the general alive," Varnum said, with unsteady voice. The Crows and Rees deserted and he fell in with Reno and went into entrenchment with him.

Crazy Horse followed the retreating troops, the officers explained, and located their position. He left a few of his warriors and some squaws to hold them in check, while he, with a large band of his young bucks, followed on Reno's track. Evidently he followed this trail until he struck the point where it diverged from Custer's and followed it until he overtook and attacked Custer's troops.

As to whether or not the party on the bluffs heard the firing of the Custer engagement, the reports of the surviving officers of the Seventh Cavalry varied. Some claimed they had heard nothing, and speculated as to what had become of Custer. Had he abandoned the idea of attack and was he off in search of Terry? Others insisted they had heard the firing on Sunday morning—volley after volley sounding the distress call of the field—and that Benteen cried, "My God, Custer's calling for help!" Reno, they said, refused to risk the lives of the men who had survived the first encounter with the hordes in the valley, though many protested with cursing.

Throughout the night and the following day the troops on the bluffs were beleaguered by the Sioux. The suffering of the wounded was increased by thirst. In the darkness small parties stole down the hills and filled the canteens. At dawn on Tuesday the valley was silent; not an Indian was in sight, while off to the east a cloud of dust drew near. The supposition was that other bands of Indians were coming to join Sitting Bull. Scouts were sent out to investigate.

The dust was raised by Terry's command riding across the beautiful plains with a line of bluffs to the east and the Little Big Horn Mountains to the west. As they approached the battle-field they saw hundreds of tepee poles, buffalo robes, a bloody glove, and soldiers' uniforms strewn on the ground. No sound broke the silence of the valley as they came upon the heart-breaking sight—Custer's battalion, officers and men, pale-faced, with set teeth, their stark forms, all but three mutilated, stretched on the earth. Custer's body was untouched; his face showed no sign of pain nor anxiety; he seemed like one in quiet sleep. It was with difficulty that his wounds were located—one in the left temple, the other in the left side. The bodies of Captain Keogh and a little trumpeter also had escaped mutilation. The dashing, golden-haired general and his battalion were buried by their companions where they lay. With the return of Reno's scouts announcing the arrival of Terry, the party on the hilltop descended the slope and joined the main command. Terry reported: "All bodies accounted for." Terry's army had subsequently pushed on to the Yellowstone looking for Sitting Bull, but instead had come upon Crook's command. Together they had continued the march after a night in camp.

Crook now sent word by courier back to his wagon train not to follow his trail but to strike toward the south end of the Black Hills—his objective. Terry was to proceed northwest, while the steamer "Far West" would carry the sick and wounded down the river.

Before the steamer started, McGillycuddy applied for a substitute for his roan horse, which was lame and sore-backed. Crook assured the Doctor there was not an extra horse in the command but, since McGillycuddy had rendered valuable service in the campaign, he would issue an order sending him down the river as medical officer with the steamer. McGillycuddy thanked the general but said he had set out with the expedition and would like to see it through. Crook said he was glad to hear him say so.

As the two commands marched together toward Cabin Creek, rain began to fall. Wind whipped the blinding gusts, which by night became a deluge. Torrents poured mercilessly on the weary men as they rode into camp. There was no shelter in the valley and nothing but dark gumbo mud on which to spread blankets for the night. Rivulets of gold streaked the black heaven, followed by blasts of thunder. No one thought of supper; a place to sleep was the only consideration.

An ingenious trooper settled his saddle in the mud and, sitting down on it, pulled his poncho over his head. One by one officers and men followed his example until the valley was dotted with hillocks—hundreds of exhausted men astride saddles, the rain rattling a staccato on their ponchos.

Before the separation of the commands on the Heart River, Terry had arranged that Crook should make a detour to Fort Lincoln, in his department, and provision his troops for the long march to the Black Hills. At the head of the Heart River, one hundred and twenty-five miles northwest of Fort Lincoln, where camp was made, as McGillycuddy strolled along the bank he saw Crook sitting alone on a fallen tree trunk, his hands clasped around his knees. Crook called to the Doctor and asked just how far it was to Fort Lincoln. It was one hundred and twenty-five miles, McGillycuddy answered, and added that it was two hundred and twenty-five miles to the Black Hills. Crook said that some of the Ree scouts had said the Hills could be seen in two days and could be reached in four. The Doctor said to make the journey in less than ten days would be impossible and probably it would take twelve with the exhausted horses. The general asked if he relied on the maps. McGillycuddy could not restrain a smile as he answered that he ought to, since he had made them himself the year before. Crook obviously was anxious to go directly to the Hills instead of making a detour into Terry's department to provision his command for the long march; but he said only: "Well, watch the guidons in the morning, McGillycuddy, and you'll see which way we are going."

The guidons of the cavalry lined to the south when the troops marched out at dawn. They were headed for Deadwood, two hundred and twenty-five miles away, with only pack-mule provisions, and not for Fort Lincoln for more supplies.

Two days passed, and the Black Hills did not come in sight. Rations were now reduced. On the distant hills small parties of Sioux could be seen watching the movements of the troops. From the peaks flashed signals to the hostiles encamped behind the hills. The horses, reduced in forage and growing weaker day by day, stumbled on the trail. Trooper after trooper asked permission to drop out of line to rest his weary mount. They chatted with the horses on the hardships of the march, as they stroked their gaunt rumps and rubbed bacon fat on their saddle-worn backs. A fallen animal often gathered courage from his master's voice and staggered to his feet, only to fall a moment later, whinnying feebly. The order to shoot all abandoned horses to prevent them from falling into the hands of the Indians was rescinded when the reports of the rifles growing more frequent each day cast a gloom over the command. Throughout the night tottering hoof-beats told that some tired animal had struggled to its goal, and at dawn an undulating line of crippled beasts, refusing to be reckoned among the vanquished, could be seen still plodding bravely toward camp.

Tom Moore, the pack-mule wizard, inspecting the mules at night, placed a white chalk cross on the saddle above any newly acquired sore, indicating the places where his assistants should cut holes in the saddle-pads. Following his example, the troopers did the same for the horses.

Rations were eked out to the fifth day, when the order was given to kill nine of the horses. Prairie dogs had been tried for food but had brought on sickness. Officers and men shared the prejudice against eating horse flesh; it seemed a betrayal of friendship. The horses were comrades, with whom they had exchanged confidences on the hardships of the trail. But sentiment had to yield when it was a question of life and death, and after some hesitation the troopers were seen trudging to the mess tent with "quarters of beef" slung over their shoulders, the metal shoes shining in the moonlight. Mush made from the prickly-pear plant gave a finishing touch to the diet.

Instead of marching in column with any particular troop, McGillycuddy acted as a sort of outrider, passing here and there along the line. One morning as he rode toward the rear he saw three men dismounted, one of whom lay on the ground. Lieutenant Huntington was doubled up with cramps. The Doctor gave him the usual prescription; but the pain continued, and he resorted to morphine. Troop after troop passed, offering assistance; but McGillycuddy thought Huntington would soon be able to mount and they would overtake the command. Instead of improving, however, Huntington grew steadily worse. The mounted rear guard marched by, gathering up the stragglers—a necessary precaution, as exhausted troopers loitering along the way were in danger of being picked up by stray bands of Indians following in search of plunder. There was no ambulance for conveying the sick officer.

By noon, when his pain had not abated, Huntington urged the Doctor to leave him and push on with the orderlies. They had better save themselves, he said—no use letting the Indians get them all. McGillycuddy refused to leave. He would not sleep well if he left Huntington alone on the prairie, he said. A dark spot in the distance suggested the possibility of a group of trees, toward which the Doctor and an orderly rode, to find the suspicion correct. Some saplings were cut and dragged to the spot where Huntington lay. After lashing them into a travois, they placed the sick officer on it. Huntington's Kentucky thoroughbred, still proud after the long march, resented having to serve as a draught-horse; and it required much persuasion to start him off with the travois at his heels.

The small party followed the trail of the soldiers, mile after mile over the ridges. As they mounted each rise of the sparse, rough country with its squat, undistinguished hills, McGillycuddy peered ahead into shadowed regions hoping to sight the main body; but the late afternoon dropped into night without his doing so. At about nine o'clock, when they had almost despaired of finding their comrades, they heard the measured tread of cavalry horses. The advancing party also heard the thump, thump of the travois on the rough ground.

"Who goes there?" came in Captain Rowell's voice through the darkness.

"The wounded train," McGillycuddy responded.

It had not been discovered until roll call that the officer, the surgeon, and two privates were missing. Crook had ordered a troop to follow back six miles on the trail and fire two signal shots. If there was then no answer, they should take it for granted that the missing party had been captured by the Indians.

The expedition was in a desperate condition by this time. Crook ordered Captain Anson B. Mills, with a detachment of one hundred and fifty of the best-conditioned troops, to push on to Crook City, one hundred miles distant, purchase supplies, and rush them out to the army, its animals worn out and its men exhausted by fifteen hundred miles of hard campaigning and having only two days' rations left.

Mills had gone about twenty miles when he was warned by Grouard, a scout, that there were Indians camped in the valley of the Slim Buttes. The sky was already darkening, and Mills decided to hide his men for the night in a canyon one and a half miles to the rear and attack at daybreak. In the fog-laden dawn a mustang stallion sniffed the air, snorted, and headed down the bank, followed by the troops. A trumpeter sounded the charge on the left, and twenty-five men raced toward the Indian village. Captain Mills and Von Leutwitz led the center infantry, Lieutenant Crawford the right. They rushed upon the sleeping redskins, firing, jabbing, and swearing at the half-clad forms which leapt from the ground and, slashing the backs of the tents, fought their way into a tortuous gorge on the west bank of Rabbit Creek. From there, American Horse Number Two, sometimes called Iron Shield, with his followers, who had been unable to flee farther, commanded a view of the valley.

The sun rose on a tattered village of thirty-seven lodges, in one of which Von Leutwitz, who had fallen by Mills' side with a slug in his knee, was laid. Private Kennedy also was seriously wounded. In the lodges were discovered several saddles from Custer's equipment, three guidons which had led the Fighting Seventh to death, and a good supply of dried meats and fruits, most welcome to the famished soldiers.

Mills ordered entrenchments thrown up on the high-cut bank against hostile bands which he felt certain were lurking near. At about ten o'clock Crook arrived with the doctors and the least unfit of his command, the remainder straggling into camp during the day.

While Von Leutwitz was being made as comfortable as possible on the ground in preparation for the amputation of his leg, McGillycuddy passed across the opening of the gulch on his way to get something from his saddlebag. He hustled back from exposure when a bullet whizzed past his head.

Mills had been satisfied to leave the Indians in the twisted gorge, but Crook determined to bring them out. He detailed two hundred men for the work, and three thousand rounds of ammunition were poured into the gulch, but the squaws had thrown up breastworks which the bullets did not penetrate. Grouard called on the entrenched Indians to surrender, promising amnesty from the general; but except for a volley of bullets no sound issued from the gorge.

Charlie White, a pal of Buffalo Bill who was known as Buffalo Chips, determined to put a bullet into the leader of the entrenched Indians. He stole cautiously up the slope, his belly hugging the ground as he reached the top of the hill and, with gun aimed, peered over the edge. The wham of a bullet cut the air, and Buffalo Chips threw his arms across his breast crying, "They've got me boys." In a moment he lay still with a shot in his brain.

Ignited poles were thrown into the gorge in an attempt to burn the Indians out; but this method met with no success. In the early afternoon a message was sent from the gulch that a wounded Indian was to be brought up. Soon two squaws were seen carrying a buck, American Horse, with a bright-colored blanket wrapped about his abdomen. He was laid on the grass, and McGillycuddy, aided by the squaws in carefully removing the blood-soaked blanket, found the Indian's intestines spilling out of a gunshot wound. The teeth of the Indian were tightly set, his lips rigid. The Doctor took out his instruments and prepared to give him a hypodermic. Some soldiers standing by began to grumble: "Put a knife through the son-of-a-bitch." "I ain't got no use for a doctor that'll do anything for a goddam Injun." But McGillycuddy's hand was steady as he administered the hypodermic. Then he turned, his Irish blood boiling, and swore as volubly as any trooper while he told them what he thought of anyone who could see man or animal suffer without giving aid.

About four o'clock, while the troops lay scattered along the valley for a mile or more, taking a much-needed rest, the surgeons were occupied in amputating Von Leutwitz's leg. The lieutenant lay on the grass, the surgeons kneeling beside him. The sun dropped below the horizon and splashed the sky with purple, gold, and crimson, tinseling the Great Plains. The doctors' eyes strained in the waning light, but their hands worked nimbly. There was a faint buzz of saw on bone. Suddenly, limned against the kindled sky, a line of yelling savages appeared at the top of

Harney's Peak
(see page 39)

Surgeon McGillycuddy
on "starvation march"

Skinning a horse on
"starvation march"

Lieutenant Huntington on
improvised Indian travois

the buttes, their war paint glistening and their eagle feathers waving in the wind. A chief, galloping up and down on a gray pony, exhorted his warriors to attack.* With wild war whoops they charged down the ridges. "Deploy skirmish-line!" shouted Crook. Instantly the sixteen hundred soldiers formed and advanced against the hostiles. The surgeons continued at their work.

The war chief now scanned the advancing troops—sixteen hundred instead of the one hundred and fifty reported by the Indians who had escaped from Mills' attack and fled to his camp on the Little Missouri. To exterminate a hundred and fifty soldiers was one thing; to battle sixteen hundred was another matter, and, after the exchange of a few shots, the Sioux, filling the air with war whoops, turned their ponies up the bluffs and disappeared into the sunset's crimson glow.

American Horse, who had slept quietly under the influence of morphine during the engagement, died soon after. Sergeant Kennedy died later in the night. A grave was dug in the lodge which had served for a hospital, the earth carefully smoothed and the tent fired in order to prevent the Indians from finding and mutilating the private's body. Buffalo Bill and some of his comrades climbed up the slope to where Buffalo Chips lay, and placed his body in a grave cautiously concealed with brush. Over it, too, a pile of ashes smoldered as the camp broke up the following morning.

McGillycuddy was now placed in charge of the wounded-train, consisting of nine travois and three horse-litters, most of them made by the soldiers while in camp at Slim Buttes. A travois was dragged by a single horse, while a litter was swung on the backs of two horses. The wounded were strapped to these rough vehicles with surcingles, pack-mules were loaded, and the army pushed on.

---

* Crook thought it was Crazy Horse who directed the attack, though the Indians were too far off to distinguish definitely. It is claimed by some that Sitting Bull led the warriors.

As they pulled out, Crazy Horse's band swooped into the abandoned camp in search of booty, then followed the command, harassing them intermittently. Three men were wounded soon after they began the march. Mills, with a picked body, pushed on to Crook City, eighty miles distant, for provisions.

A rear guard was deployed in skirmish-line formation to pick up any troopers who had lingered by the way. The heavy cavalry boots were torturing. Too exhausted to care what happened to them, men hid in the brush or behind rocks, praying they would be unobserved and gain a chance to rest. Now, roused by the guard's "Git out'a there," a weary soldier pleaded: "For Gawd's sake leave me be, can't ye, sergeant. I can't go on; my feet's so sore."

"Damn it, don't y' know what'll happen t' ye if I leaves ye here? D' ye want t' be scalped by the goddam Injuns?"

"I don't care. All I want's rest."

A prod of the heel or a prick of a bayonet forced the exhausted man to his feet.

The horses carrying the litters were worried frequently into breaking step, which eased the bouncing of their loads. McGilly-cuddy rode or walked beside the hospital train, adjusting bandages, dealing out medicines, and offering encouragement to the patients.

Suddenly, over the prairie, supposedly devoid of game, raced four antelope toward the troops. Without waiting for permission, the troopers opened fire and the antelope fell riddled with bullets. The men broke ranks and rushed upon the torn animals. Those first on the spot seized them by the legs, lifted them from the ground, and slashed off pieces of flesh from the still quivering creatures and thrust the morsels in their bags.

"Goddamity, goddamity," issued often from Von Leutwitz' lips on the forty-mile march from Owl Butte to Crow Creek, the longest march which had been attempted in a day. To add to the discomfort of the troops, a drizzling rain set in. As darkness came on, the wounded-train halted.

"We've got to shtop," roared Von Leutwitz, "so I can rest. I'm worn out."

The Doctor said he was sorry, but they couldn't stop; and he repeated the order to push on.

"This sergeant belongs in my troop and he'll take orders from me," Von Leutwitz shouted.

"I'm in charge of the wounded-train and am the only one to give orders," the Doctor said.

A mob of dismounted cavalry, wet to the skin, passed by, ready for trouble. Among them was a sergeant, his chevrons scarcely visible in the darkness, who apparently had gone crazy. He jumped up and down in the mud, screaming: "I'm tired; I'm damn tired; I was never so goddam tired in my life; but by God I'd walk forty miles further to dance on the grave of the idiot who got——"

A voice in the darkness interrupted his raving: "Ain't you ashamed of yourself to talk like that about the——"

"Put a head on the fool that's interferin'!" a soldier yelled from the rear line. Exhaustion alone prevented a general row.

At ten o'clock the last of the bedraggled trops reached camp on Crow Creek. Canvas was laid on the slimy mud and blankets were placed on top. The weary men crawled in; but the beds became soaked, and there was little sleep that night.

There was wild rejoicing when Mills arrived the following morning with provisions from the Hills. The famished soldiers tore open the flour sacks, shouting at the prospect of flapjacks; but their faces turned grim when they found there was but a limited supply of baking powder. They decided to make the best of it and mixed the batter, when there came the realization that there was nothing on which to fry them. An enterprising trooper then suggested making a skillet by melting the solder joining the two sections of a canteen. The experiment proved successful, and the camp feasted on sodden flapjacks. Only the doctors ate sparingly, while they warned against the orgy and reminded the others that all would be asking for pills.

After forty-eight hours of doling out laxatives the surgeons again urged the men to use caution when they came upon an oasis of wild plums and berries; but it was of no avail. McGillycuddy was glad it was not a laxative that was needed this time, for the supply had been exhausted.

As the ragged army marched into Crook City they were greeted by a delegation from Deadwood, among whom was Calamity Jane, dressed in her usual cowboy costume, a Winchester rifle slung across her saddle, the saddlebags vibrating with the bucking of her bronco. Also California Joe, as quiet and undemonstrative as ever, had come out on foot with his hound at his heels to meet his old friends.

General Crook and Calamity Jane led the grand march at the dance given at the McDaniels Theatre to celebrate the arrival of the troops in Deadwood. Calamity planted a kiss on the Doctor's cheek as they danced a schottische, shuffling through the crowd on the dance floor. Her legs still were steady, for she carried her liquor like a man. McGillycuddy scarcely could keep his balance as they cavorted through the half-drunken mob, Calamity shrieking at old pals and slapping them on the back as they passed. The Doctor was glad to rest when the raucous music stopped and a corporal jerked Calamity into his own arms.

Seth Bullock now sat down beside McGillycuddy. Seth, tall and spare, with a long, flowing, blonde mustache, was the first sheriff of Deadwood. He had come from Montana, where he had served in the territorial legislature and on the vigilance committee. He was typical of the finest men of the West. He remarked that Calamity Jane was a star performer—as tough as they make them but, with the tenderest heart in the world, she would help anyone in trouble. One evening, he said, Calamity, drunk as usual, had joined a street-corner crowd to see what was going on. A man was holding forth from a dry-goods-box platform. Calamity had drawn closer, wondering what brand of patent medicine the orator was peddling. She had stood listening for some time, catching phrases strange to her ears: "Come to Jesus . . . . Save your souls from the hell-fires that's waiting for sinners." Calamity had shifted from one foot to the other—it was a habit of hers. Finally, she seemed to catch on: "Gee, fellers, he's a sky pilot frum God's country," she cried. "Lissen t'him . . . . get on t'what he's sayin'. He's tryin' ter git ye for Jesus . . . . he says Jesus needs money . . . . Jesus needs help . . . . dig inter them pokes o'yours and git out th'dust!"

She had grabbed a hat from the man standing nearest and passed among the crowd, screeching, "Dig up. Jesus needs money. Jesus needs help. Dig up!" When she had finished the canvass, she had gone to the preacher and had poured two hundred and fifty dollars' worth of gold dust into his hat.

It was late when Calamity jostled up to McGillycuddy again and asked him if he had heard about Wild Bill's murder. He told her he had not heard of it until he had reached Crook City. She then said: "It wus that good-fer-nothing loafer, Jack McCall, done it . . . . shot 'im in the back, the only way anybody'd ever uv got Wild Bill, he wus that quick on the trigger." She went on to relate how Bill had gone into the Number Ten saloon one afternoon when Bill Utter and two men were sitting at a table. They had called him to come and take a hand at poker, but Bill had shaken his head. There was but one empty chair at the table and that was back to the door. It was Bill's custom to face doors; he also stood always at the end of the bar—never in the center. After his refusal to join the game he had sauntered over to the table, sat down, and taken a hand. Jack McCall had passed the saloon where the door stood open wide enough for him to see Bill sitting there, back to him. He had slipped up to his room over a saloon a few steps down the street, seized his revolver, and returned to the Number Ten saloon. There he had swung the door farther open and yelled, "Look out fellers!" The four men had sprung up; but before Bill could turn, the bullet had hit him in the head. "He just sprawled over the table—never said a word. He was dead when they turned him over."

Since there was no organized court in Deadwood at the time,

McCall had been tried by a committee of citizens assembled hurriedly. McCall had claimed that Wild Bill had killed his brother and threatened to kill him also and said he had promised his mother to shoot Bill in revenge for his brother's death. He had been found not guilty and had left the town immediately. Some of Wild Bill's closest friends had arrived in Deadwood soon after and had taken up the matter before the grand jury in Yankton, with the result that McCall had been indicted for murder. A deputy marshal sent to Texas where McCall had been located had brought McCall back for trial in the United States Court at Yankton, where he had been found guilty of murder and hanged.

"They found him guilty 'cause he shot him in th' back, the son-of-a-bitch," Calamity said, the tears rolling down her cheeks. She was drunk. She rambled on about Preacher Smith, whom the Indians had killed as he walked out of Deadwood alone with his Bible under his arm. He was a good man who had come to Deadwood to save the souls of the frontiersmen, "and they sure need savin'," she added.

When the last stragglers came out of the hall, McGillycuddy was among them. Tired as he was, he had enjoyed the happy crowd after the hardships of the march. He liked to dance, and he did not know that he danced badly. He had had little time for amusement. Besides, his medical services had been enlisted many times during the night—women as well as men drunk—a black eye—a smashed nose. He had made up for lost time by staying to the last. Calamity Jane left the hall at the same time, looking young in spite of the sickly gray dawn, though drink was hardening her face. Her slim body was boyish in chaps and leather jacket. She walked down the street with the Doctor and dropped into Al Sweringen's dance hall, where gamblers still sat at poker, while McGillycuddy continued his way to the camp.

After a brief rest Crook's command set out on the march to Fort Robinson, where the various regiments were distributed among the posts in the department, and McGillycuddy was assigned to duty as assistant post-surgeon at Fort Robinson.

Chapter 6

THE KILLING OF CRAZY HORSE

With the disbanding of Crook's command in October a new expedition with fresh troops of the Fourth Cavalry commanded by General Ranald McKenzie, with California Joe as chief scout and guide, was organized to go north and round up scattered bands of Sioux and Cheyennes operating along the base of the Big Horn Mountains. On the afternoon of the day before the expedition was to leave Fort Robinson, McGillycuddy dropped in to the barroom of the sutler's store, where miners, cowboys, soldiers, hunters, and scouts were congregated. Joe was among them and already under the influence of liquor. Tom Newcomb, a butcher employed in the Quartermaster Department, came in. For some time there had been bad blood between him and California Joe, growing out of charges and countercharges as to the killing the previous winter of a well-known French squawman, John Richard, proprietor of a whisky camp on the Niobrara River. The two men had threatened to shoot on sight.

As Newcomb saw Joe standing at the bar, he pulled his gun. The crowd scattered, yelling, "Look out, Joe!" Joe whirled, pulling out his gun; but neither fired. "Oh, hell," he said, "put up yer gun and hev a drink." The crowd, seeing Joe and Tom shake hands and drink together, gathered again at the bar.

As McGillycuddy left the saloon, Joe joined him and they walked together toward the hospital. Joe asked the Doctor if he were not going out with the expedition, and McGillycuddy said he was not, adding that he had had enough roughing it for a while. Joe said he had better come along; he reckoned there'd be some fun. The Doctor went up the steps of the hospital and sat down in a rocking-chair on the porch, and the old scout disappeared around the corner of the quartermaster's corral several hundred feet farther on.

Only a few minutes elapsed before the Doctor heard a shot in the direction which Joe had taken. He started off and met a soldier, who saluted and said, "Joe's shot, sir." The old scout was lying on his face when the Doctor reached him. A crowd had collected, talking excitedly. From the confusion McGillycuddy gathered that Newcomb's "making up" had been only a bluff. He had come around the corner looking for Joe and, seeing the scout, had fired. Some soldiers near by had seen Joe throw up his hands, exclaiming, "My God, what is it?" as he fell on his face. He was dead when the Doctor got there.

The body was carried to the hospital and McGillycuddy performed an autopsy. In an inside pocket of Joe's coat, wrapped in a piece of old oil silk, he found a worn card bearing Joe's real name and the date and place of his birth. Until then his real name had been a mystery. As McKenzie's expedition marched past the hospital the following morning, with guidons flying and trumpets sounding, California Joe's body lay in a coffin, wrapped in the United States flag, in front of the building. He had been out on his last expedition. He was buried on the bank of the White River, a red cedar board bearing the inscription:

MOSES EMBREE MILNER (CALIFORNIA JOE)

BORN IN STRATFORD, KENTUCKY, 1829

MURDERED OCTOBER 29TH, 1876

Tom Newcomb was arrested and confined in the guardhouse. Under the government laws established over the unorganized frontier lands, in the absence of a court of justice, a criminal was to be placed in the nearest guardhouse and the authorities of the adjacent organized county to the east were to be notified. If the prisoner was not called for by those authorities within four days, he was to be released. No one called for the murderer of California Joe. Except for the rigid discipline of the army, Newcomb would have been lynched upon his release. He disappeared immediately from that region.*

McGillycuddy now applied for leave of absence without pay. He wished to go to Detroit to bring his wife to the post. General Crook arranged instead that he should be commissioned to take an insane soldier to the National Asylum in Washington, thereby furnishing him traveling expenses and salary. The Doctor wired Fanny to meet him in Chicago. They would enjoy a visit together in the capital.

Upon his return to Fort Robinson with his wife the Doctor resumed his duties as assistant post surgeon, which consisted of caring for patients in the post itself, in two outside cantonments, and in two Indian camps. Dr. Munn, the surgeon in charge, confined his practice to the hospital.

The round of sick calls began at seven in the morning. On a bitterly cold day in December as the doctor paid his visit to one of the cantonments and had gone into a cabin, he was startled by a shot near by. He hurried to the door, and the orderly pointed to the cabin in which the shot had been fired. The guard was rushing in. McGillycuddy followed. Sergeant Casey lay wounded on the floor, and a private crouched in a cot. Casey was carried to the hospital, and the private was taken to the guardhouse. Casey explained that he had disciplined the soldier the previous day for drunkenness. When the man was absent at reveille, Casey had gone to discover the reason. "I made a foine target," he said, "standin' there in the doorway. The man nivir sed a wurd, jest let fly." The ball had entered the Sergeant's left side under the collarbone, shattering two ribs. A cough developed and grew worse steadily; fever set in; and at the end of six weeks Casey was dead.

* Fifty years later, in Berkeley, California, McGillycuddy was visited by an old acquaintance who told him that, happening to mention the Doctor's name to a man he had met recently in Montana, the stranger had asked if it was the Dr. McGillycuddy who had served with Crook in 1876. When told that he was, the stranger had remarked: "If you see him again you might mention that you met Tom Newcomb; but he won't be pleased to hear of me."

In performing an autopsy McGillycuddy scratched his finger on a splintered rib but thought nothing of it until his hand began to swell. The swelling extended up his arm; he turned a greenish color, and his pulse ran up to one hundred and twenty—a clear case of blood-poisoning. The temperature out of doors was about twenty-five below zero. There were five sick calls to be made daily, the most distant at a camp three miles away at the Red Cloud Agency. Surgeon Munn was ill frequently; McGillycuddy could not ask him to take his calls. On the contrary, it was necessary often that he should attend the hospital cases as well as his own. He decided that he might as well keep going; he would recover or be dead in a few days. His head reeled. He staggered when as reveille sounded Fanny helped him into his clothes and brought him a dish of canned pears, the only thing he could eat. His skin, the whites of his eyes, and his nails turned tobacco color. His teeth chattered as Hocksmith, the orderly, helped him to his saddle. For a week his life seemed hanging in the balance; but then he improved, his pulse slowed down, and his rainbow-tinted body resumed its natural color.

He had scarcely recovered when, on his return from one of the cantonments, he found the trader from the Red Cloud Agency waiting to see him. His wife was very ill, he said; had been sick since five o'clock; the baby wouldn't come. As he rode with the trader to the Agency McGillycuddy remarked that it was not usual for an Indian woman to have a doctor in confinement. The trader said it was not. Many a time he had seen a squaw drop out of line in a long march and disappear in the bushes with one or two women following. It wouldn't be more than an hour or two, after they had gone into camp, before the squaws would come trudging along, the new mother carrying her papoose on her back. The trader didn't know what was the matter with his wife.

A heap of sagebrush burned outside the trader's lodge. A group of medicine men crouched around it droning incantations to Wakantanka. A drum beat out its solemn tum, tum, tum, as the doctor bent his long, lean body and passed into the lodge. The smell of the tent was stifling. McGillycuddy told the trader to fasten back the tent flap. The girl lay on a pile of buffalo robes, half a dozen old squaws around her. Her mother was among them. Their bodies stank. Sweat rolled down the girl's face. One hundred and thirty—the Doctor counted her pulse. He would have to make an examination, he said. The squaws muttered their disapproval. He asked the girl's age. The trader said she was eighteen. The Doctor repeated that an examination was necessary. After the trader had argued some time with the squaws, they stopped their mutterings.

The child was dead, the Doctor said presently. He would have to make a delivery with instruments. The squaws grumbled and shook their heads. McGillycuddy told them the girl would die if he did not take the child. "It will bring down the anger of the Great Spirit," the trader interpreted their protests. The Doctor told them to think it over; he would come back when they sent for him, but they must remember the girl would not live long unless the child was delivered.

At midnight a young buck, holding a sweating pony, tapped at the Doctor's door and by signs which McGillycuddy understood urged him to hurry to the trader's lodge. The Doctor's surgical case stood on a table in the hall. He jumped on the bare-backed pony and was off, leaving the courier behind. The bridge over White River creaked as he galloped across. The sagebrush fire outside the lodge emitted but fitful coils of holy smoke as the Doctor rode up to the lodge on the panting horse. The medicine men were silent.

A fire burned inside the tent. Sweat poured from the faces of the squaws. Telling them to put out the fire, McGillycuddy pulled off his coat. There was a hissing and a splattering of ashes as Calloff poured water on the flame. The girl lay unconscious on the buffalo robes. Then, piece by piece, he removed the bones of the skull of the child. "Hump-hump-hump," the squaws muttered. McGillycuddy worked on. When he had finished and the girl slept quietly, he asked them what they did when babies didn't come.

"They always come," the mother answered.

"This time it didn't," the Doctor said.

"That's because she married a white man," the mother explained. "Their heads are too big. It serves her right."

The medicine men outside the lodge spoke in low tones as the Doctor came from the lodge. He asked the trader what they were saying.

"They are saying, 'How Wasicu Wakan.' They think you are a miracle man."

Fanny and the Doctor were enjoying life at the post when in March a report came of attacks made on settlers in the Black Hills by Indians. Four troops of the Third Cavalry under Major P. D. Vroom, with McGillycuddy as surgeon, were ordered to the Hills to protect them. Fanny preferred to go with the Doctor rather than remain at the post, though she would be the only woman in the camp; and she rode out with the command on a cold morning, wearing a long green riding habit. A beaver jacket and cap protected her from the bitter wind that whistled up the gulches as they journeyed the one hundred and eighty miles to the foothills and went into camp on False Bottom Creek, fourteen miles from Deadwood. Their tents were pitched and their Sibley stoves set up before nightfall. After a dinner of roast beef and vegetables cooked in Dutch ovens and served in the mess tent, the Doctor and his wife crawled into their beds of buffalo robes spread on the ground and slept soundly.

Snowbirds twittered merrily as the sun rose next morning and Fanny left the tent at the summons of the Doctor. An old buffalo bull stood solitary on a cliff—driven out of the herd, the Doctor explained, superseded by younger animals. He gazed dumbly across the snow-covered valley as if in search of his former comrades.

Weeks passed without any engagements with the hostiles. The snowdrifts thawed under the spring sun by noon, only to be frozen over again on cold nights. To break the monotony of camp life the Doctor proposed one morning that he and Fanny ride to Deadwood, make a few purchases, and return the following day. Their horses were fresh, and they galloped up the hills and across the valleys until they reached the top of a high mountain sloping precipitately to the town. Melting snow flowed slushily as the riders zigzagged down the slope. Occasionally the horses slipped and floundered in the mud, but invariably they regained their footing. As they rode down into Deadwood Gulch and up the street to the hotel, a man standing on the rough boardwalk remarked that he had been watching them come down the precipice and all he'd got to say was that they had more sand than sense.

It was pleasant after the life in camp to wander along the walk on Main Street with its rough, squat buildings and watch the people going in and out of the little shops, hurrying here and there. Beautiful bleached blondes with painted faces ambled wistfully here and there. Long bull-teams shambled down the streets of the town, the bull-whackers cracking their whips and swearing loudly—the only language bulls understood. Children dragging their sleds up Forest Hill to the west of the town or sliding down at breakneck speed frequently slipped into melting snowdrifts. The limestone peaks of the White Rocks toward the east glistened in the sunlight. Low log houses perched on the sides of the hills or huddled on the narrow streets. The mining town overflowed with youth and hope. It seemed to the two young people who had camped for several weeks on False Bottom Creek to be bursting with life.

Seth Bullock, the gentlemanly sheriff, came down the street and greeted the Doctor, who introduced him to Fanny. Seth's long blond mustache flared in the wind which whistled up the gulch. He gave the Doctor the latest news of the town, which he had seen only three months earlier after the "Starvation March" with Crook.

Long sociable tables stood in the dining room of the hotel. As McGillycuddy and his wife went in to supper, Seth Bullock sat at one of the tables with a man with long, sandy whiskers and blue eyes. Seth introduced the newcomers to him, General Dawson, the revenue collector, who talked of the difficulty of collecting taxes from people who were not exactly citizens—people who had stolen into the Hills in defiance of the treaty with the Indians.

The young town looked drab as the Doctor and Fanny rode away at dawn. Men and women dragged heavy steps from the dance halls and saloons, looking pallid in the gray light. At the street corner some people were congregated, and they rode up to see what was the cause of interest. McGillycuddy recognized Calamity Jane, with bleary eyes, standing on one foot and then the other. A young boy sat on the sidewalk with his feet in the gutter. One felt he was young, though his face was buried in his hands. The crowd stood aloof and stared at the forlorn figure. The Doctor heard Calamity's drink-befogged voice: "Say, fellers, whazze matter wizze kid?"

He's got the smallpox, someone answered.

"Geez," she exclaimed, her voice thick, "ain't that hell! What're goin' ter do wiz him?" No one answered. Smallpox was greatly dreaded in the mushroom metropolis, which possessed no hospital.

Calamity balanced on one foot and then on the other and eyed the bent young back with the solemn look of the half-inebriated, then stepped over to the boy and touched him on the shoulder: "Heven't ye enny place ter go? Ain't there ennyone ter take ker o'ye?"

"Ye ain't cryin' is ye, kid?" She turned to the crowd and said: "Say, boys, put a coupla shakedowns in that ol' cabin up the hill and I'll take ker o'him."

She raised the boy from the sidewalk and, with her arm around him, climbed the hill to the shack.

The Doctor and Fanny rode on—there was nothing they could do about it. For some time, neither spoke. Then the Doctor recalled incidents of his former acquaintance with Calamity. He spoke of her kindness to anyone in trouble, as well as of her utter recklessness and lack of morals, expressing his opinion that there was much more real feeling in the hearts of the average rough human beings of the West than in those of more cultured centers. He was still relating some of Calamity's exploits when they reached a ranch along the trail back to False Bottom Creek. They stopped to ask the best way to proceed to the camp. Should they follow the trail or was there a less precipitous route? The rancher said there was no easier way than the trail they were following, but warned against their going on. There were two men in his cabin who had been wounded by the Indians—the hills were full of them. McGillycuddy said he was a doctor and asked if there was anything he could do for the men. The rancher was delighted and invited them into the cabin.

The men were not seriously wounded; each had received a bullet in his leg. McGillycuddy dressed the wounds, while the rancher continued his protests against the continuance of their ride to False Bottom Creek: The Doctor certainly would not be so foolish as to take his wife through the Indian-infested country. But McGillycuddy said his wife had no more fear than he, and they went on their way. They saw no Indians as they galloped over the hills, and they reached the camp in time to share a meal of venison.

Camps were moved several times into regions from which reports of Indian invasions were received, but by the time the troops arrived depredators were nowhere to be seen. The Doctor inquired of a rider from Deadwood as to the fate of the boy ill with smallpox. He learned that each morning a fresh supply of food, fuel, and water was left near the cabin by some of the miners, but no one ventured inside. The fever ran high. The boy became delirious. He muttered of fears on the lonely mountain trails beset with dangers, of the silence of nights unbroken save by the cries of wild animals; and always he babbled of his search for gold. Calamity moistened his parched lips and tried to console him. The fever broke at last, but through the slow convalescence the youth fretted to be off once more in search of gold. The rider said he was in a saloon one morning when Calamity came in, bedraggled and unhappy. She had wakened to find her patient's bed empty. "He's gone looking fer gold," she said, "stinkin' gold."

The order to return to the post was rescinded when the troops, rejoicing to be off, had gone but a short distance to Gardiner's ranch. Complaints had been raised against their withdrawal, and an order had come for them to return to the troubled area. The continuance of the scare was unwarranted, however, and they were soon again on their way to Fort Robinson.

There was much talk at the post concerning the surrender of some of the Indians who had been engaged with Sitting Bull the previous summer. Many of them had been willing to exchange the life of hardship on the plains for a comfortable and well-fed existence at the agencies. Touch the Clouds, Roman Nose, and Red Bear, acting under the advice of Spotted Tail, had surrendered with one thousand of their bands and were located at the Spotted Tail Agency, while one hundred Cheyennes had surrendered at Fort Robinson.

Yet months of solicitation on the part of Crook had failed to induce Crazy Horse, the victorious warrior of the campaign, to come in. Spotted Tail, with two hundred of his head men, had been to Montana in the dead of winter to urge the advisability of surrender for the fugitives entrenched in the mountains; but Crazy Horse was still undecided, though he knew he could not remain long in his retreat. Only one of two courses lay open to him—surrender, or flight to British America.

Owing to the hardships of the winter, Crazy Horse's wife was seriously ill. The medicine men had practiced all their arts; but neither the sweat tepee nor their smoke pyres had brought relief from the cough which racked her body. This swayed the balance in favor of surrender rather than flight, for at an Indian agency doctors might perform some magic on his sick wife. There was also the consideration that the buffalo herds in the northwest were decreasing; these were fast yielding their empire to civilization.

At last, in May 1877, Crazy Horse, the young war lord, consented to come in. His arrival was anticipated with great interest, couriers daily reporting his approach. The prairies were covered with buffalo grass, dotted with innumerable spring flowers, when his band marched out of the serrated cliffs of the Rocky Mountains, and meadow larks burst into songs that did not ease the pain in the heart of the warrior as he pushed on to Fort Robinson with his thousand followers and surrendered. Yet the surrender was not made with submission; nor was it unconditional. It was with provisos, rather than petitions, that the war chief made terms with the white man. He had not been conquered; and even if his capture in the States had impended, there had been always the possibility of escape to British America. For the present he had chosen to come to Fort Robinson and was willing, for the time at least, to live on government beef instead of trusting to the precarious bounty of the plains and to relinquish his wornout skin lodges for handsome new duck tents.

Crazy Horse's first request was that an army doctor come to see his sick wife. McGillycuddy attended the ailing woman, his wife often accompanying him on his professional visits to the camp. Fanny aroused much curiosity on her visits to the Indian villages. The squaws hunched themselves from the ground and approached her, exclaiming with low, guttural grunts. She greeted them with a friendly smile, shook hands with the squaws, and patted a papoose slung in a beaded bag from its mother's back. But their attention was riveted on her long green riding skirt as she sat on her horse. At last the most venturesome of the women lifted her skirt a trifle and peeked under. She nodded to the others. Their suspicions were correct; the white woman had but one foot. They looked commiseratingly at her. When the Doctor came out from the lodge of his patient and helped Fanny off the horse, asking her to go inside, the commiserating looks turned to amused surprise. The white woman had two feet. They had not seen the leg under the third horn. Fanny was well known in the camps by the time Crazy Horse's wife was one of McGillycuddy's patients. Their daily calls became half social, and a friendship developed between the Doctor and the Indian war chief while Fanny chatted with the women and children.

But Crook, a past master in his dealings with the Indians, had a new problem in the victorious warrior of the Sitting Bull campaign. The young leader was neither a politician nor a diplomat. He was a fanatic, whose sole interest was the cause of his people. And, since his surrender, a new situation had arisen among the Sioux. The two chiefs, Spotted Tail and Red Cloud, had become jealous of the adored warrior. They had not anticipated the hero worship which invariably follows the return of a successful military leader. Victor in the Battle of the Rosebud, and eight days later in the great Custer Battle, Crazy Horse became the idol of the young fighting element of the Sioux and Cheyennes, numbering many thousands, and suffered from the jealousy of his old friends. He became restless.

To solve the problem, Crook contemplated the appointment of Crazy Horse as head chief of the Ogallalas, thereby supplanting Red Cloud. It was not long, however, before he realized that agency life palled on the young warrior, who asked no tolerance, sufferance, or protection from the white man. Though Crazy Horse had agreed to a treaty of peace, he retained the right of free life on his hunting grounds and the privilege of living on the game which those lands supplied—lands long possessed by his ancestors.

Unostentatious, unself-conscious, fanatical, Crazy Horse showed the sufferings of his people on his mystic face. With no ornaments symbolic of his chieftainship—no eagle feathers or warshirt, no paint or beadwork—his silent figure passed among the camps, invariably alone. Only his eye betokened the power of the leader. Indian youths rolling their hoops or engaged in a game of shinny stopped their sports as the silent warrior passed, apparently unconscious of their homage or even of their presence. The problems of his race engrossed him. He longed to be roving again with his people over the great prairies and mountain ranges, hunting buffalo and deer or fishing the streams. Agency life with its regulation of rations was no life for a warrior accustomed to the satisfaction of maintenance by effort. Even to return, empty-handed, from the chase and to feel the pangs of hunger while awaiting a more successful hunt was better than living the life of a squaw, sitting about a campfire. His restlessness was increased by messages continually brought him by runners from Sitting Bull, who had crossed the British American line in the month of his own surrender, urging him to escape and join Sitting Bull in the north. Always there were tales of the herds of buffalo, of venison cooked on campfires, and of trout leaping in the sunlight. The young warrior laid plans to be off, counting on a following of about two thousand Indians.

Crook, aware of Crazy Horse's restlessness, in a council held soon after his surrender promised the Indians a big buffalo hunt in the fall. The prospect had kept the chief more or less contented until the time for the expected hunt arrived and he saw no move toward the fulfillment of the promise. By that time the general had become doubtful of the advisability of allowing the Indians to indulge in their favorite sport. Also Spotted Tail opposed the plan. It was more than probable, he said, that many of the malcontents would leave the hunting party and escape into British America to join Sitting Bull. And the promise of the buffalo hunt, like many others made to the Indians, remained unfulfilled.

Crazy Horse's wife steadily improved in health; and as the friendship between him and the Doctor grew, he was led at last to talk of Indian wars. Though he seemed unwilling to speak of the campaign on the Little Big Horn, he was finally induced to do so. He told his story with no sign of boasting.

"No one got away," he said, "but the officer who put spurs to his horse and galloped to the east, and the Crow scout." Several warriors pursued the officer, but his horse was powerful and fleet and they soon gave up the chase to return to the fight. Just after they turned their horses a shot rang out in the direction of the fleeing officer and, looking back, they saw him fall from his horse. His foot caught in the stirrup, and the war-maddened animal plunged across the prairie dragging his rider behind him. If he hadn't shot himself, the chief said, he would probably have reached Terry's camp the next day.

Crazy Horse said there were two thousand women and children in the Little Big Horn Valley when Reno surprised them. He was reticent when asked concerning the mutilation of the bodies of Custer's command but finally said that all but three suffered mutilation. He had given strict orders that Custer's body should be untouched because he was the soldier-chief. There was some difficulty in deciding which was his body, since two other officers also were dressed in buckskin. Besides, Custer no longer wore the long hair nor the red shirt which had distinguished him from the rest. He at length was identified when maps and papers were found in his pockets.

Captain Keogh's body escaped mutilation for two reasons—the Indians knew and liked him well, and they found around his neck, when he was stripped, a silver charm, the Agnus Dei, which they looked upon as a holy charm.

The third unmutilated body was that of the little trumpeter who had visited the camps on the Missouri River and had become friendly with the Sioux. The squaws, to whom the rite of mutilation belonged, spared his corpse.

McGillycuddy asked Crazy Horse what had determined the abandonment of the stronghold in the Little Big Horn Valley. The chief explained that they had heard of the nearness of Terry's army through their scouts and had known that, once his forces joined with those of Crook's, which they had lately encountered, they would be overpowered. When told that Reno's command had seen the dust of his retreating party from their entrenchment on the bluffs Tuesday morning, the war-chief said: "It was not the dust we raised in our retreat which they saw. We left the valley as soon as darkness came on Monday night. It was the dust of *Wicanpi Yamini*'s army."

When Crook realized the disappointment as well as resentment in the heart of the war chief at the abandonment of the plan for the buffalo hunt, he shrewdly evolved a scheme of enlisting his services against another tribe of Indians, with whom Crazy Horse was not on friendly terms. These were the Nez Perces under Chief Joseph, whose reservation was in the Wallula Valley in Washington. Until that year their treaty rights had been observed, but in 1877 the settlers living on the fringe of the reservation waxed greedy for the lands in the fertile valley, and a reduction of their territory resulted. This led to a revolt of the hitherto peaceable tribe, who attacked the settlers, resisted the soldiers, and fled across Idaho into the mountains of Montana, where they were entrenched at this time.

Some old grudge existed between the Nez Perces and the Crazy Horse band. Crook recognized the value of this antagonism and hoped to enlist Crazy Horse's services against the common enemy. It not only would aid the military in their invasion of the retreat but would keep the young warrior occupied; and the general went to Fort Robinson on September 2 to formulate plans for co-operation. On the following day he proceeded with his staff to Crazy Horse's camp, taking the scout, Frank Grouard, as interpreter in the council which had been called.

There was unfriendliness between Crazy Horse and Grouard because of the latter's desertion of Sitting Bull, who had brought him up, early in the spring of 1876 when Sitting Bull went on the warpath. Grouard was despised by the Indians, who claimed that Sitting Bull had treated him as his own son. Grouard had doubly outraged them by taking service with Crook against them. It was unfortunate for Crazy Horse that this renegade scout acted as interpreter in the council, which broke up in misunderstanding and suspicion.

While the council was in session at the Indian village, McGillycuddy started for the camp on his usual professional visit. When halfway to the village, he saw an ambulance approaching at a rapid pace. General Crook leaned out as he neared the Doctor and ordered him to return at once to the post, saying it would not be safe for him to go on, since the Indians were in a hostile mood and were threatening to go on the warpath. McGillycuddy said he had seen the chiefs every day and they had shown no hostility. He pleaded for permission to go on; but it was refused.

Soon after dinner the Doctor was visited by Louis Bordeaux, who exclaimed, "There's goin' to be the devil to pay if this thing ain't straightened up." He went on to say that Grouard had misinterpreted Crazy Horse's words in the council. After the general had asked if Crazy Horse would go to Montana and fight for the government, Crazy Horse had risen and answered: "Myself and my people are tired of war. We have come in and surrendered to the Great Father and asked for peace. But now, if he wishes us to go to war again and asks our help, we will go north and fight till there is not a Nez Perces left." He had sat down amid a chorus of *"How, How,"* from the other chiefs. But Grouard had not interpreted the last part of the warrior's speech correctly, Bordeaux said. He had quoted Crazy Horse as saying: "We will go north and fight till there is not a white man left."

Bordeaux had wanted to tell the general of the mistake, but as soon as Grouard had finished speaking Crook and his staff had got up and walked out of the council lodge. The chiefs had not understood: They had been asked to become allies of the Great Father and had agreed to do so. They wondered why the white chief did not remain and make plans for the campaign. Bordeaux said that Grouard was afraid the Indians would kill him because of his desertion of Sitting Bull and, for that reason, wished to engage them in trouble with the government.

When Bordeaux departed, McGillycuddy went to Crook's quarters to tell him what he had said. But Crook had confidence in Grouard, who had served him as interpreter for a long time, and did not trust Crazy Horse. He departed the following morning for Fort Laramie, a distance of sixty-three miles to the west.

McGillycuddy asked permission to make his regular visit to the camp the next morning, hoping that in a private talk with

Crazy Horse he might get at the truth of Bordeaux's statement, which he thoroughly believed. Colonel Bradley, in command, refused his request, saying it would be unsafe for him to go to the village. McGillycuddy said he would take his wife with him to prove his faith in the chief. Bradley said he was crazy.

The second evening after his departure Crook sent orders to Bradley to send troops to the hostile village the following morning, arrest Crazy Horse, and hold him prisoner until further orders. McGillycuddy was detailed as surgeon with the command, which consisted of eight troops of cavalry, four hundred friendly Indians, and one piece of field artillery under Lieutenant Philo Clark.

Dark clouds scuttled across the sky; the hooves of the cavalry horses clattered up the valley, accompanied by the rumble of cannon wheels as the troops marched toward Crazy Horse's village. At a narrow defile entering the camp they encountered a lone horseman whose war bonnet of eagle feathers towered above his head and extended to the end of the horse's tail. The animal stood across the road leading into the camp. As the troops advanced, the warrior raised his hand crying: "This is the village of Crazy Horse; it is his ground; no soldier comes here."

It was a futile gesture. He was pushed roughly aside, and the troops marched on to the village or rather to the spot where, on the previous evening, the village had stood. Now, instead of a camp alive with fifteen hundred bucks, squaws, and children, not an Indian nor a lodge was in sight: Crazy Horse had got wind of the movement and, in the dark hours of night, silently had vanished with his band.

Bradley ordered a search among the Indian camps, but Crazy Horse was not to be found. It seemed that this land which he had fought to save for his people had opened its arms and encompassed him.

Early the next morning a courier arrived from the Spotted Tail Agency, forty-three miles to the east, with a message from Major Daniel Burke, commanding the troops at that agency, saying that

Crazy Horse had come to Spotted Tail's village. Bradley sent orders to arrest the chief and return him to Fort Robinson where he belonged. The courier reached the Agency at sundown. Burke summoned Spotted Tail and told him of the order. Spotted Tail replied that Crazy Horse was his guest: he was a chief, and he could not be taken prisoner; but if the soldier-chief wished to speak with him, they would come together and hold council. Burke asked that he bring Crazy Horse to his office at nine o'clock the next morning.

The two chiefs arrived according to agreement, and Crazy Horse was informed that General Bradley requested his return to Fort Robinson for a council. The warrior replied that he was willing to counsel. Burke asked Lieutenant Jesse M. Lee, Acting Agent at the Spotted Tail Agency, to accompany Crazy Horse to Fort Robinson, withholding from Lee the information that the chief was under arrest. Louis Bordeaux was sent as interpreter with the two, who left immediately for Fort Robinson in an ambulance accompanied by a mounted Indian escort.

Halfway to the post they lunched under the trees on Chadron Creek. After the meal was finished, Crazy Horse, sauntering along the stream, heard the tread of moccasined feet behind him. A look of surprise crossed the warrior's face as he said: "I see I am a prisoner." Without a word of protest he retraced his steps to the ambulance.

At Fort Robinson, Lee, Crazy Horse, and Bordeaux went to the adjutant's office and were received by Captain Kennington, officer of the day, to whom Lee reported that he had brought Crazy Horse to counsel with General Bradley. Kennington said he knew nothing of a council; his orders were to put Crazy Horse in the guardhouse. Bordeaux whispered to Lee that they had better get away. If they tried to put Crazy Horse in the guardhouse, the Indians would blame them for bringing him there. Lee suggested they go to see the Colonel; and they struck across the parade ground to his quarters, leaving the warrior with Kennington.

McGillycuddy was crossing the parade ground from his quarters on his way to the adjutant's office when he met Lee and Bordeaux, who seemed greatly disturbed. Lee remarked to the Doctor: "I'm not going to be made a goat of in this affair." As McGillycuddy approached the office he noticed a number of officers standing near. Before he reached the door it opened, and Kennington, Crazy Horse, and Little Big Man, who was serving as scout, came outside and turned toward the guardhouse. As Crazy Horse passed the Doctor, he greeted him with the friendly salutation, *"How kola."* The guardhouse door opened, the three entered, and the door was quickly closed. One of the officers said to the Doctor that the arrest had gone off smoothly enough; he guessed there would be no trouble after all.

Hardly had he spoken when the door flew open and Crazy Horse dashed out brandishing a knife in either hand. Captain Kennington grasped his left arm, Little Big Man his right, as Kennington cried, "Call out the guard!"

The officers scattered to company quarters, while the double guard of twenty men who had been stationed near the guardhouse drew in. Kennington loosed his hold on Crazy Horse and jumped to one side, while the guard immediately surrounded him. The chief lunged from side to side in his effort to escape through the circle. McGillycuddy saw one of the guard, a private of the Ninth Infantry, make a pass at him, and the chief fell to the ground writhing and struggling. The Doctor pushed his way through the guard and knelt by the warrior. Blood trickled from a wound above his right hip where the guard's bayonet had entered to traverse his abdomen. Froth oozed from his mouth; his pulse dropped rapidly; he was evidently mortally wounded.

McGillycuddy worked his way out of the crowd and explained to Kennington Crazy Horse's condition. Kennington replied that his orders had been to put the chief in the guardhouse and into the guardhouse he would go—the Doctor should take one leg, he'd take the other, a guard would take his head, and they'd put him in.

Several hundred Indians, mounted or on foot, were closing in on them, menacing in their attitude. The Doctor saw Grouard peering around the corner of the commissary building and beckoned him to come; but the interpreter shook his head and disappeared. McGillycuddy then saw his own interpreter, Johnny Provost, not far off, who answered his summons.

During the commotion Colonel Bradley had been pacing up and down the porch of his quarters several hundred feet across the parade ground. As Kennington and the Doctor started to raise the wounded chief, one of his warriors placed a hand on McGillycuddy's shoulder and motioned him to desist. At the same time the hostiles began loading their carbines and drawing toward them. Kennington accepted the Doctor's offer to report conditions to Bradley, who, after the situation was explained, answered that his orders were to be carried out. McGillycuddy returned and delivered the message.

Not far away, American Horse, one of the friendly Indians, sat mounted on his pony. The Doctor repeated the Colonel's message to him with the assurance that if the chiefs would consent to their taking Crazy Horse into the guardhouse he would care for him personally and give him every attention. American Horse replied that Crazy Horse was a chief and must not be put in prison.

Again McGillycuddy crossed to Bradley's quarters and reported the refusal of the friendly as well as the hostile Indians to allow the chief to be imprisoned. He suggested that, owing to the friendliness of the Indians toward him, he might be able to bring about a compromise and put the dying chief in the adjutant's office. He would not last the night, he said. Bradley consented to the compromise.

McGillycuddy then rejoined American Horse, who, when he heard of the change of plan, jumped off his pony and spread his blanket on the ground beside Crazy Horse; and, motioning some of the young bucks to come forward, he helped them lift him gently on the blanket and carry him into the adjutant's office.

"It was one of the knives on the soldiers' guns that wounded me," the warrior said, writhing in agony. "It passed across my body. I shall die before sunup." Morphine relieved his pain for a time.

On account of the general disturbance among the fifteen thousand Sioux surrounding the post, the entire garrison of eight hundred men was kept on picket all night. Attempts at reprisal were feared.

Until sundown the Indians were allowed in the post; they came continually to the office to inquire Crazy Horse's condition. After retreat, only his father, an old chief of eighty years, and his mother's uncle, Touch the Cloud, a chief of the Minnecoujou Sioux whose name was inspired by his great height of nearly seven feet, were allowed to remain.

On a pile of blankets in a corner of the office the young chief lay dying. His father stood near, his face drawn. "We were not agency Indians," he said. "We belonged in the North on the buffalo ranges. We did not want the white man's beef; we asked only to live by hunting and fishing. But during the winter the Gray Fox* continually sent runners to us saying, 'Come in, come in.' We have come in, and hard times are upon us. My son was a brave man; only thirty-six winters have passed over him. Red Cloud was jealous of him. We were getting tired of his jealousy and would not have remained here long." The old man stood with arms folded across his breast, his eyes fastened on his son's face.

The long evening wore on. The office, dimly lighted by an ill-smelling kerosene lamp, was dismal. The monotony of the watch was broken occasionally by the entrance of the officer of the day and the officer of the guard. The Doctor scarcely left the side of the patient.

As the effect of the morphine wore off, a look of recognition appeared in Crazy Horse's fast-dimming eyes. A half-stifled

* General Crook.

groan passed his lips, as he said feebly, *"How kola."* Another hypodermic eased his pain. It was no use to let him suffer, the Doctor said to the two old chiefs, who sat on the floor at the far end of the room; he would die soon. The old men grunted approval.

Outside the office could be heard the rhythmic march of the sentry, his measured tread mocking the stertorous breathing of the dying warrior. At last through the chill night air taps sounded from the sentry before the guardhouse. Now Crazy Horse roused from his lethargy. The significance of the notes he was beyond understanding. A bugle call now meant but one thing to the half-conscious warrior—the summons of the white soldier against his people. Perhaps in his dimming eye he saw the fair-haired general with his army charging on their stronghold in the valley of the Little Big Horn. On his failing brain may have been pictured the tragedy of his race, whose God-given lands and herds were being stolen from them, leaving them paupers in the hands of their conquerors. He raised his hand a trifle as his rallying cry to his braves on the banks of the Little Big Horn was repeated feebly, this time from pale lips: *"Okici ze anpetu waste . . . ."* His head dropped. The Doctor thought he would not speak again; but after a few seconds the words came faintly: *"Cante wasaka . . . ."* and, once more leading his soldiers against the intruders, the greatest of the Sioux warriors rode into the happy hunting ground in search of the white buffalo.

McGillycuddy gave the Indian sign announcing to the watchers that Crazy Horse was dead. Touch the Cloud strode across the room to the corner where the body lay and drew the blanket over the head of the slain chief; then, drawing himself to his full height, he pointed to the slim figure outlined beneath the cover and said: "That is the lodge of Crazy Horse." Then, seeming to grow yet taller in the dim light as he pointed upward, he added: "The chief has gone above."

At midnight the adjutant's office was closed. McGillycuddy crossed the parade ground to his quarters. Touch the Cloud followed silently, rolled himself in his blanket, and lay down outside McGillycuddy's door, on guard lest any harm come to the man who, in after years, was known as *Tasunka Witko Kola,* Crazy Horse's friend, while he slept. In some mysterious manner word of the death of the war chief spread in an incredibly short time into the surrounding camps of the Indians, and from miles about arose the death wail, hideously gloomy in the darkness. In the early morning Crazy Horse's body was given to a delegation of Indians from his own band to prepare for burial. It was embalmed by a process of drying and placed on a platform on selected ground at the Spotted Tail Agency near Fort Sheridan. For three days his parents sat without food, beside his resting place; then Lieutenant Lee discovered them and sent food to them. The great warrior who by his loyalty to his people in fighting for their rights had become *persona non grata* to the white man did not know that a detail had been ordered to take him that night to the Dry Tortugas in Florida, the St. Helena of the Indian; death had spared him the ultimate humiliation.

Chapter 7

THE TRAGEDY OF THE CHEYENNES

AFTER the death of Crazy Horse it was determined to increase the distance between the Spotted Tail and Red Cloud bands, many of them hostile, and the Sitting Bull band in British America by moving the former to the Missouri River in Dakota, a distance of about two hundred and eighty miles to the east. The protests of the red men availed nothing, though they were based mainly on their preference for the highlands. And the long caravan left the Agency, under command of Major Peter D. Vroom, in the autumn of 1877, with the body of Crazy Horse on a litter forming part of the straggling procession.

McGillycuddy was detailed as surgeon for the escort which accompanied the Indians to their new home. Fanny, the only white woman in the party, rode with the escort, leaving the ambulance assigned for the surgeon's use to the two alley cats which had attached themselves to their ménage. The cats sat in a dignified manner on the back seat of the ambulance.

The stark prairies, long stretches seared by fire or browned by blazing sun, were dust-clouded from the thousands of tramping feet as the cortege left the highlands and marched down the gentle slope toward the Missouri River, across miles of land too compacted by the tread of countless numbers of buffalo to allow for the germination of the seeds of trees or grass. Only soap plants and cactus bushes contrived to grow on it.

Among the Sioux traveling to the new agency were the three hundred warriors whom Crook, with a stroke of genius, had organized and enlisted into a band of scouts for the purpose of allaying the restlessness pervading the Crazy Horse band after their surrender. Their duties consisted of watching for runners

88

from Sitting Bull's camp and picking up whatever information would be valuable to the army. On the march to the Missouri River these scouts were detailed with the military escort.

Little Hawk, a subchief of one of Crazy Horse's bands, was one of the scouts. He often visted the Doctor's tent in the evening and related tales of fabulous wealth stored in spots in the Black Hills unknown to anyone but himself. He promised that when spring came he would take the Doctor to those places and they would become rich.

Indian summer was nearly gone when, after a month on the trail, the troops reached their destination, the Red Cloud Post. But the Indians were not with them. The Highland Sioux, who had protested violently against their removal to the lowlands, had refused to proceed beyond the forks of Medicine Creek, though they were then sixty miles from the agency to which they had been assigned. Spotted Tail went even farther down the river to the Ponca Agency, and the troops passed on to their post.

At Red Cloud Post the Doctor's quarters, in which lived the only woman at the post, became the center of the limited social life. Visits frequently were exchanged between the residents of the Red Cloud and Fort Hale posts, the latter commanded by Colonel Robert E. Hale, a blond-bearded bachelor with a lisp. The only woman at Fort Hale was the wife of Captain W. E. Dougherty.

When a freezing fog spread over the river and the endless stretch of plains was blanched with snow, visits back and forth occurred less often and none but men shared the fireside in the Doctor's quarters. But Fanny was never idle. One of the young officers had suggested that he give her Spanish lessons during the Doctor's hours on duty. Fanny agreed that that was the time when she most needed occupation and settled down to serious study, for she was not a frivolous person. The lieutenant sometimes appeared too much engrossed with the lesson to answer the Doctor's greeting when he came in, and Fanny, looking up from the book to welcome him, did not notice the omission.

One day as the lieutenant passed McGillycuddy on the parade ground he failed to salute him. The Doctor halted him and asked if the lieutenant had ever thought that some day he might be ill and that he, McGillycuddy, was the only surgeon within easy reach—it might be awkward not to be on speaking terms with the Doctor. When he returned to his quarters he related the incident to Fanny, who had been unaware of any rudeness on the part of the officer. She immediately discontinued the Spanish lessons and the visits ceased. The lieutenant took particular pains to be courteous to the Doctor whenever they met thereafter.

The Indians came regularly each week throughout the winter to receive their rations which were issued at the Red Cloud Agency. At intervals their threats of striking out for familiar haunts caused uneasiness at the small garrison. With the coming of spring Sitting Bull resumed his tactics of sending runners, regardless of the distance they then had to travel, to induce the bands to escape and join him in the North. It required but little persuasion to lure them back to the homeland, and as the river thawed and the trees leaved the most adventurous of the homesick exiles set out.

The fugitives included the entire body of three hundred scouts who had been armed with carbines or rifles at the expense of the government. This fleeing band of red men, renegades in a sense, in their attempt to join Sitting Bull had to cross hundreds of miles of country through Wyoming, Dakota, and Montana before reaching the British Northwest. They naturally expected to be pursued by troops sent from the various posts along the route to intercept them and force them to return to the lowlands. To furnish resistance against interception, arms would be invaluable; yet not a single gun belonging to the government was taken with them. This nostalgic band made the attempt at escape practically unarmed rather than take advantage of the guns furnished by the power whose authority they opposed. They did not proceed in a body, but broke up into small parties; and though some of the groups encountered the cavalry sent out against them, nearly all succeeded in reaching Sitting Bull's camp.

The Indians who remained on the river continued in a state of unrest and resentment. A promise of their return to the hill country was granted at last by the Indian Office; yet time passed and nothing was done toward effecting the shift. September came, yet still there was no order for the westward march of the Sioux. In another month the cold weather would set in. The roller-top-desk gentlemen in Washington gave no thought to the exigencies of a journey in the wilderness at forty degrees below zero.

Spotted Tail's band was divided into a war party and a peace party, with the former in the majority. Red Cloud's men threatened war. To the tom-tom of the drums they danced the Omaha dance, while they told tales of heroic deeds performed in the North, the details of the destruction of Forts Phil Kearney and Reno calling forth the wildest beating of the drums. But before any definite trouble arose came the order for the return of the Sioux to the hill country. There was no necessity for an escort on this journey; the homesick Indians would travel as speedily and peaceably as possible back to the homeland, led by their heartstrings. Their new agency was in the same general region, though not the one they had occupied before their transference to the river. Pine Ridge, as it was named, was even more to their liking than the agency near Fort Robinson, since it was located fourteen miles from an army post. Again the body of Crazy Horse was a part of the procession, which this time traveled westward; when Pine Ridge Agency was reached the Indians buried it in a ravine near by in a spot known only to themselves.

Soon after the departure of the Indians from the Missouri River, McGillycuddy received an invitation from the Army Medical Board to take the examination for a commission in the Medical Corps. He accordingly wrote the Medical Director of the Department of Dakota asking for release from his contract and received orders to report in person to the Medical Director in Omaha. He was about to leave when suddenly, in the dead of winter, the War Office awoke to the fact that troops with which he had been stationed in the Missouri River Valley were serving no purpose. To terminate this foolish waste of money the order was issued for their immediate return to Fort Robinson. A successor to McGillycuddy could not be secured on short notice, and his offer to serve on the march was gladly accepted.

But the Doctor would not hazard the journey across the frozen country for his wife; and it was decided she should go to her home in Detroit by stage and train. It was a bitterly cold drive to the Brûlé River Agency, twelve miles farther down the river, whence the stage carried them to Yankton. Though wrapped in fur coats, wool stockings, overshoes, and buffalo robes, the freezing gusts of wind which swept the plains while the stage plowed through deep snowdrifts chilled its occupants to the bone.

After seeing his wife on the eastbound train McGillycuddy returned to the post just before the troops were ready to leave for Fort Robinson on December 9. The country rivaled Siberia in the severity of its winters. Mounted, the command made excellent targets for the howling wind, which whipped the snow falling from heavy skies across their faces. Every hour the order to dismount and lead was given. The sound of crunching snow hummed in the air as officers and men stamped the circulation into their freezing feet. They beat their hands and rubbed snow on their frosted ears and noses.

Only when night darkened the seemingly endless plains was the bottle passed around. It had been agreed before setting out that the whisky should be placed in a locker containing the medical supplies, the key to which was in the Doctor's pocket. He had warned them that the overstimulation produced by liquor resulted, when the stimulation had passed, in lowered vitality, making it more difficult to resist the cold. Frequently some member of the command weakened and begged for a drink, but the key to the locker remained in the Doctor's pocket until camp was made at night on the frozen plains. For more than one hundred miles fires had burned over the country, leaving no wood for campfires. Smothered sounds of wolves howling in the distance often broke the silence of the plains as the command tried to sleep on the snow-blanketed ground. Only one private succumbed to the bitter weather, though the command reached Fort Robinson on January 3 with every officer and man frostbitten. There they were located in Camp Canby, a mile from the post.

One subject chiefly occupied the mind of each person at Fort Robinson—the plight of the Cheyennes from the Indian Territory. McGillycuddy, who since his earliest experiences in the West had felt deeply the injustice of the treatment of the Indians, listened sadly to the full details of their sufferings.

The Cheyennes, after their capture by McKenzie in the autumn of 1876, had been quartered in Indian Territory, contrary to their earnest petitions. These Northern Indians then appealed to the Great Father for permission to return to the homeland, saying they would provide for themselves—they would release the white man from his promise to support them in remuneration for the thousands of square miles in their territory taken from them—they would live by hunting and fishing and would molest no one. The Indian Territory was to them nothing but a desert; no herds of buffalo roamed its desolate sands; neither elk nor deer stalked the arid land. They were accustomed to mountain air, cool breezes, and cold, starlit nights. In the humid lowlands they had become infested with malaria. They were homesick and lonely—lonely for their old friends, the Sioux. But their supplications were refused.

Four of the chiefs—Dull Knife, Old Crow, Tangle Hair, and Wild Hog—with a band of about one hundred fifty, determined upon flight. Under cover of night, in the full of the moon on September 9, this intrepid band fled from the Agency. As soon as their absence was discovered, troops from Fort Reno in the Territory set out in pursuit, while word was flashed to army posts in various locations to join in the search for the fugitives. Troops of two entire departments were placed in the field to track down the little band, who asked nothing but the privilege of living in the land of their birth, the only land to which they were accustomed, the land where lay the bones of their ancestors.

They stole along toward the homeland, concealing themselves as best they could from town-dwellers by skirting the villages and hiding in the underbrush. Mile after mile was left behind as the fugitives crossed three states and two railroads, frequently encountering troops, while those who escaped death continued the flight with the one hope of reaching the Sioux at the Red Cloud Agency. Quietly their moccasined feet trod the most sequestered trails leading to the north. Many times they were attacked by bodies of ranchers organized against them and, in defense of their women and children, met assault with assault. But they had no desire to fight; nothing could destroy more easily their hope of concealment and the attainment of their aim.

At last, surviving attack, hunger, and weariness, they reached the northern part of Nebraska, only fifteen miles from where their friends lived across the line in Dakota at the Red Cloud Agency, three miles from Fort Robinson. They had traveled six hundred miles under conditions which made this one of the most remarkable feats ever accomplished by Indians, with the one purpose of reaching home.

On October 6 the Cheyennes succeeded in getting into the Sandhills of Nebraska, a trackless desert piled with drifting sand—a desert extending ninety miles north and south and two hundred miles east and west, within which were only a few isolated lakes where water could be obtained. Into this arid country the Cheyennes, ragged, hungry, and footsore, fled from the horde of troops hot on their trail. The tragic story of their wanderings in the Sandhills is a story of hardship almost beyond compare. At length, on October 27, with the aid of a field gun brought up from Fort Robinson by Lieutenant G. F. Chase, the decimated ranks of the exhausted wanderers were shelled into surrender. In a blinding snowstorm the remnant of the fugitive band was taken into Fort Robinson at night and quartered in one of the barracks in a corner of the parade ground.

Here, soundlessly, after the warriors had surrendered a few worthless guns to their captors, the floor boards of the barracks were loosened and beneath them were hidden twenty-two good rifles and some ammunition which had been concealed under the blankets of the squaws. The doors and windows of the impro- vised jail remained unbarred and only a small guard kept watch over the prisoners.

No one knew what to do with these indomitable red men— neither the Indian Bureau nor the army. General Sheridan in his report of 1878 put in a strong plea for fair treatment for the worthy foes. Red Cloud petitioned their release and permission for them to live among his people. But the states of Nebraska and Kansas urged holding them in custody in the hope of receiving indemnification for the killing of their citizens in encounters during the northern march.

In December a great council, with Captain W. F. Wessels pre- siding, was held, in which the Sioux, the Cheyennes, and repre- sentatives of the army participated. Worn with his sixty winters and the hideous march, dressed in rags, Chief Dull Knife pleaded for the right of his tribesmen to live in the land of their people according to treaty promises. They were homesick, he said. The trees in the South were hollow and the earth nothing but sand. Disease stalked among the tribe; many had died, and they had chosen to risk death on the trail rather than continue in the fever-infested country in the South. They would be good, he said, as he had promised the Great Father when petitioning him from the Territory. They would not ask even for rations; only let them remain in the home of their birth. Wessels promised to communicate Dull Knife's plea to the Great Father.

But the petition was denied by the departments of War and the Interior. The Cheyenne chiefs were again summoned to council. It was the day following the arrival of the troops from the Mis- souri River. McGillycuddy attended the council and listened to the rendering of the report from the departments.

Again Dull Knife pleaded for permission to remain in the highlands, reiterating his promises of good behavior and self- support. The commanding officer was under orders; he repeated that they were to be taken back to the Territory as soon as they were able to travel. Old Crow gathered his tattered blanket about him and spoke: "We are old," he said, "and our fighting days are over. If the Great Father tells us to go back we should be forced to obey because our blood burns no longer. But we cannot answer for our young men; their brains whirl and their fighting blood runs warm. We will go back to the guardhouse and consult them."

The chiefs were returned to the barracks. After some hours a sergeant was sent to learn their decision—would they go peaceably, or must force be used to return them to the Territory? The prisoners refused to leave. For five successive days the same question was put to the imprisoned Cheyennes. The answer was always the same: they would not go again to the country where they had suffered so much, where they were dying of chills and fever; it was better to die in their own land than to return to death in the lowlands. Rations were cut off in the hope that hunger would force them into submission. For five days the prisoners subsisted without food, in the unheated barracks, with the thermometer below zero. The death-chant rose faintly at first, then was picked up by another voice, until the wails floated like a blast of wind across the desert. The offer to remove and feed the children was refused; all would die together, they said.

During the afternoon of the fifth day the chiefs again were summoned to council. Only Wild Hog and Old Crow responded, the Cheyennes refusing to imperil the life of their old chief, Dull Knife. Upon their final refusal to surrender, the two chiefs were seized. In the scuffle which followed, Wild Hog, raising the war cry, wounded Private Ferguson of Troop A. All was confusion in the council-room. The war cry was heard in the barracks, where the prisoners loaded the salvaged guns, and awaited attack. But nothing happened.

Regardless of the excitement of the day the guard stationed outside the barracks was not increased. Whether the guards slept or simply were heedless, no one knew. The wild dash of the Indians was planned with military precision—in the night the entire band poured forth, lunging through doors and windows, armed with the guns which the squaws had concealed under the floor and with pieces of broken flooring and stove iron; and before the astonished guards knew what was happening they were fired upon by the Cheyennes, who fled toward a sawmill a mile from the post.

So perfectly were they organized that, even in the hasty flight, they maintained their formation. Lots had been drawn before the exit to decide which ten of the young bucks should form the extreme rear guard, thus affording protection for the rest of the band from the military guard which followed in hot pursuit. All of these ten, as well as many others, were pierced by flying bullets and fell in the snow that frostbound night, January 9. Their bodies, frozen stiff, were loaded into wagons like cordwood and brought into the post the following morning. All but a few of the band were rounded up and returned to the post.

McGillycuddy left for Washington that night, wiring his wife to meet him in Chicago. On reaching the Capital he called on the Commissioner of Indian Affairs, E. A. Hayt, who eagerly questioned him concerning the situation at Fort Robinson. McGillycuddy gave him details of the councils he had attended and spoke bitterly of the hardships the Cheyennes had endured, as well as of the cruelty practiced on the wards of the nation. Early the following morning he received a message from Mr. Hayt asking him to call again at his earliest convenience, for the Secretary of the Interior, Carl Schurz, wished to meet him. When Commissioner Hayt and McGillycuddy went into Secretary Schurz's office Schurz spoke at once of the trouble at Fort Robinson. The Red Cloud Indians were stirred by the excitement over the Cheyennes. The agent at Pine Ridge had been a success as agent for the peaceable Shoshones but was hardly the man to handle the semi-hostile Sioux. In the unsettled state of affairs on the frontier a different type of man was essential. McGillycuddy had been mentioned prominently as a man qualified for the position, the

Secretary said. He had been recommended by officers of the army as well as by members of the Department of the Interior.

Schurz remarked, as he closely studied the face of the Doctor, that he looked very young to handle eight thousand Indians, many of them lately engaged in the Sitting Bull campaign, scattered over four thousand square miles of territory. Would he accept the position if it were offered him? McGillycuddy said he would like to have time to consult his wife before giving his answer. Schurz asked if he might have it by two o'clock that afternoon, it being then eleven o'clock.

At the specified hour the Doctor returned to the Secretary's office and accepted the position as agent for the Red Cloud Sioux. His appointment would be made by the President and rushed through the Senate, Schurz said. Things were in bad shape in the West, and he was anxious to have the change of agents made as speedily as possible. He was busy every day until four o'clock, and suggested that the Doctor drop in to see him as often as convenient after that hour, since he wished to talk over frontier matters with him. Meanwhile McGillycuddy paid a visit to the Surgeon General and told him of his change of plans—why he was not to take the examination before the Medical Board of the Army.

News of the situation at Fort Robinson now poured into Washington. The remnant of the valiant band of Cheyennes which had escaped from the post—nine living Indians, two of them wounded—after untold hardship, were finally captured in a washout near the head of Warbonnet Creek, forty miles southeast of Fort Robinson, on January 21. Twenty-two frozen bodies lying there beside the icebound stream were taken into the post. After due consideration by the Washington authorities it was decided that these survivors offered no menace, and they were given leave to remain in the North—nine red men, a fraction of the dauntless one hundred and fifty who had earned as well as inherited the right to live on the Great Plains.

Carl Schurz, stretched on a couch, his hands folded behind his head, proved by an interminable flow of questions during the Doctor's visits to his office after four o'clock that his interest in the West was insatiable. No detail of the frontier was too trivial to concern the Secretary of the Interior.

When McGillycuddy's nomination was made by the President and approved by the Senate on January 29, he was advised by the Secretary to remain a few weeks in Washington in order to study the system of the Indian Bureau. Fanny had rejoiced in her short visits in Washington, and was happy to have this one extended, though life on the frontier attracted her. She did not fear hardships, and the Indians whom she knew at Fort Robinson had become her friends. She would be glad to be among them again, though she knew that life at an Indian agency would be unlike that at an army post. She wondered if the coming years held as varied and exciting experiences as the Doctor's last decade had supplied, feeling that the best things in life were won by venturing.

The little railroad station at Sidney, Nebraska, dismal enough in mid-March with the wind howling across its snowcovered platform, did not dampen the spirits of the young couple about to take the stage for Pine Ridge Agency, where, as we have seen in chapter one, they arrived on schedule.

PART
2

McGILLYCUDDY
AND RED CLOUD

Chapter 8

THE BIG COUNCIL

THE MOST important occurrence in McGillycuddy's first month at Pine Ridge was the big council. The old chief presided at the council. After McGillycuddy went in with his interpreter, Johnny Provost, Red Cloud lighted a long pipe, blew a puff through his lean nostrils, and, rising from the bench which circled the room, passed it to his new "Father." After taking a puff, the Agent handed it back to Red Cloud and it was smoked in turn by each of the assembled chiefs, coils of kinnikinnick smoke rising to the ceiling and filling the council room. Then in an opening address which showed no animosity toward the Agent, Red Cloud advised the Indians to listen to what he had to say.

McGillycuddy fastened a map of the reservation on the wall and pointed out the small part of their great lands which were then occupied by the bands—the small area in which they were huddled about the Agency, where there was little chance to farm and to live independently. He advised them to scatter out in the fertile valleys, plow the land, and earn a living.

Red Cloud rose and said: "Father, the Great Spirit did not make us to work. He made us to hunt and fish. He gave us the great prairies and hills and covered them with buffalo, deer, and antelope. He filled the rivers and streams with fish. The white man can work if he wants to, but the Great Spirit did not make us to work. The white man owes us a living for the lands he has taken from us."

McGillycuddy saw that he could never erase from the mind of the aging warrior his memory of the old life on the plains. All such effort would be useless. He assured him, however, that the white men would live up to the treaties only so long as they had to. There would come a time, he said, when they would cease to think it necessary; then the Indian would have to work.

Little Wound said that no Indian wanted to move from the Agency lest those near by receive more rations. The Agent said he would increase the rations according to the distance of the camp to which any band moved. It would be only fair to do so, he said, since those living far off would have to exert themselves more to get them. No further objection was offered, though no one proposed moving to an outlying district.

McGillycuddy then suggested that fifty young bucks chosen from the different bands be organized, uniformed, and equipped as a mounted police force. When that was done he would ask the Great Father to take away the white soldiers from the vicinity and they would handle their own affairs just as the white man did. In white men's cities and towns each community had a government of its own. That was what he wanted the Indians to have—a government with a body of counselors.

Red Cloud grunted approval of the plan but assured him there was no necessity for organizing a new police force since there were several thousand warriors whom he would turn over to him to enforce the law. McGillycuddy asked the chief if the soldiers were not responsible to him as head war chief and if they must not accept orders from him. Red Cloud grunted affirmation.

The agent then said he had no wish to weaken Red Cloud's authority provided he used it for the advancement of his people. If, however, he continued to exercise it arbitrarily in the line of a communal, tribal system which necessarily was opposed to civilization, he might be obliged to employ the Indian police against the chief himself. Would his young warriors carry out his orders? Red Cloud knew they would not. If there was to be a home government at Pine Ridge, its agent must have men sworn to serve the Great Father and no one else.

Many of the chiefs approved the plan. Red Cloud and his followers dissented. But McGillycuddy determined to have an organized police force. And so the council ended.

McGillycuddy likewise made an inventory of government property at the Agency and took a trip to the Missouri River Landing, one hundred and fifty miles away, to sign for supplies.

One April Sunday as he sat in his office there was a tap at the door. McGillycuddy called, "Come in," and was surprised when a Catholic priest entered. He was Father McCarthy, he said; he had come to establish a mission at Pine Ridge. McGillycuddy greeted him cordially and asked his authority for establishing a mission. Had he a letter authorizing him to do so? The priest drew a letter from his pocket and handed it to him. It was from the Bishop of Omaha. After reading it, the Agent returned it to Father McCarthy saying he was sorry but permission to establish a mission at any agency must come from the Secretary of the Interior. Father McCarthy protested: he knew no authority but that of the Church. McGillycuddy told him that by an act of Congress only one denomination could be represented at an agency—diversified teaching only confused the minds of the savages, it had been decided. The government had complete authority in the matter; he was powerless in the case.

"Faith!" exclaimed the priest, and repeated that the only authority he knew was the Church of Rome. McGillycuddy said he regretted his taking that attitude, since if Father McCarthy attempted to start a mission at Pine Ridge he would be obliged to put him off the reservation. It was not a question of religion; it was merely one of carrying out orders. His instructions were that Pine Ridge was an Episcopal agency and no other church could be represented there.

The priest looked astonished and asked if the Agent really would put him off the reservation if he started a mission. McGillycuddy replied that he did not wish to seem inhospitable—the priest was welcome to remain at the Agency as long as he liked—but if he attempted to establish a mission his only recourse would be to remove him. "Come over to lunch with me," he added, "and we'll talk about it; but there is no possibility of a change in the decision."

The priest expressed surprise when they went into McGilly-cuddy's house. Fanny greeted him with her usual cordiality. He said he had never seen so comfortable a house at an Indian agency. A thick gray Brussels carpet with a flowered border covered the living-room floor. In a corner stood a square piano, an ornament only, since the keys if touched emitted but a hollow sound. Yet it stood proudly as if confident that listeners to the music pouring from a large music box standing near by would believe it issued from its own rich mahogany case with its yellowed ivory keys. The music box, the size and shape of a coffin, had four large cylinders, each of which played six numbers. The price of the box had seemed high—two hundred and fifty dollars—but not when measured by the Doctor's love of music. His taste was eclectic; he liked almost anything from the classical to the tom-tom of the Indian drum. Fanny had wound up the box before the two men came in. She usually did so when she expected the Doctor. Now it began playing "I Dreamt I Dwelt in Marble Halls."

Through double doors one could see into the bedroom, with its blue carpet bordered with pink. The bed was suspended from the ceiling by four iron rods fastened to huge iron hooks. Under a molding above the bed were hung net curtains with a hand-darned, patterned border, edged with torchon lace, and lined with pale blue silk. A spread and pillow shams of the same materials covered the swinging bed.

At lunch the Doctor remarked that personally he would approve of the Catholic Church at all Indian agencies. It had an appeal for the red men greater than any other form of worship. They liked the chanting, the burning of incense, and the bell-ringing; it was like medicine-making to the Indian.

"Then why not let them have it?" the priest urged.

McGillycuddy explained that the regulation of churches on Indian reservations, known as the Grant Peace Policy, had been decreed to avoid confusing the heathen mind. With a touch of humor he said that it had been ordained that the Red Cloud Indians should travel to heaven by the Episcopal route; the Catholic

Church was detailed to save the souls of the Sitting Bull Indians; the Presbyterian method was prescribed to lead the Yanktons to salvation; while to the Congregationalists was assigned the responsibility of Christianizing the Lower Brûlé Sioux. It had all been mapped out so that each church had a mission to perform and the minds of the red men were spared the difficulty of choosing among them. Even the white man, he said, often found difficulty in deciding on which creed to base his hope of salvation.

"Not you," the priest said confidently. "A McGillycuddy, an Irishman, of course you're a Catholic."

"Religion is the only bone of contention in our family," the Doctor answered. "My father is a Protestant, my mother a Catholic." He went on to say that his father's ancestors had abjured the faith upon the accession of James II to the English throne in 1685 when the government of Ireland was overthrown and the lands of the Catholics were forfeited to the Crown. To save their estates the McGillycuddys and those nearest of kin had accepted Protestantism.

"My mother is an ardent Catholic," the Doctor continued. She and his father had met on the vessel which brought them to America, she bringing a letter to the Archbishop of New York which she had never presented because of her marriage to a Protestant when the ship reached port. "Would you like to read the letter?" the Doctor asked. "It is my most prized possession."

He left the table and soon returned with the letter. The priest read:

LONDON
11th July, 1842;

MY DEAR AND RESPECTED LORD.

This letter will be handed to you by the Miss Trants who have determined to leave this country and to live in America.

The idea is their own—their parents are dead—and they exercise for themselves the right of visiting where they chuse.

I want for them the advice of the wise and the countenance of the exalted and the good. I therefore respectfully solicit for them from you advice and countenance.

If they did not merit the latter as in a strange land they will want the former I should not address you on their behalf nor make the claim on your goodness which I do at present.

I can of course most distinctly assure you that they deserve all the respect that can be shown them. Their mother was an O'Connell—a most aimiable and cherished gentlewoman giving me a claim of relationship upon them.

Their cousin german is married to my loved daughter Kate and thus I have a claim of the nearest affinity to them.

They are well educated, religious and I need not say of spotless purity and propriety of conduct. There cannot be young ladies found fulfilling all the duties and performing all the virtues of their rank and station more completely than they do.

My wish is that you should be acquainted with them—that you should be able to pledge yourself when any need may be for the truth of these assertions to the strictest accuracy of which I most solemnly pledge myself to you. But they will not be troublesome to you. All they desire is that there should be a person of your dignified rank in New York who could answer for it that their representation of themselves is true in every respect.

I have the honour to be with esteem and veneration

> Your most faithful
> and devoted servant
> DANIEL O'CONNELL

My Lord
Rt. Rev. Dr. Hughes.

"What a pity you did not follow the religion of your mother," Father McCarthy said when he had finished reading the letter. "Your father may be responsible to Almighty God for the loss of your soul and the government for the loss of the souls of many Indians." And he added that perhaps it was his Christian duty to remain at Pine Ridge in spite of orders.

"Look here, Father," McGillycuddy said. "If I should be obliged to put you off the reservation there might be bloodshed. Many of the older Indians including Red Cloud, on account of their friendship for Father de Smet, have a leaning toward the Catholic Church. They might resist if I removed you. Would you like to read in the press that a priest of the Church had caused an outbreak among the Sioux while opposing the government?"

Father McCarthy scratched his head. "Faith, McGillycuddy," he said, "I guess you're right. I'll go tomorrow."

When lunch was over, the two men left the house, the Doctor telling the priest to remain at the Agency as long as he liked. He was a welcome guest, though he could not establish a mission. Father McCarthy set out for Red Cloud's village, and McGilly-cuddy returned to his office.

There was little in the first months of McGillycuddy's service at Pine Ridge to indicate what seethed beneath the surface. His every move was watched by Red Cloud and his followers, among whom was a group of disgruntled squawmen who feared for their prestige and for the support granted by the government through their squaw wives. They distrusted the innovations taking place at Pine Ridge—it was becoming too orderly; there was too much organization; the attention given to the numbers in each band offered little hope of a surplus of rations and annuities.

But McGillycuddy was no less assiduous than the dissident members of the tribe in his watchfulness of their movements, and keen observers among the friendly Indians kept him well advised. His steel-blue eyes, softened by the droop of the left eyelid, seemed to ferret the thoughts of the thousands whose destiny for the time had been placed in his care.

Some of his plans must await the organization of the police force; but one required immediate attention, and that he would give. Among the squawmen was one whom he well knew was doing more than any other to hinder his every innovation. He was inciting the Indians to rebellion and instigating many offenses. McGillycuddy had known Nick Janiss for some time. He had been a member of Red Cloud's band at the Red Cloud Agency; he was married to the chief's sister, a fact which gave him prestige with a certain element. He was known as the intriguer of the camps, setting the ball of discord rolling and hiding behind the perpetrators of the acts he inspired. McGillycuddy would not wait for the organization of the police force to clip the wings of Nick Janiss; and, having formed his resolution, he acted promptly.

It was Nick's custom to lounge around the traders' stores during the day in touch with members of all the bands of Indians as well as squawmen and other loafers. At five o'clock he usually passed the Agent's office on his way to Red Cloud's village, where he lived at government expense.

On the first evening after having made his resolution, McGillycuddy watched from his office window for Nick's coming. He recognized the slatternly walk of the squawman ambling down the hard-baked road; a bandy-legged bitch with sagging dugs followed at his heels. When he reached the office McGillycuddy stepped out and swung into step beside him. Nick frowned.

"I have something to say to you, Nick," the Agent said.

Nick's shifty eyes glowered. He said nothing, but spat some tobacco juice. It dribbled down his black beard.

"I've had it in my mind for some time, but I waited to make sure of my suspicions before doing so," McGillycuddy continued. "You are stirring up mischief among the Indians and the half-breeds. You have some influence over them, not because you are a big man but simply because Red Cloud's sister is your squaw. On that account you are carried on the payrolls and fed."

Nick rubbed spittle from his beard with the back of his hand. He started to speak but stopped. McGillycuddy went on.

"You have been responsible for attacks on settlers and for many deaths on the borders. You've had your way long enough—don't reach for your gun, Nick—you'd be dead before you could get it." McGillycuddy's hand was in his pocket. They had reached the bridge across the White Clay Creek near Red Cloud's camp. It was dim-lighted. Willow trees overhung it. Wild clematis climbed the banks of the stream, its scent mingling with that of roses. There was no one in sight. "You've got to give up your deviltry, Nick," the Agent said, "or you'll be ordered off the reservation. And if you're ordered off and don't stay off—well that's all I have to say, Nick. I've given you warning. Good night."

Nick said nothing. McGillycuddy watched the slouching figure until it reached the end of the bridge and disappeared into the
bushes which lined the path to Red Cloud's village. "Perhaps it
would have been wiser to have brought a gun," he thought, as he
withdrew his hand from his pocket and whistled his way back to
the Agency.

In the dim light as he drew near his house the Doctor saw
Fanny standing on the lawn, her golden head scarcely visible.
Some Indian boys were close by. He stopped whistling when he
saw her. She noticed the cessation and called to him: "Come and
see what the boys brought me."

Two small buffalo calves were nuzzling her skirts when the
Doctor joined the group. They had been brought by some Indians
to whom he had given a permit to go north on a buffalo hunt.
The calves had been captured and then readily accepted by one
of the domestic cows taken with the party. Tethered and held by
an Indian not far off, the cow now restlessly watched the young
buffalo until they were returned to her, when they dashed immediately for her udder, butting it violently. The doctor proposed
lending another cow to the Indians until the calves were old
enough to wean.

Days passed with unaccountable rapidity, and the new organization had taken shape by the time summer walked upon the
endless prairies pouring sunshine on the cliffs to the south, decking
the land with flowers, spawning wild roses and clematis along the
banks of the streams, and filling the air with the song of birds.

Fanny as well as the Doctor was busy from morning to night.
Her garden was yielding fresh vegetables; and there were young
turkeys, ducks, and chickens to care for. Tommy, an Indian boy
engaged to assist her, cleaned the chicken yard and weeded the
garden; but there was much that she attended to herself. She took
care of the nests and gathered the eggs, which were her special
pride after the stale, frozen ones shipped from the Landing which
they had used for a time. She paid frequent visits to the paddock,
set off from the Agency enclosure by a barbed-wire fence, in which

roamed the cow and the buffalo calves until the young animals learned to nibble the fresh buffalo grass, when the cow was returned to its owner.

Shortly after the buffalo were weaned, two Indian boys who had been wandering in the pine bluffs brought in a pair of young eagles and presented them to the Agent. McGillycuddy reproached the boys for robbing the nest, but they had come a long way and he did not insist on having them taken back, though the wild look in their eyes made him feel that the netted cage made for them was a poor substitute for the native crags. He fed them chunks of meat; but the wild look in their eyes never softened, never showed a sign of friendliness. With raucous voices they screeched as they grabbed the food; but this showed not gratitude but only the natural reaction to the sight of a meal.

Outwardly the Indians were calm, and McGillycuddy was satisfied that things were coming on well at Pine Ridge.

Chapter 9

THE VENEER OF CIVILIZATION

On the advice of Young Man Afraid, McGillycuddy appointed Miwakan Yuha, an Indian of about twenty-seven years of age, to select young bucks for the police force. This Indian known as Man Who Carries the Sword, while still very young, had shown great skill and courage in horse raids during wars with other tribes. He was tall, straight as a poplar, and of military bearing. His movements were easy and his tread soft. His cheekbones were particularly high. He understood the necessity of civilization for his people, and he was brave enough to dare their most bitter opposition to the establishment of a native police force.

McGillycuddy promised Sword the commission of Captain of Police when he had succeeded in getting fifty bucks of about twenty years of age to constitute the force. He believed that when an Indian took a soldier's oath, wore a soldier's uniform, and drew government pay he would be incapable of treachery to the Great Father and would even hunt and kill members of his own tribe rather than betray his trust.

As Sword set about acquiring any Indian for the force, Red Cloud applied all his persuasive power as well as threats to prevent that brave's acceptance. Sword suggested to the Agent that he be allowed to have a barbecue, to which he would invite some of the young bucks whom he desired to enlist. McGillycuddy issued the order for beef, and the party was held. The following morning Sword came to the office, almost in tears, to say that members of Red Cloud's band had swooped upon them, seized the roasting beef, and devoured it. McGillycuddy issued an order for more beef and advised Sword to assemble his party in a more secluded spot.

McGillycuddy felt the necessity of a local police force as much or more to protect the Agency against the depredations of horse thieves, outlaws, and desperadoes who infested the sparsely settled region along the Niobrara River in Nebraska at this time as to preserve order among the Indians. These outlaws frequently committed depredations on Indian stock; with but a short distance to travel before reaching the uncertain Nebraska line, beyond the jurisdiction of the Agent, they concealed themselves among the cattle ranches.

Conversely it was the Agency which furnished sanctuary for criminals from northern Nebraska and the Black Hills country who, when pursued by authorities, took refuge on the reservation. Pine Ridge caught the bad men coming and going, besides having the lawless group of squawmen who continuously incited the Indians to rebellion. A well-supplied whisky ranch almost within gunshot of the reservation supplied liquor to Indians and halfbreeds, causing the Agent to make periodic trips into Nebraska to gather up those killed or wounded in drunken quarrels. McGillycuddy keenly felt the necessity of protecting the Indians from the bad men on the frontier.

One of the Agent's most valuable assets in the handling of the Sioux was his interpreter, Johnny Provost, the half-breed who had served him at Fort Robinson and whom he had engaged when he came to Pine Ridge. Johnny was the son of "Old Man Provost," a French-Canadian trapper who lived with his Sioux wife in the Cache la Poudre Valley in Colorado. Johnny was a white man in dress, appearance, and sympathy; he spoke the white man's language; he seemed absolutely trustworthy.

His brother Charlie, who spent desultory periods at the Agency, was two years his junior. The two brothers were as unlike as if no drop of blood in their veins derived from the same source and they had not suckled at the same breasts. There was but one evidence of consanguinity—a common preference for the home of their mother's people. While Johnny had inherited the best qualities of both races, Charlie possessed the worst characteristics of each. A blanket Indian, he confederated with the worst class of Indians and squawmen, and spoke only the Sioux language. His habits were bad. Many times he had been suspected of causing losses in various herds; but he was slippery, it was difficult to prove his guilt. By taking a short ride over into Nebraska and selling the horse to some easy bidder, he rid himself of telltale ownership.

One day in July, three months after McGillycuddy had assumed charge at Pine Ridge, a Brûlé Sioux came from the Rosebud Agency to report the theft of one of his horses by Charlie Provost. The Agent summoned Charlie to the office. The boy came in, and Johnny, his brother, interpreted. McGillycuddy told the half-breed that he had given much trouble: his influence was bad; it was felt not only at Pine Ridge but along the border; he was a regular troublemaker. He must wait at the office until the return of the Brûlé Sioux sent with witnesses to Charlie's camp in order to identify the pony. The Brûlé soon came in and said his pony was in Charlie's herd. McGillycuddy then reminded Charlie that he had warned him several times to mend his ways or expect to be punished. He would give him one more opportunity to change his habits; for the next offense the threat would be put into execution.

Charlie wrapped his blanket around him and without a word left the office. He crossed the enclosure and went to the blacksmith shop in the rear corner. There he asked the blacksmith to lend him a pistol; he wanted to shoot a rabbit, he said. When the gun was in his hand he said his "Father" had scolded him—his heart was bad—he was going to kill someone—maybe his Father, maybe himself. He stalked toward his lodge, a short distance back of the enclosure, while the blacksmith hurried to warn the Agent.

Fanny, standing in the back yard, saw Charlie striding toward his lodge and, as he reached it, she saw him throw off his blanket, raise the revolver to his head and fire. His body trembled; he staggered a few steps, and slumped to the ground. She ran toward the office to tell McGillycuddy what had happened. Not more than ten minutes had elapsed since Charlie had left the office, and the Agent and Johnny, who were still conferring, had heard the shot. McGillycuddy sent the interpreter for the Agency doctor, while he hurried outside and met the blacksmith, who stammered breathlessly: "Charlie took my gun—said he was going to shoot you or himself—guess he's shot himself." Fanny, who had joined them, said she had seen him fall.

McGillycuddy hurried to the spot, turned over the motionless body lying face downward, and saw the mortal wound in the temple. Charlie would give no more trouble, he thought, as he covered the boy's face with his blanket. Just then another shot rang out in the direction from which he had come. He hurried past the stables and his own house and saw Johnny in the midst of a group in the center of the enclosure. Two men were trying to wrest a gun from his uplifted hand. Then he saw Fanny push her way through the crowd and heard her voice, quiet, commanding: "Give me the gun, Johnny; you've done enough harm already."

Without a protest Johnny relinquished the weapon. But a few feet away Clementi Bernard lay dead. Johnny's Indian blood, which had lain dormant in his veins until he heard the shot, which intuitively he knew had killed his brother, had awakened to Indian traditions. Somewhere back in his brain, latent until then, was the memory of a tribal custom: The dead must have company on the long journey to the happy hunting grounds. The road was lonely—it was difficult to find—the wrong ones led to great dangers and insuperable difficulties—someone must keep his brother company while he traversed the weary distance.

Instead of going for the doctor as McGillycuddy had directed, Johnny had gone to the desk and taken a gun from the drawer. As he had left the office, Clementi Bernard had been passing. He and Johnny had been friends since childhood. There had been no quarrel between them. But Charlie would be lonely on the long trail. Clementi must go with him. Without a word Johnny had raised the gun and fired.

There was no court nor guardhouse at Pine Ridge; there was

no law but that administered by the Agent. Among the crowd which had gathered stood Ott Means, the stableman. McGillycuddy told him to hitch up his team and bring it to him. There was a tautness in the air as the mob waited for Means' return. Scarcely a word was spoken. Johnny seemed dazed. Ott returned in a short time. McGillycuddy got into the light buckboard and, taking the reins, told Johnny to get in. There was no trace of the Indian in the half-breed's face as he took his seat beside the Agent. There was no need of sheriff nor shackles, as the two young men —friends, as friendships were made on the frontier through a sharing of common dangers—drove in the late afternoon to Fort Sheridan. The Doctor's heart was heavy. Johnny had been faithful to him; but there must be law at an Indian Agency as well as elsewhere. Besides, the half-breed's life would be in constant danger if he remained at Pine Ridge, for Clementi's relatives would not allow his murderer to go unpunished.

The Doctor's whistle, which usually accompanied his horses' hoofbeats as he drove across the plains, was silent. "I'm sorry, Johnny," he said, as they drove along shoulder to shoulder; "but there is no other way. Lives can't be wiped out like that."

"My brain whirled," said Johnny in a muffled voice.

Night fell on the plains before the two men drove into the post, where prison doors closed on the interpreter, McGillycuddy promising to do all he could to help him as they shook hands at parting. The Agent refused Captain Crawford's invitation to dinner. Having no heart for sociability, he drove out alone into the night. Most of the long return drive was through a light rain. At length he drove over the short bridge across White Clay Creek and the horses quickened their pace, nearing the Agency. A faint sound reached McGillycuddy's ears, grew louder, and resolved itself into wild wailing as he drove into the enclosure and left the team at the stable, not stopping to ask Ott Means the cause of the wailing going on in front of his house. He knew without asking that the squaws were mourning Clementi Bernard and Charlie Provost. He went in through the back door and found Fanny sitting in the front room embroidering. He asked how long the wailing had been going on. Since six o'clock, she told him, and exclaimed that he was drenched; he must take off his wet clothes.

The Agent paid no attention to what she said. He went to the front door. The wails of the squaws rose to a higher pitch as they saw him standing there. They seemed unmindful of the rain pouring down or of the late hour. The Agent waved his arms and shouted, *"Henela, hunta."* The voices of the mourners almost instantly were hushed, as they accepted the order to clear out and slipped away into the thick darkness.

When McGillycuddy was summoned to Deadwood on the case of the murder of Clementi Bernard, he went to the jail as soon as he arrived, to visit the prisoner. Confinement had been bad for Johnny. He was pale and looked worried, though he brightened up when the Agent went in. He was not accustomed to being indoors, he said; he had nothing to do but sit and think; he wished he had not killed Clementi; he had had nothing against him—his brain had whirled.

At the trial, McGillycuddy, though called by the prosecution, testified in favor of the defense. He said there were extenuating circumstances in the case. Johnny was a man of exemplary character, was especially friendly to the whites, and had borne no ill-will toward the murdered man. He said that the mental state of an Indian with a "bad heart" was comparable to insanity, and he asked that the circumstances be thoroughly considered. A verdict of manslaughter was brought in, after the judge had also made a plea in Johnny's behalf. Accordingly the prisoner was sentenced merely to five years in the Detroit House of Correction.

When McGillycuddy went to the jail to bid him good-bye, Johnny thanked him for what he had said in his favor. His head had felt queer, he said, ever since he had killed his friend. McGillycuddy promised to speak to the prison doctor about it. As he left the jail, he thought he would never see Johnny again.

Red Cloud protested against the sentence; but McGillycuddy explained that since Johnny was not a full-blooded Indian he was under the jurisdiction of the United States Court. And Billy Garnett, the half-breed son of General Richard Garnett, succeeded to the position of interpreter for the Agent.

Shortly after McGillycuddy's return from Deadwood, as he and Fanny sat at the breakfast table, there was a sound of wild wailing outside. The maid, Louise, rushed in from the kitchen. Her dark skin was blanched. Almost immediately the back door opened and moccasined feet moved across the kitchen floor. McGillycuddy went out and saw Little Big Man with knives protruding from wounds in his arms and legs, down which the blood streamed. The diminutive chief's wails rose higher as the Agent came through the door.

"*Taku?*" McGillycuddy inquired the cause of the Indian's "bad heart."

"Papoose fall in fire," the little chief moaned. "*Sica! Lela sica!*" The burns were very bad. McGillycuddy promised to send the Agency physician immediately. "Cook some bacon and eggs for Little Big Man," he told Louise, who, with Fanny, had followed him to the kitchen. The Indian stopped his wailing and ate his breakfast, but refused to take the knives from his bleeding arms and legs. He hoped to get more than a breakfast out of his "bad heart." Louise wiped the blood from the floor.

When he finished eating, the little chief went out and, mounting his pony, rode toward the traders' stores, his renewed wails rising higher and higher as he reached George Blanchard's place. Up the five steps leading to the open door Little Big Man lashed his pony and rode inside the store. The semicircle of Indians squatting on the floor paid no attention to the howling chief. They smoked on in silence. The clerks dodged behind the counter.

The trader came from his office back of the store at the sound of the outburst. "Jarchow!" he called, seeing no sign of the clerk who spoke the Indian language. Jarchow's head appeared above the counter. "Come here," Blanchard said. "We've got to find out what's the matter with Little Big Man." The story was now repeated to the new audience. Blanchard tried to persuade the

Indian to remove the knives from his self-inflicted wounds, but he refused. His grief was somewhat assuaged, however, when the clerk weighed out ten pounds of sugar from a barrel, measured off five yards of blue Indian blanket, and filled a paper sack with twisted sticks of candy for the burned child. The chief packed the articles on his pony's back and rode quietly out of the store, only to resume the wailing as he whipped his horse toward the other store. Stragglers on the road fled as the howling Indian came in sight. Doors were locked and window shades pulled down in the homes of the few white families at the Agency. After receiving gifts at the second store also, Little Big Man rode off to his camp, where he found the physician binding up the child's burned hand.

All was quiet for the rest of the day; but as McGillycuddy and his wife drove past the little chief's camp in the evening they noticed an Indian sitting stonily by the roadside, his body and head completely enveloped by a blanket. They drove past the silent figure. Fanny, turning for another glance at him, saw him running after them, his blanket thrown aside, a gun pointed at them.

"He's coming after us," she gasped. "He's going to shoot."

The team broke into a gallop at a sudden stroke of McGillycuddy's whip.

"He was just trying to frighten us," McGillycuddy said, as the Indian seated himself again on the ground.

Chapter 10

THE INDIAN POLICE

By STRENUOUS endeavor fifty young bucks were at last persuaded to join the police force and were duly sworn in to serve the Great Father and him only. Sword received the promised appointment of captain. He was a born soldier and was proud of his position. McGillycuddy was convinced that he would see to it that law was enforced but would never abuse his power. Two lieutenants and ten noncommissioned officers were appointed, with James Oldham as chief of police. There were no uniforms available; but Sergeant Donald Brown, an ex-cavalry soldier whom the Agent had known at Fort Robinson, while paying a visit to Pine Ridge consented to act as drillmaster and master of transportation. There was nothing in the way of military tactics that Brown overlooked in the training of the police. Unsmilingly he put them through the strictest drills, apparently unconscious, as were the Indians themselves, of their scantily and incongruously clothed bodies— occasionally a gee-string became entangled in a pair of naked brown legs; but its owner quickly re-established his step.

In response to his request, McGillycuddy received permission to go to Washington, where, among other important matters, he wished to obtain arms and uniforms for his police force. Stopping over night at Fort Robinson, he was entertained by Colonel Stewart van Vleet, in command of the Third Cavalry, to whom he communicated his intention. Van Vleet said there were some Spencer rifles stored in the Quartermaster Department, and if McGillycuddy could get authority from General Sheridan to use them he would transfer them to him.

When McGillycuddy arrived in Washington he called on the Secretary of the Interior and explained his need. Schurz said uniforms would be issued immediately, since there were some on hand; but as for arms they could not be supplied until an appropriation was made. He then asked the Agent why he did not arm his police with clubs—police always carried clubs, he said.

McGillycuddy, restraining a smile, replied that clubs were all right in a civilized country and in dealing with pedestrians; but that on the frontier, where nearly all the citizens were mounted and carried guns, a policeman couldn't get near enough to an offender to club him. He thought of the amusing cartoon Nast would draw for *Harper's Weekly* if the subject got into the press —a lone cowboy driving the whole Indian police force out of the country, vainly brandishing their clubs. Schurz saw the point but said there was no possibility of getting guns immediately. McGillycuddy then told him of Van Vleet's offer and asked permission to make the request of Sheridan. The Commissioner of Indian Affairs, who was present, said he did not think it possible for anyone in the Indian Bureau to obtain a favor from the War Department. The Agent said he had assured the Indians, in enlisting their services, that they should be properly equipped for the discharge of their duties. He could not consistently ask them to risk their lives arresting criminals armed only with clubs. Schurz said he had no objection to his asking the favor of Sheridan if he did not mind meeting refusal.

When the situation of the unarmed police force was explained to Sheridan he hesitated and then said: "Well, McGillycuddy— well, yes, I'll give you an order for the guns; but I want you to understand I'm doing this for you personally. I'll be damned if I'd grant any favor to that Indian Bureau." He went on to explain the recent cause of his animosity toward that Bureau. Indian agents were being instructed to make a list of the half-breeds at their respective agencies. "You see the point?" the General asked. "They want to ascertain their paternity. It's a reflection on the army officer." He asked if McGillycuddy had not received his instructions to this effect. The Agent said this was the first he had heard of it.

The trouble between the Interior and the War departments had arisen after the Custer battle, when there was a strong movement over the country generally, and widely discussed in the press, for the transference of the Indian Bureau from the Interior to the War Department and for the appointment of army officers rather than civilians as agents. Many of the bands still remained hostile, and agents who had been efficient under previous conditions weakened after the Sitting Bull campaign. There was argument in favor of military discipline. The Department of the Interior had resisted the transfer, claiming that the future of the Indian depended upon his becoming civilized, an undertaking which belonged naturally to a civil branch of the government. While the issue was pending, some pragmatist conceived the idea of arousing a prejudice against army officers as Indian agents by introducing a moral question. Whatever bearing this matter had on the subject, the Department of the Interior retained the Indian Bureau.

Soon after his return to the Agency, McGillycuddy received word that the uniforms for the police were at the Missouri River Landing. He sent a few Indians with newly acquired wagons to fetch them. As they neared Three Bears' camp on the return journey, one of the cases fell off a wagon; it broke open, revealing gray uniforms. Tod Randall, an ex-Confederate, one of the most bellicose of the squawmen, was standing near.

"So the Indian police are to be dressed in Confederate uniforms," he sneered, "the uniforms of the Great Father's enemies."

There was consternation among the police when this information was repeated to them. These uniforms were a portion of those furnished the Columbian Guard at the Centennial Exposition in Philadelphia in 1876, McGillycuddy explained to the police. But they refused to wear them and, continued in heterogeneous costume until at length the gray uniforms were replaced with blue.

Hardly had this been accomplished when the opportunity to test the efficiency of the force arose. One morning in early September, Young Man Afraid came to the office to discuss the restlessness of the hostile bands. Couriers were continually arriving

from Sitting Bull's camp, he said, with messages from the chief
urging the young warriors to strike out and join him in the north.
He was provoking trouble in Montana and Wyoming as well as
in Dakota. McGillycuddy assured the chief that he knew all that,
but nevertheless the police were keeping close watch on the hostile
villages at Pine Ridge.

"How, how," Young Man Afraid said. "But Spotted Wolf,
with twenty-five of his young bucks, passed through my village
last night on their way north. It is a war party."

"Well, I'll be damned," McGillycuddy exploded. He would
see who was running that Agency—he or Sitting Bull. He sent
for the police captain.

"Damn these Cheyennes," he spluttered as he waited for Sword
to come in. "They're always plotting mischief."

Three minutes later Sword arrived and was informed of the
flight of Spotted Wolf's party. He must go after them with twenty-
five of his best men mounted on their swiftest ponies.

"Spotted Wolf must return," he said. "You understand, Captain. Bring him here to my office, alive—or dead."

The Captain saluted and went out.

Ten days passed without a word from Sword. McGillycuddy
feared that alarming reports of the fugitives would reach the press
and trouble would be stirred up along the frontier. What had
happened to the police? Had they been wiped out in an encounter
with the Cheyennes or had blood called to blood and were they
fleeing together, Spotted Wolf and Sword, with their followers,
toward the White Mother's country? On the eleventh day after
the departure of the police, as evening fell, the mournful wail of
the death chant floated up the valley of White Clay Creek. Mc-
Gillycuddy went to the door of his office and met Billy Garnett
coming in.

"Sword's coming back," he said.

Streaks of red cooling into paler tints colored the sky as the
captain of police with his twenty-five men came up the valley,
followed by a mob of howling Indians—Sioux, Cheyennes; bucks

and squaws—singing the death song. As they drew near the Agency, McGillycuddy saw that fastened to the saddle on one of the ponies was a travois bearing a lashed bundle. The procession halted in front of the Agent's office. Sword and his men dismounted, the captain telling Sergeant Pumpkin Seed and Corporal White Feathers to unlash the bundle and carry it into the office. The death song rose more shrilly as the bundle disappeared through the doorway. There was the sound of dull, dead weight on bare boards as Sword said, pointing to the roll on the floor, "There is the body of Spotted Wolf."

The Indians thronged into the office, lamenting. The Agent raised his hand, commanding silence, and asked Sword how this had happened. They had come on the Cheyennes, Sword explained, one hundred and eighty miles from Pine Ridge, in Wyoming. The fugitives had traveled in the beds of the streams wherever possible, in order to hide their tracks. Only two or three at a time rode along the banks. "But," Sword said, "me know Injun ways; me Injun too." Many times he had picked up the trail and lost it again, until at the end of five days he had overtaken the fleeing band. He had then informed Spotted Wolf he must come back; but the Cheyenne chief had said he would not come back. This was the hunting ground of the Indians; he would take no orders from an agent or from police. Sword had told him if he did not come he would carry him back. At that Spotted Wolf had reached for his gun; but Sword had been quicker—he had fired, and the chief had fallen. The others had seen it was useless to fight and had surrendered.

McGillycuddy commended the captain, saying if the police had not got the Cheyennes white soldiers would have been despatched to capture the band, and many people, both Indians and whites, would have been killed. As it was, the Cheyenne chief had been the only one to die. He gave the Indians permission to take the body: they might continue the death song until morning; then it must stop. "And remember this," he said: "You have seen the power of the police; they represent the Great Father. *Hunta.*"

The Indians filed out of the office after picking up the body of Spotted Wolf. A dull wail pervaded the valley throughout the night, and at dawn they laid away the Cheyenne chief. Later in the day Sword came to the Agent with a troubled face. According to the custom of his people, he said, he had been fined fifteen ponies for the killing of Spotted Wolf. It was the price for killing a chief. He was a poor man, and he had no ponies. McGillycuddy told him to send the complainants to him; it was his affair, not Sword's. No one came to demand the ponies.

The red men began to respect the Indian police; but criminals from Nebraska still paid visits to the reservation. McGillycuddy petitioned for an executive order to withdraw a strip of country five miles wide and ten miles long in Nebraska along the uncertain border on which no one should be permitted to take residence —a sort of no man's land. The President favored the plan, and the order was issued. A re-survey of the country was ordered, which determined that Pine Ridge was five miles from the Nebraska line and Little Wound's village was in Nebraska. Little Wound was an irascible old Indian, and the Agent anticipated trouble when he found himself forced to communicate the news to him that he would be obliged to pull up stakes and move into Dakota. He was wholly unprepared for the philosophical point of view with which the red man accepted the ultimatum and passed judgment on the white man.

"Father," he said, "I want to tell you something about that line. Myself and my band lived many winters ago on the Platte River over by Fort Laramie, Wyoming. We were not interfering with anyone or causing any trouble. One day a number of white men came along carrying a spyglass set up on three sticks. They looked across the country and began putting little stakes in the ground; then they put up some posts. Then I was called for a council with the Agent, who said I and my people were not on the reservation and we must pull down our lodges and move our camp. They took us about a two days' ride to the northeast to the White River. We set up our village near Fort Robinson, and we lived there several winters, not interfering with anyone nor making any trouble.

"Then one day some white men came with the spyglass on three sticks and began looking over that country, same as the other white men. They drove stakes and set up posts, and again we were told that we were off the reservation. We were in Nebraska, they said; and they moved us down to the Missouri River.

"One winter ago they sent us here and we thought we should have a rest—that this was to be our home as long as we lived. We are getting along nicely; we have been happy here; but again the white men have come with the spyglass and now you tell us we are off the reservation. Father, we are getting tired of this; we should like to settle down and never move again, but before we pull down our lodges I want to ask you a question: When the Great Father puts boundaries around an Indian reservation, why doesn't he take a range of mountains or a river which the Great Spirit marks the country with and which never moves? These stakes that the white man puts up are all the time rotting away and when he puts them back he never puts them in the same place; they always move closer to the Indian and cut off some of his land. Where shall we move now, Father?"

McGillycuddy advised him to move his camp to the northeast, on Medicine Creek. The following day the lodges in Little Wound's village were pulled down and, after loading their possessions on the backs of the ponies and the squaws, the band set out. They pitched their tents sixty miles from the Agency in the fertile valley; and the Agent increased the rations of the wayfarers. Other progressive bands followed the example of Little Wound and selected camps on lands bordering the creeks and streams.

The Indians seemed manageable; but the horse thieves and bandits were a problem. In order to increase his authority, McGillycuddy secured through Judge G. C. Moody of the United States Territorial Court an appointment as United States Court Commissioner, the Judge saying that he did not know whether or not the appointment was valid, while McGillycuddy trusted that at least it had the appearance of validity. The Agent was somewhat Jesuitical in this, believing that the end justified the means.

The appointment, if valid, empowered him to issue warrants for the arrest of offenders, place them on trial, and, if necessary, bind them over for final trial before the United States Court in Deadwood. The newly erected guardhouse thereby became a United States jail and the chief of police, as deputy marshal, was authorized to arrest any lawbreaker.

The Department of Justice in Washington, hoping to rid the country of its horde of outlaws, contributed to the innovation by the appointment of W. H. Llewellyn as a special agent to assist McGillycuddy. In addition to these certified officers of the law the Union Pacific Railroad, which had suffered greatly from the unrestrained element of the community, offered the services of one of its best deputies to aid in the clean-up. "Whispering Smith's" appearance suggested nothing of the "wild West." His voice was gentle; he never indulged in liquor; he was not a quarrelsome man; yet he had no regard for human life and was known on the frontier as a killer.

Two hundred miles to the north of Pine Ridge was the new gold reservation of the Black Hills. Bullion from the mines was shipped weekly to the railroad in treasure coaches guarded by messengers known as the Shotgun Brigade in the employ of the Wells-Fargo Express Company. This transportation of gold over the three hundred miles to the railroad afforded endless temptation for the illegal acquisition of wealth. Thus the United States government, the railroad, and the express company were equally eager that McGillycuddy should effect some change in the conditions on the frontier.

It happened, however, that the first chance for reformation was afforded when McGillycuddy received word that two notorious horse thieves, Harris and "Lame Johnny," were in the Black Hills on their way to Pine Ridge to steal Indian stock. He communicated with Captain Emmet Crawford, commanding Fort Sheridan, situated between the Agency and the Black Hills, giving a description of the bandits and asking his assistance in their capture. A few days later word came from Crawford that he had arrested two men answering the description of the thieves.

Whispering Smith was at the time in Sidney, Nebraska, on the Union Pacific Railroad, about one hundred and fifty miles south of the Agency. McGillycuddy sent a messenger to Fort Robinson with a wire to Whispering Smith asking him to come to Pine Ridge by way of Fort Sheridan and, if possible, to identify the prisoners. Three days later Whispering Smith put in an appearance at the Agent's office and informed him that he had seen the two men; they were the ones McGillycuddy was after, Harris and Lame Johnny, all right. McGillycuddy said it would be a blessing to the country to have the bandits under lock and key. They had been a worry to him ever since he had taken charge at Pine Ridge. He gave Smith a warrant of commitment to the nearest jail in the Black Hills, where they would be held for trial before the United States Court.

"All right, Major,"* Smith said. "But I have a kind o' feelin' in my bones that I'll lose one o' them fellers on the way to the Hills. I have that feelin' come over me sometimes and when I do I always lose the man."

McGillycuddy warned him then to be unusually careful.

Ten days later Smith reached Pine Ridge. McGillycuddy asked him if he had turned in the prisoners.

"I'm sorry, Major," Whispering Smith said, "but I lost one o' my men jest as I expected. I lost him; he's dead."

McGillycuddy asked how it happened.

"Well, it was like this," Smith said. "We left Fort Sheridan and struck west to the stage line and got the stage in the afternoon 'bout four o'clock. There was no passengers but me, Harris, and Lame Johnny. We made Buffalo Gap at 'leven o'clock and

---

* A title often applied to an Indian agent.

changed horses. There's a little crick crosses the road 'bout ten miles north of Buffalo Gap Station. The grass there is very tall, and there's a lot o' trees growin' 'long Whiskey Crick.

"It was 'bout midnight; the stage was rollin' along and I was dozin' a bit, when all of a sudden the stage stopped. I looked out but didn't see no station and I was just wonderin' why we'd stopped when I seen six fellers on horseback on the other side of the stage. They was drunk. One of 'em asked if there was a man named Lame Johnny inside. I told him there was; I was takin' him to Rapid City. They said he was a pal o' theirs and they wanted to see him. Lame Johnny didn't seem anxious to see his pals, but one o' the men got off his horse and reached in the door and grabbed Johnny by the shoulder and begun t' pull him out.

"I said, 'Say, that's my prisoner; y' can't take him out'a here.' But the man didn't pay no 'tention and kept draggin' Johnny out. Since he was my prisoner I objected to havin' him taken away from me, so I jumped out of the coach after him. The six fellers stood there and they all had their guns pointin' at me. I grabbed Johnny, but one o' the fellers had hold of him and we begun scufflin'. The grass along Whiskey Crick's very high."

McGillycuddy reminded him that he had said that before.

"Well, in the scuffle I dropped my knife. It was a knife I'd had a long time and I set a store by that knife, so I looked 'round in the grass for it; and, would you believe it, when I looked up there was Lame Johnny hangin' to one of the trees and the six men was ridin' off up the road. There was nothin' I could do; so I went on up to Rapid City and turned Harris in the guardhouse as I was told to do. Here's the receipt for him."

Later in the day the commissary clerk, Frank Stewart, told the Agent that Smith had confided to him that he had an idea McGillycuddy would be glad to have Lame Johnny put out of the way but didn't like to say so. Hence he had wired the Shotgun Brigade in Deadwood to meet him near Buffalo Gap Station.

Though McGillycuddy had no intention of pursuing so drastic a course as that taken by Whispering Smith, he was determined

YOUNG MAN AFRAID

CAPTAIN SWORD

to do what he could toward getting rid of trespassers on the reservation. He told the chief of police, Jim Oldham, to forget all about the Nebraska line when going after a culprit operating on Indian territory and to continue the chase until he was captured. Shortly after the order was given, a raid was made on Indian stock; and the police chief, with a posse, set out on the trail of the horse thieves. They traveled sixty miles into Nebraska, caught the leader of the gang at a ranch, and brought him to Pine Ridge, where he was locked up.

McGillycuddy anticipated trouble. Without delay he held a United States Court Commissioner's investigation and found the prisoner guilty of intruding on the reservation and stealing Indian stock. He issued a warrant of commitment and placed him in charge of Whispering Smith, who rushed him through to Deadwood for trial in the United States Court. Trouble was not long in coming. The people of Nebraska wakened to the fact that the agent at Pine Ridge had invaded their sovereign state with his Indian police and arrested a citizen. An appeal was made to the Nebraska delegation in Congress.

The Secretary of the Interior sent word to McGillycuddy that he had exceeded his authority and that the prisoner must be released. The Agent replied that he regretted exceedingly that he was powerless to act, since the United States Court Commissioner (not mentioning the fact that he was the commissioner) had bound the prisoner over for trial before the United States Court in Deadwood; that he had been tried and convicted and was now serving his time. McGillycuddy heard no more of the incident, and the number of raids on Indian stock diminished rapidly.

But there were other troubles for the Pine Ridge agent. About eight miles south of the Agency, in Nebraska, a trading store engaged in the sale of liquor. An employee of the trader, who was also a United States mail subcontractor, made it a practice to come to the reservation for the purpose of supplying whisky to the Indians. McGillycuddy remonstrated without effect, and the bootlegger was ordered off the reservation.

The trader now came to the Agency, his face looking ugly as he demanded that the order be rescinded. McGillycuddy refused. The trader threatened to swear the man in as a mail carrier, thereby guaranteeing him immunity from arrest. McGillycuddy warned him that, regardless of the capacity in which the bootlegger might return to the Agency, he would be arrested and placed in the guardhouse. The irate trader shouted that McGillycuddy would get into trouble if he interfered with a mail carrier.

When McGillycuddy received word from Fort Robinson soon after that the bootlegger–mail carrier was en route to Pine Ridge, he ordered the Agency postmaster to swear in a new carrier prepared to take charge of the mail without delay.

The buckboard carrying the mail clattered up to the post office on Saturday evening as usual. The sergeant of police, Pumpkin Seed, who stood placidly near the counter, arrested the carrier as soon as the sacks of mail were delivered. Wild protestations were offered and these increased in volume when the carrier saw another policeman removing some bottles of liquor from the buckboard; but in spite of the wrangling the carrier was lodged in the guardhouse. But the mail went out according to schedule.

A war between departments was now instigated. The tradition that any man carrying the United States mail—even if outlaw, thief, or murderer—was exempt from interference had been violated.

Post Office Inspector Furey, informed of the untoward event, arrived from Omaha in haste and peremptorily demanded the release of the prisoner. McGillycuddy as peremptorily refused to comply. A message was then sent to the Postmaster General informing him of the indignity put upon the department by the young Indian agent. The matter was taken up with the Secretary of the Interior, who telegraphed the Agent that he was making himself liable by his interference with the United States mail. McGillycuddy wired back—the messages having to be sent to Fort Robinson—that the mail had been conducted by authorized means and on scheduled time. The situation, he added, involved the question as to which department controlled an Indian agency, the Interior or the Post Office Department, and whether or not horse thieves and bootleggers could escape the law by virtue of functioning as mail carriers. His telegram was signed: "McGilly-cuddy, Agent." The interdepartmental question was thereafter ignored, while the offending mail carrier served his sentence in jail.

Matters of the sort just related were greatly delayed by Mc-Gillycuddy's having to send telegrams to Fort Robinson by messenger for transmission to Washington. McGillycuddy now wrote the Commissioner of Indian Affairs that a telegraph station at Pine Ridge not only would facilitate Agency affairs but would provide greater safety to residents along the frontier. He suggested that materials for the line be furnished by the government and Indian labor be employed in its construction. The suggestion was acted upon, and the Indians were set to work digging holes for the telegraph poles, the line to extend from Fort Robinson through Pine Ridge to the Spotted Tail Agency.

Affairs were moving now rapidly at Pine Ridge, the old chief, Red Cloud, viewing all innovations with suspicion. During this period Spotted Tail paid a visit to his quasi friend, the Oglala chief. He was greatly impressed with the improvements being made at Pine Ridge and the advanced condition existing there. No detail escaped his eye. He wanted the same things at his Agency; he heartily approved of the seven villages scattered along the streams and of the five schoolhouses on the Oglala reservation, as well as of the log houses under construction, with Indians hauling the logs in wagons furnished by the government and the understand-ing that, if not used to advantage, they would be transferred to other Indians, also on trial. Windows, doors, a cook stove, a bed, and some chairs were furnished by the government for each of the new houses. Spotted Tail admired the Indian police in their blue uniforms and, with perspicuity, studied Red Cloud's disgruntled behavior and said:

"Brother Red Cloud, you'd better do as this boy the Great

Father has sent you tells you to do. He has a long head and he knows what is best for the Indian. If you don't do as he says, Brother Red Cloud, he'll break you up." But the old warrior paid no heed to the advice: his "heart was bad."

The press reported a flourishing condition at Pine Ridge, saying: "Dr. McGillycuddy . . . . is fast breaking up the tribal system which is the first great stride in the direction of civilizing the red men. . . . The Rosebud Indians [Spotted Tail's band] are anxious to be transferred to Pine Ridge. . . . . It would not be a bad policy to consolidate the two agencies as McGillycuddy is thoroughly competent to handle the entire reservation."

Though old Red Cloud grumbled and frequently sent messages to the Agent that he was likely to be assassinated, he paid friendly visits to McGillycuddy and, squatting on the floor with his long pipe in his mouth, talked with him as though he approved of the innovations. Sometimes he rubbed his belly, indicating a pain in his stomach, and cupped his hand to his mouth, inviting the Agent to give him a drink. When in his most tolerant mood McGillycuddy sometimes went to the dispensary and brought him a small glass of whisky, which Red Cloud received with a *"How kola"* and solemnly gulped. McGillycuddy almost was led to believe at times that the old chief approved of the Indian police.

Chapter II

BAD BLOOD

QUARRELS between drunken men carrying guns about the Agency had frequently resulted in bloodshed. For that reason McGillycuddy had a notice, printed on heavy cotton material, posted at intervals over the Sioux reservation:

NOTICE—
PINE RIDGE AGENCY
DAKOTA.

Strangers visiting the agency except on
PORCUPINE HIGHWAY
are requested to report and register at the OFFICE.
The carrying of FIREARMS of any description, by white men,
half-breeds or Indians, in the vicinity of the AGENCY, is
PROHIBITED.

McGILLYCUDDY—AGENT

Most of the cowboys conformed to the new order and during their visits to the Agency left their guns at the Agent's office. Several of them, however, when depositing their weapons, remarked that it was all right with them—they were perfectly willing to comply with regulations—but if McGillycuddy ever tried to round up that man Quantrell and make him give up his gun, he'd have trouble. Quantrell, they said, was a dangerous man. He was the nephew of the famous guerrilla leader who had made the raid on Lawrence, Kansas, during the Civil War and killed a lot of women and children. Quantrell himself enjoyed breaking laws.

McGillycuddy accordingly "laid for" Quantrell. Frequently he was informed that Quantrell had heard of the notices and had sworn that he'd "like to see any goddam Indian agent make him give up his gun—he'd never been parted from his gun since he was 'leven years old and didn't intend to be."

Some weeks passed before McGillycuddy, while eating his lunch, received word that Quantrell was in his office. He told the messenger that he would be over as soon as he had finished his meal. When the message was repeated to Quantrell he asked who in hell this man thought he was; he wasn't "in the habit of waitin' for folks." However, he waited. When the Agent walked into the office he saw a hard-looking man sprawled in the armchair in front of his desk. He wore the usual cowboy costume, consisting of chaps made of cowhide, a shirt open at the throat around which hung loosely a red bandanna, and high-heeled boots. A forty-five Colt revolver was stuck in his belt. Pumpkin Seed stood beside him.

Quantrell looked up and asked if this was the Agent. McGillycuddy said he was, and in turn asked his name.

"My name's Quantrell," the cowboy answered sulkily.

McGillycuddy asked what he was doing there.

"That's what I want t' know; that damn Injun brought me here."

The Agent pointed to the gun, saying: "Oh, I see, Mr. Quantrell. You're carrying a gun; that's against orders."

Quantrell said he didn't know anything about the orders; but McGillycuddy informed him that he had been told many times of his threats to ignore them, adding that Quantrell would have to give up his gun.

"How in hell 'll you make me give it up?" Quantrell asked. There was a look of suppressed rage in his eyes, though his voice remained cool, insulting. McGillycuddy's voice too remained calm as he said he would make him give it up all right.

"What d' ye think I'll be doin' about that time?" the cowboy asked and McGillycuddy answered that he probably would be dead. He drew his watch from his vest pocket and said that when the second hand had made one revolution, the cowboy must give up his gun. McGillycuddy was unarmed. Quantrell grunted. Pumpkin Seed's carbine was slung across his arm; his wooden countenance exhibited no particular interest. Without taking his eyes off Quantrell, McGillycuddy told the sergeant that when he said "Ready" he was to take the gun.

With his eyes on the watch and on Quantrell also, the Agent counted off the seconds, announcing them at intervals. Quantrell's body slumped a trifle lower in the swivel chair as the Agent announced that fifteen seconds had passed. He pulled the knot of the bandanna tied about his throat when told that half the time was gone. He changed the crossing of his knees and spat on the floor when the Agent announced that but fifteen seconds were left. There was a muttered oath from the cowboy when five seconds only were left; and as McGillycuddy said "One sec——" the cowboy took his gun from the holster and handed it to him. Pumpkin Seed blinked.

McGillycuddy told the cowboy that a lot of stuff that passed on the frontier for bravery wasn't bravery at all; it was just damn foolishness. There was no use in having hard feelings, he said. When Quantrell was ready to leave the Agency he could have his gun. McGillycuddy extended his hand, and Quantrell accepted it with no surprise. Both men were accustomed to frontier ways; there was no personal quarrel between them; it was only a question of authority.

Though McGillycuddy heard frequently of the espionage practice at Pine Ridge by the Indian Ring, there was no open evidence of it except in the continued hostility of some of the bands. He paid slight attention to their animosity, being engaged still in trying to eliminate the bad influence of white men on the frontier.

A ranch in Nebraska ten miles from the Agency and two miles from Fort Sheridan was owned by a man named McDonald, who dispensed liquor to Indians and soldiers alike. On a visit of Captain Crawford at Pine Ridge to witness the receipt of Agency beef cattle, a government requirement, after seeing some drunken Indians at the corrals McGillycuddy talked with Crawford concerning McDonald's ranch, each declaring it was causing much trouble in the community and each advising the other to close up the place, though it was outside the jurisdiction of both of them. They finally agreed, however, that if McGillycuddy performed the act, Crawford would testify, if trouble ensued, that according to the best of his knowledge and belief McGillycuddy had acted within the law.

On Sunday, a week later, McGillycuddy ordered the captain of police, with ten men and a spring wagon, to report at his office at half-past one for special service. They set out for McDonald's ranch, which lay in a draw surrounded by low hills. Just before reaching the draw McGillycuddy told the captain to keep his men under cover and place himself where he could see without being seen. If McGillycuddy should wave his handkerchief, they were to swoop down on the ranch.

Behind a bar running the length of the room which McGilly-cuddy entered alone stood a red-faced, tough-looking man serving drinks to perhaps a dozen cowboys, several of whom invited the Agent to drink with them. When he declined, McDonald asked what he had come for if not to have a drink. McGillycuddy said he had come to close up the saloon—liquor could not be sold on the reservation. McDonald protested he was not on the reservation and the Agent had no authority to close him out. All the same he intended to do so, McGillycuddy answered; the saloon-keeper was causing a lot of trouble and his stuff was to be confiscated.

McDonald then leaped over the bar, grabbed McGillycuddy by the collar, yelling, "Get out'a here you goddam liar," and pushed McGillycuddy toward the door. The onlookers saw no reason to interfere; the scene added to the excitement of a regular Sunday afternoon in the barroom. The Agent was shoved through the door, and only his foot, wedged in the opening, prevented its being closed behind him. But the concealed guard answered McGilly-cuddy's handkerchief signal and descended the hill, the spring wagon clattering behind. McGillycuddy told them to load up the liquor. McDonald, by that time helpless in the grip of two of the police, watched the shelves in the barroom cleared and the bottles loaded into the wagon, while he poured forth threats and male-dictions on the heads of the intruders.

"I'll hev the law on ye," he bellowed, as the spring wagon clat-tered down the draw to White River Valley, the police following, McGillycuddy and Sword riding side by side.

That very night the Deadwood stage, carrying bullion from the Black Hills to Sidney, Nebraska, was held up at midnight a mile from Buffalo Gap Station in Dakota. Two Wells-Fargo deputies lurched forward as the stage came to a sudden halt, the leader of a gang of bandits crying, "Hands up!" The deputies, outnumbered three to one and with guns staring them in the face, offered no resistance, as the stage was emptied of the treasure. From the near-est telegraph station word of the holdup was soon wired to head-quarters.

A week later McGillycuddy received a letter from the United States Marshal for Nebraska stating that a man named McDonald was being held in custody in Omaha on the charge of holding up the Wells-Fargo stage at Buffalo Gap on the previous Sunday night. McDonald claimed that the Pine Ridge Agent had seen him at his ranch in Nebraska, eighty-five miles from the scene of the holdup, at four o'clock that same afternoon, definitely estab-lishing his alibi. Was McDonald correct in his statement? Mc-Gillycuddy felt he had squared with the illicit whisky dealer when he wrote that it was impossible for McDonald to have been at Buffalo Gap on the night of the holdup.

Chapter 12

AN IMPORTANT VISITOR

The Philadelphia Mint, eager to facilitate the circulation of silver dollars, had arranged with the Indian Office that the ten thousand dollars apportioned for the monthly obligations at Pine Ridge should be shipped in that coinage. The silver, clumsy, bulky, and cumbersome, was packed in kegs, each weighing six hundred pounds, and shipped to the Missouri River Landing, a distance of two hundred miles from Pine Ridge. The Agent made the trip monthly in a buckboard, with only his driver for company, and transported the money to the Agency.

On one of these trips, as he was preparing to go into camp for the night, he saw a party of Indians already camped near the spot where he proposed to stop. He drove up and, discovering it to be Spotted Tail with a hunting party, told the driver to set up his tent near by. McGillycuddy and the chief, with the aid of the half-breed driver, talked beside the campfire until it burned low. As goodnights were exchanged, McGillycuddy remarked that he supposed the money in the wagon would be safe. There were ten thousand dollars in the kegs, and the Indians all knew it.

"Oh, yes, Father," the chief answered. "There isn't a white man within twenty miles."

The Missouri River Landing as the shipping point for Pine Ridge was abandoned soon after this episode and the money was thereafter sent to Sidney, Nebraska, thus cutting off many miles of transportation by wagon. Still the silver dollars in kegs wrapped in gunnysacks were the cause of extreme annoyance to the stage drivers. Curses synchronized with the hoists and shoves which eventually established the cumbersome freight in the front boot of the stage. From Sidney it was taken to Fort Robinson and turned

over to McGillycuddy. Whereas the distance from the Missouri
River Landing was much greater than the one now to be traversed and the former journey was almost entirely within the
reservation, making it practically a safe undertaking, the trip from
Fort Robinson, with the exception of the last nine miles, was in
Nebraska. Yet McGillycuddy saw no reason to change his method
of transportation.

The first consignment was safely conveyed by the new route.
But word leaked out, unknown to the Agent, that he had made the
journey alone except for his driver with the precious cargo. It
reached the ears of "Doc" Middleton and his followers, one of
the most notorious gangs in the country, who by luck and cunning
had so far escaped the clutches of the law. Their grief was abysmal
when they learned of their lost opportunity to add ten thousand
dollars to their ill-gotten gains by the mere overcoming of two
men. They were determined not to lose another such chance.

A month passed. McGillycuddy left Fort Robinson as before
and, on reaching Fort Sheridan, was surprised and not a little annoyed when Sergeant Potega, a brother of Captain Sword, with
ten of the police, rode up to the buckboard and saluted. He asked
what they were doing there; he had not ordered an escort. The
sergeant explained that their "Mother" had sent them. McGillycuddy's annoyance was assuaged but little with the information;
he wondered that his wife had assumed so much authority. The
buckboard now continued on its way, with the escort riding behind. At the crossing of Bordeaux Creek the party forded the
stream and, turning a bend of the road, saw four horsemen
galloping toward them. The escort at once surrounded the buckboard. The strange riders, seeing themselves outnumbered, thereupon turned their horses to the northwest and fled up White
River Valley.

When he reached home, McGillycuddy asked his wife why she
had sent the police to meet him. Jim Murray,* from E. S. New-
man's ranch, she said, had come to the Agency to give information

* Later known as James Dahlman, for many years Mayor of Omaha, Nebraska.

that Doc Middleton was going to be on the lookout for him on his return trip with the money. "Well, your prompt action doubtless saved the government ten thousand dollars," the Doctor said. But she answered that she had been much more interested in saving her husband's life.

Never was money a source of greater inconvenience than were the silver dollars which flooded the country. The Agency employees, teamsters and laborers, with great alacrity, exchanged them for articles at the traders' stores. The bulky commodity, to the tune of curses, was hustled back to the railroad towns, where it inundated the banks. The banks tried to work it out of the country back to its original source in the East; but as fast as they got rid of one supply a fresh shipment flowed in.

Tod Randall, seeing an opportunity to complicate matters for the Agent, persuaded some of the Indians that they should receive remuneration for their services in gold rather than silver. "Gold's wurth a lot more'n silver," he told them. But when, at the Agent's request, a portion of the monthly remittance was forwarded in gold, the preference for the yellow metal soon languished when the Indians discovered that the loss of a single piece of gold was heavy; and the silver dollars continued to pour into the country.

In his effort to engage the Oglalas in self-sustaining labor McGillycuddy himself was doubtless the hardest-worked individual at the Agency. From morning to night he wandered about the place, inspecting the stables, the carpenter and blacksmith shops, and the commissary, as well as visiting the camps and inspecting the farms which were springing up at many of the villages along the valleys. He supervised the hauling of logs for the houses which were fast going up in the villages.

As he rode with his interpreter one day on an inspection tour, examining the crops and looking to see that farm implements were properly cared for, and they were following a lonely trail up White Clay Creek, suddenly the death song reached their ears. An Indian with a "bad heart" was coming down the trail.

"We'd better get off and hide in the bushes," Billy Garnett

said. But the Agent insisted upon going on. The wailing voice drew nearer; the mourner's naked body, painted black, gleamed like satin in the sunlight. Streams of blood ran down his slitted legs, in which knives stuck. Billy edged off the trail, but McGillycuddy rode on unconcernedly.

The Indian's eyes stared straight ahead, apparently unseeing; he appeared not to wink; he was like one hypnotized. McGillycuddy's horse swerved as the muzzle of the Winchester lying across the Indian's saddle struck his flank. The wailing Sioux gave no sign of recognition as he passed the two men and continued down the trail. They turned their horses and followed.

The mourner rode straight to the Agency, dismounted in front of the office, and sat down on a hummock. The employees hurried into their quarters and locked doors and windows. Louise rushed in from the kitchen with scared face, yet believing somehow that Mrs. McGillycuddy could protect her. Fanny was calm as always. She had not pulled down the shades but was looking to see where the wailing came from. She was reassured, after seeing the Indian on the hummock, when the Agent came in sight.

McGillycuddy told the interpreter to send the Indian into his office. Billy said he did not like to tackle the fellow; but he called to him that his "Father" wanted to see him. The Sioux rose from the hummock and went in, wailing.

McGillycuddy asked him if his heart was bad and what had happened to cause the mourning.

"*Lela sicha*," the Indian answered and continued to relate his trouble, while Billy, who had followed into the office, interpreted. His wife was dead; her body lay in the lodge; he was very lonely.

The Agent expressed sympathy for him but told him it was a foolish custom to slash one's body and to parade about with guns when one was in trouble. It was unwise to carry a gun when one's heart was bad; foolish things might happen; he would keep the gun for him until his heart was good again. The Indian relinquished his weapon unprotestingly and, a week later, returned to claim it, apparently recovered from his sorrow.

When, in the latter part of the month of August 1879, word was received that the Secretary of the Interior would visit the Agency in September in accordance with his promise given on McGillycuddy's visit to Washington, the Pine Ridge agent anticipated Schurz's visit with great pleasure. Not content with awaiting his arrival, he drove to the Rosebud Agency to meet him, stationing a relay halfway between the two agencies.

After a two-day inspection of the Spotted Tail Agency, Secretary Schurz was ready, with his party—consisting of his private secretary, Webb Hayes, son of the President; Count Dernhoff, of the German Legation; Gaullier of the *New York Times;* and some clerks—to leave with McGillycuddy for Pine Ridge. The journey of one hundred and three miles was made in a day by changing teams at the halfway point. Ten miles from the Agency they were met by a police escort, McGillycuddy having warned his guests not to be alarmed if the greeting of the young bucks resembled an attack. The party reached Pine Ridge at midnight and were welcomed by Fanny, who, after assigning their rooms, told them dinner would be served as soon as they were ready.

A cot had been set up in her room, which the Secretary and Count Dernhoff were to occupy. The bathroom was furnished, though the water system had not been installed—pitchers of hot water stood at hand. Webb Hayes and Gaullier were given the spare bedroom; the other guests were to be housed in the employees' quarters. No one saw the Agent climb up the built-in ladder in the hall and crawl through the trap door in the ceiling to a room which he and Fanny would occupy during the Secretary's visit. When he had washed he came down the ladder as agile as a cat. Fanny had wound up the music box and it was playing "Listen to the Mockingbird" when he came down to the living room, where the guests soon joined them. After cocktails the party sat down to dinner.

The Agent was pleased to see the admiring glances given his wife, who wore a black lace dinner gown, her hair in a French twist, from which two blonde curls hung on her shoulder. Her simple, unaffected manner was most attractive. She talked if necessary, but was at her best as a listener. Her attention was given entirely to her guests. She showed no nervousness as to whether or not the dinner was being served properly. Curtis, a young Negro boy engaged for the period of their guests' visit, was getting on splendidly; the fish which McGillycuddy had sent some Indian boys to get from White Clay Creek was delicious. They had brought in some ducks as well. The sauterne and the claret were excellent. The guests expressed astonishment that such a meal could be served in the Indian country.

Matters of public interest were discussed. At length the Agent announced that he had despatched runners to the outlying villages to summon the Indians to a council the following morning. There was little lingering for conversation when dinner was finished at half-past one; the travelers were tired after their long journey beyond rails and Pullman cars.

When the guests were safely behind closed doors, Fanny followed the Agent up the ladder to the furnished room in the attic, giving him her hand as she crawled through the trap door.

Indians began flocking into the Agency at an early hour on Tuesday morning, the enclosure filling rapidly with bucks, squaws, and children, the bright blankets and beadwork worn by the Indians splashing color over the brown autumn grass. Outside the wire fence swarmed thousands of redskins, the young bucks amusing themselves before the opening of the council by racing their ponies across the plains.

The Secretary and his party, with their hosts, seated themselves on the porch of the Agent's house. The chiefs, some on chairs, others on the ground, faced the porch. Red Cloud wore a black broadcloth suit, a gift from some of his Eastern friends. Young Man Afraid, as usual, wore a blue blanket and a single eagle's feather standing upright in his hair. The other chiefs were blanketed also. Two young deer, recent gifts from the Indians, roamed over the grounds, occasionally stretching their necks to reach Fanny's hand as she fed them carrots fresh from her garden.

As the council opened, Red Cloud lighted a pipe and, holding it at arm's length, invoked the guidance of the Great Spirit. He then drew a whiff from the pipe, after which he passed it to the Agent,* the Secretary, and each of his party. The chiefs in turn were handed the peace pipe. When the round was completed the bowl held only ashes.

Red Cloud then addressed the council, saying that the Indians never had received payment for the land north of the Platte River; that they wanted assurance of annuities and rations in compensation for the Black Hills as long as there was an Oglala left to wear the clothes and eat the food; and that they wanted one thousand each of four-horse wagons, two-horse wagons, and spring-wagons, and more cows, sheep, hogs, and chickens, also more houses and farm implements. His requests for additional possessions were legion; but there were a few things of which he would like to be relieved. He did not like the Agent; he wanted the Great Father to take him away; he was tired of him and he wanted a new Father. The Indian police also he could dispense with. Young Man Afraid then spoke with great praise of the work that was being accomplished at Pine Ridge. And Three Bears repeated Red Cloud's condemnation of the Agent and the police.

The Secretary now told the Indians that, according to the treaty, they were entitled to annuities and subsistence until they became self-supporting, and that as long as he had authority he would see that every article of the agreement was fulfilled. In regard to the police, he said they were soldiers of the Great Father, and if any Indian interfered with them his ration would be discontinued and his annuity withheld. If the offender were a chief, he would be deposed. Then, addressing the old chief, he said: "Red Cloud, the Great Father is a very wise man. He knows everything. If there is anything wrong with your Agent he will know it before either you or I know it."

---

* It was the custom among the Indians to offer the pipe first to the Agent, as well as to shake hands with him first, no matter who was present.

(*Above*) Red Cloud, war chief of the Sioux. (*Left*) Red Cloud under arrest at Fort Robinson.

At the close of the council, Three Bears, fearing his ration would be cut off because of his having expressed objection to the police, apologized, saying he had not meant what he said. To prove the sincerity of his retraction he brought forth two of his finest young bucks and asked the Agent to enlist them in the force.

After lunch, as the visitors were shown about the Agency, they were much entertained by the game between Buffer, the dog, and the sand-hill crane, the latter stepping sedately by the Agent's side while Buffer attempted to dislodge him. The eagles' cage, the stables, the buffalo enclosure, and the chicken yards were inspected, Fanny feeding all the animals and the fowls morsels of their favorite foods.

The Secretary was interested in a rope which hung within easy reach through a hole in the ceiling of the office. McGillycuddy explained that it was a device for summoning himself or his employees without waste of time. A list of calls was tacked on the wall near the swaying rope. One ring of the bell signaled the Agent, two the captain of police, three the chief of police, and so on through the list of employes. Fanny remarked that one ring of the bell always aroused interest. Wherever she happened to be, as the bell ceased after a single stroke, white people and Indians alike invariably commented: "I wonder why the Agent is wanted." Two bells for the captain of police and three for the chief caused momentary alarm. All interest ceased if the bell continued to toll—no one being concerned but the carpenter, the blacksmith, or any other employee whose number was rung. In the clear air of the plains, unbroken by hills, trees, or tall buildings, the sonorous tones rang out across the prairies and could be heard for nearly a mile.

In the evening the bucks and squaws vied with each other to receive the approval of the Easterners for the Omaha and squaw dances. Fresh beef roasted on a huge campfire supplied a feast which concluded the ceremonies. The two following days were devoted to the inspection of the villages, Schurz expressing great satisfaction in the number of acres under cultivation and the houses already finished or under construction.

At the camp of the Man Afraid family, Old Man Afraid greeted the visitors. With trembling lips the withered old warrior spoke:

"*How kola.* I am Old Man Afraid. More than eighty winters have passed over me. I am old—I am no use now to my people. My fighting days are over—I shall soon go on the journey of the four sleeps to the happy hunting ground of my people." It made his heart good, he said, to meet the man who sat beside the Great Father. He wished to give him a present to show his happiness.

He thereupon despatched a young buck to his lodge, who soon returned bearing a war shirt. The decrepit warrior took the trophy with uncertain hands and fumbled lovingly the black-tipped ermine tails which hung in clusters from its blood-stained folds. His fighting days were over, he repeated. He had been a friend of the white man for many winters and had counseled his people to live at peace with them. He tottered to the white chief and laid the treasure across his shoulders, saying: "It belonged to my father and his father before him. It has been in many battles against Indians and white men. *How kola.*" The wind soughed among the lodges, hissed through the dry grass, scuttled across the prairies, and sent a cloud of dust down the furrowed road, as the Agency carriage bore the party back to the Agency.

At the end of five days the Secretary and his party left Pine Ridge, but not before he had promised to see that McGillycuddy's request for a twenty-thousand-dollar appropriation for a boarding school had been granted.

After their departure McGillycuddy issued a permit to Young Man Afraid with eighty of his braves and their women and children to go north on a buffalo hunt. A squad of police in uniform were to serve as a guarantee of the good behavior of this band, in reality as trustworthy as any group of white men. The Agent wrote the Deadwood papers: "Will you please give notice that Chief Young Man Afraid leaves here today with a party of one hundred Oglalas for a buffalo hunt north of the Hills. He is our best chief, and I bespeak kind treatment for him and his party."

Now it happened that Boone May, a treasure-coach messenger, scout, and hunter, was hunting in that same section of country when Young Man Afraid's band set out. After seeing McGilly-cuddy's notice in the paper, some troublesome whites sent messengers from Deadwood to warn May that the Agent had issued orders for his arrest and that a party of Indians accompanied with a police force was out to get him. Reinforcements also were despatched to his aid, and word sped from coast to coast that war was impending on the frontier. One paper reported: "The Indians turned loose by Agent McGillycuddy at Pine Ridge have got as far north as the Little Missouri River and cleaned out the camps of several hunting and trapping parties. The hunters in that country have organized into a band comprising seventy members and purpose making red angels of some of the agency pets. The agent had a warrant sworn out for the arrest of Boone May and one of the liveliest fights ever seen in the West is predicted if the Indians attempt to carry out the order. The reds have done enough harm already to justify the boys in cleaning them out and Major Mc-Gillycuddy had better recall his pets or they may be hurt."

But the hunting parties of Boone May and Young Man Afraid did not meet. Neither was looking for the other, and at the expiration of the allotted time the Indians returned to the Agency, having interfered with no one, unfortunately not even with the buffalo themselves. But for weeks the frontier was in a state of agitation.

A Texas cattle company in their shipment of a herd of cattle for Indian beef included a goat as a gift to the Agent. Billy was a great curiosity to the Indians, many of whom had never seen a goat. They flocked into the enclosure to inspect the queer animal, the children taking flight when he uttered loud, piercing bleats. The goat was allowed the freedom of the Agency. Complaints of his depredations were ceaseless, but his liberty was never curtailed. McGillycuddy even laughed when told that little

Johnny Alder, son of the chief clerk, had run screaming to his mother when Billy had pulled the buttons off his shirt while he lay on the grass.

Only one of the many presents offered to Fanny did she refuse, though she had to empty the cookie box to appease the feelings of the Indian children—when she told them she would rather not have skunks about the place. Though the animals looked like innocent black and white kittens, she foresaw a time when their advantage over human beings would be indisputable.

A temporary calm at the Agency was interrupted when McGillycuddy received a copy of a letter sent to Secretary Schurz containing a list of charges against him—charges of fraud, tyranny, and cruelty. The letter was signed "L. T." and was followed by the signatures—crosses, dashes, and so forth, with the names of the signers written after them—of nearly all the chiefs at Pine Ridge. The letter stated: "if they persist in upholding this rotten agent, why, let them be held fully responsible to the country for the good behavior of the Oglala Sioux in the future. And I will state to you here in plain terms, that if the Interior Department does not act in this matter within the time specified [sixty days] by the Indians, why, they are fully determined to act themselves in the matter, as nothing short of a new agent will restore quiet here."

McGillycuddy called a council of chiefs. The letter was read and interpreted to them. Blank faces stared at the Agent. Not an Indian had ever heard of the letter. Even Red Cloud disclaimed any knowledge of the contents of the paper—which the chiefs had signed upon being told that it was a request for more farming implements. The author of the letter was not discovered; but McGillycuddy's exoneration was complete. The Indian Ring was crafty.

Chapter *13*

OLD GLORY OVERHEAD

According to arrangements made when Secretary Schurz had visited Pine Ridge, McGillycuddy and his wife went to Washington the following winter, stopping off at Carlisle, Pennsylvania, to see how the sixteen children who had been sent from the Agency to the Indian school were faring. Captain Pratt, an old friend, showed them about the buildings. Tommy, the Indian boy whom Fanny had employed during the first months at Pine Ridge, was overjoyed to see them. He had taken the name of Tommy McGillycuddy. He was homesick, he said; he wanted to go back to the Agency. The Agent assured him it was much to his advantage to remain at the school.

When they returned to the office Captain Pratt told them that some visitors at Carlisle had been attracted by Tommy and had asked his name. The boy had answered stolidly that he was Tommy McGillycuddy. The visitor had turned to Pratt: "I've read a lot about that agent at Pine Ridge," he said, "and I always thought he was a bad lot."

Another stop was made in Philadelphia, according to instructions from the Indian Bureau, for an interview with the Quaker City Indian Peace Commission, which had great influence in Indian matters. McGillycuddy had notified the Commission of his coming and a meeting had been called. Arriving at it, McGillycuddy went in and presented his card. The chairman looked surprised and asked if he were the agent at Pine Ridge. When told that he was, the chairman looked keenly at him and asked: "Art thou the man who has been having so much trouble with Red Cloud lately?"

McGillycuddy smiled an amused smile as he answered:

151

"Red Cloud thinks I am the man with whom he has been having much trouble lately." The *New York Tribune* had published a scathing article the previous week on McGillycuddy's tyrannous handling of the Sioux. The chairman studied the face of the slim figure before him and said: "Thou art not a bad-looking man." McGillycuddy wondered if he had expected to see a border ruffian with pistols hanging in holsters from his belt.

One of the commissioners now asked the Doctor why the Indian could not be civilized as the Negro had been. McGillycuddy answered that it was because there was as much difference between them as between the American eagle and the goose, the grizzly bear and the buffalo. A wild goose or duck hatched under a domestic bird would become a barnyard fowl; a buffalo raised among farm animals became as gentle as they. But you could not tame an eagle into a domestic bird nor make a pet of a grizzly bear. There was that difference between the American Indian and the Negro, he repeated. Hunger alone had forced the red men to surrender, and though they had been subdued they had never been conquered.

He related a story of the nestling eagles which had been brought to the Agency the previous summer. He had kept them in a netted cage until winter, when he had turned them loose in the commissary building, the tallest building at the Agency, where they flew among the rafters. One day, with the thermometer thirty degrees below zero, Cloud Shield, a police sergeant, had run to his office exclaiming breathlessly: *"Wambli kiela!"* Someone had opened a window while sweeping the commissary, forgetful of the eagles in the rafters, and one of them had flown out. Days had passed; snow had fallen unceasingly, making an unbroken, white expanse. There seemed no sky but only snow falling silently in large, soft flakes. At the end of a week pale patches of sky had appeared through the white clouds. As he had plodded through the deep snow on his way from his home to the office he had met the police sergeant running toward him, shouting as he pointed upward, *"Wambli cuwa; wambli cuwa!"* High in the air and circling lower and lower, the great bird had taken his bearings. The circles had grown smaller as he had neared the earth until at last he had settled on the snow-covered ground. An Indian who stood near had thrown his blanket over the unresisting bird, and the sergeant had carried him back to the commissary, the Agent following. There had been no hint of affection in the eagle's eye as the blanket had been removed. Though he had remembered where he had been fed he had no feeling of affection for the hand that had fed him; there was no suggestion of the conquered in his cold, hard stare. He had found himself a lone warrior in a land where his accustomed prey did not winter; the cliffs were but jagged mounds of snow; he was hungry, and he had come back to be fed.

It was the same with the Indian. There was little left of their accustomed subsistence on the plains; systematically the railroads and the corporations, as well as the government itself, had despoiled the West of its game, largely for the purpose of forcing the Indians to surrender. They had done so. Like the eagle they had come in to be fed, but they were not conquered.

The commission seemed satisfied with the explanation. McGillycuddy went on to Washington and at once called on the Commissioner of Indian Affairs, who told him that Secretary Schurz had reported excellent conditions at Pine Ridge—by far the best of any of the agencies he had visited. He expressed surprise at the varying reports concerning him that came to his office from Indians, as well as the radically opposite opinions of the press. The Spotted Tail Indians clamored to be transferred to Pine Ridge, while Red Cloud continually petitioned for a change of agents. Many newspapers upheld his policies with enthusiasm, while others condemned his tyrannical handling of the Sioux.

McGillycuddy explained that the question of the Indians hung on a single issue—that of progress or reaction. As to the press, he thought the antagonism toward his administration was due to sentimentalism and to ignorance of what was being done at Pine Ridge as well as to propaganda on the part of the Indian Ring.

Hayt referred to the list of charges recently preferred against McGillycuddy, saying it was doubtless a sample of the difficulties he had encountered.

Fanny was occupied continually in Washington, making purchases in the shops and visiting old friends. There were also new friends whom they had entertained at the Agency, all of whom offered hospitality to her and her husband. For a dinner at the White House, attended by the members of Secretary Schurz's party at the Agency, she bought a new gown of pale blue silk. The President and his wife expressed great interest in Indian matters, saying their son had talked of little else since his visit among them. Webb Hayes insisted that McGillycuddy should repeat the stories he had heard the previous summer—the death of Crazy Horse, the Starvation March, Calamity Jane's experiences in the Black Hills Exploration, and incidents of the Boundary Survey. The company listened with interest to the story of the eagle's flight and return and to the Agent's analogy between bird and Indian.

When McGillycuddy paid a parting visit to Commissioner Hayt they laughed over the difficulties of the Department, and McGillycuddy felt that the Indian Bureau understood his aims and ambitions better for the month he had spent about the offices. He was made happy by Hayt's assurance of the appropriation for the greatly desired boarding school at Pine Ridge.

On his return from Washington, McGillycuddy, after organizing a hundred-wagon-train—wagons drawn by Indian ponies and driven by Indian teamsters—notified the shipping clerk at the government warehouse in Sidney that Indians on a certain date would arrive for their supplies. Contractors for the transportation, having taken the contracts with the understanding that as soon as the Indians were qualified to handle their own freighting they would do so, rebelled at losing their opportunity of making money and were upheld in their contention by the Sidney citizens. Threats of burning the wagons if they arrived were made—Indian labor should not interfere with white labor. McGillycuddy replied that the wagons would be in Sidney as scheduled, with one hundred teamsters well armed, and accompanied by twenty-five mounted police. Besides, he said there were eight thousand Sioux at the Agency and the force could be augmented if necessary to accomplish his purpose. The wagon-train at length drove up to the warehouse and was greeted by a mob of citizens, who threatened and cursed while the freight was loaded; but, with the armed force present and the possibility of thousands more to be reckoned with, they offered no physical opposition to the Indian teamsters.

But this incident only added to the wrath of the Indian Ring, which was becoming more convinced daily of the impossibility of enriching itself at the expense of the Indians. With thousands of dollars spent monthly on the Sioux not a penny had been added to the coffers of the ring, though their efforts in that direction had been unceasing. They must find something of which to accuse the Pine Ridge agent. They searched for some irregularity in his actions.

At last, Clay Deer, the trader across the Nebraska line, and George Bernard, a squawman who had been in jail in Deadwood for horse stealing, both of whom had been ordered off the reservation for selling liquor to the Indians, claimed that a man named Heister had seen forty sacks of corn, the sacks bearing the Indian brand, taken from the warehouse and delivered to trader Cowgill between the hours of midnight and four o'clock—in fact, had assisted in emptying and burning the sacks.

A thorough investigation was made by an inspector sent from Washington; but no one could be found to corroborate the charge, not even Heister himself, who, when duly sworn in, said he knew nothing of any corn-stealing—he was in debt to Clay Deer, and was given the choice of signing the paper or being kicked out on the prairie. He was hearing the affidavit for the first time. The charge was pronounced "a clear case of persecution."

The *Sioux City Journal* wrote that "the charge of corn-stealing was perfectly absurd . . . . the quarters of the police force join on to the commissary and their instructions have always been to arrest any person going in or out of the government warehouses after night; besides, there is an Indian night watchman who walks over the grounds within the enclosure where all of the government buildings are—all night, and it would be impracticable to say the least, to try to get a plug of tobacco or a can of baking powder out of any of the storerooms after night . . . . This corn story, manufactured without any raw material by the gentleman from Deadwood and the gallant guerilla is too thin and comes with poor grace from two fugitives from justice."

The ring had not succeeded in its first open attack on the Pine Ridge agent; but it was not discouraged.

McGillycuddy, however, was too much interested in the progress being made at the Agency to lose any sleep over the efforts to catch him in irregularities. He had been anxious for some time to have a flag at Pine Ridge, and when he was notified that Fort Sheridan was to be abandoned he wrote Crook to ask if he might have the flagstaff from the post. Crook readily agreed to the proposal, and immediately after the departure of the troops two wagons arrived to bear the staff to Pine Ridge. McGillycuddy felt no more apprehension concerning the establishment of the flag at the Agency than over the threatened disestablishment of the post. As to the former, he knew of the relinquishment of the attempt to raise the flag at the Red Cloud Agency in 1875 because of the alarming objection encountered, in spite of the fact that a troop of cavalry had guarded the men who had been sent to set up the staff. But with so large a percentage of the Indians at Pine Ridge in favor of progress, he felt no anxiety about this innovation. As to the removal of the army post he was thoroughly acquiescent, believing that in case of trouble with reactionaries in his Agency the greatest catastrophe would be the arrival of troops. It would cause a revolt among even the friendly Indians, inciting them to join forces with the malcontents against the army. He believed that confidence was reciprocal and he trusted the progressives.

Low grunts of disapproval from the hostile bands arose as the wagons bearing the staff drove into the Agency enclosure. It was placed on a trestle beside a six-foot hole in the center of the grounds. The entire police force, in full regalia, attended on the following day when it had been announced the staff would be set up. A crowd of Indians gathered on the lawn. Red Cloud shouted to the bystanders that he did not want a flagstaff that had stood on the parade grounds of an army post. The flag represented the white man's victory over the Indian. But the captain of police drew up his men beside the trestle, and McGillycuddy spoke to the crowd, raising his hand for silence.

Red Cloud had a wrong idea of the flag, he said, and what it stood for, Billy Garnett interpreting his words. He and some of the other Indians thought it stood for war; but it equally represented peace. The flag floated over the home of the Great Father, and wherever it flew the protection of the Great Father was assured.

At a signal from the Agent the staff was raised from the trestle, a murmur of disapproval rising from the reactionaries; and it was lowered into the hole, which was quickly filled with earth. Unmindful of the dissenting voices, McGillycuddy handed to Captain Sword the large flag which had been sent from Washington at his request. The flag was then attached to the ropes, the signal was given, a salute was fired, and the Stars and Stripes rose for the first time over an Indian agency. A grumbling was heard from sections of the crowd; but no further protest was offered, and the Indians departed to think it over.

Newspapers opposed to McGillycuddy's "tyranny" over the old warrior, Red Cloud, were harsh in their criticisms of this last act; while one of the many which approved his methods wrote: "If all agencies were handled as Pine Ridge is being handled there would be no more trouble with the Indians of the United States."

McGillycuddy chuckled over the praise as well as over the anathemas poured upon him. He was more interested in the protests raised by another innovation at the Agency—a reservoir under construction for water works. The squawmen were filling the minds of the malcontents with false ideas. Nick Janiss said: "Ye allus find them things at railroad stations. Fust thing you know ye'll hev a railroad a-runnin' through your reservation and then where'll ye be? Off to the Injun Territory same as the Cheyennes. You got to look out for this here agent." McGillycuddy laughed when he heard of the warning.

There were many amusing things happening at the Agency. He was entertained one day when Three Bears followed him into the engine room of the new sawmill. The forty-horsepower engine was roaring. The Indian kept at a respectful distance from the revolving wheel. He stood still and gazed at the machine, while McGillycuddy pottered about, examining every detail, his whistle inaudible above the roar of the engine. He had forgotten the presence of Three Bears, when he felt a touch on his arm as he passed the stationary figure.

"*Ta——*"

McGillycuddy yelled to him to speak louder, since he couldn't hear what he said.

"*Taku iapi?*" the Indian shouted, pointing to the roaring engine.

The Agent yelled that it was an engine.

"*Taku iapi mia?*" Three Bears screeched.

McGillycuddy, unmindful of the puzzled look on the Indian's face, answered that he was called an Indian. The Doctor's attention was now riveted on the engine with its smooth roar; machinery fascinated him. Three Bears nudged him again and, pointing repeatedly to the engine and then to himself, he shouted: "Injun—injun—injun—injun. Oh, hell!" He left the sawmill wondering why he and the roaring machine were called by the same name!

McGillycuddy stopped at the carpenter shop on his way back to the office to see how some work he was eager to have finished was progressing. Mr. Higgs, the carpenter, whistled almost as unceasingly as the Agent but in a different tempo. As McGillycuddy drew near the shop he heard Higgs whistling the strains of a hymn, his saw keeping its rhythm "Near—er—my—God—to—Thee"—and whining dolefully in its tardy movement. McGillycuddy felt impatient, for the carpenter by his apathy was delaying work in other departments. The Agent restrained his temper and asked politely if Mr. Higgs, who was never addressed by his first name, could whistle any other tune. The carpenter said he could whistle almost any hymn in the hymnbook. McGillycuddy no longer endeavored to keep his temper; he spoke roughly: "Damn it," he said, "can't you whistle 'Yankee Doodle' and whistle it fast? Your saw might keep as good time to that tune as it does to the hymns you whistle." Mr. Higgs looked hurt as McGillycuddy took the saw from his hand. The tool now moved swiftly back and forth to the strain of "Yankee Doodle" as the Doctor plowed through the board, his whistle echoing from the roof and filling the shop with the spirit of activity. He was sure Mr. Higgs could work faster if he would try that tune, the Agent said, as he left the shop and went off to see how work in other departments was progressing.

As wailing winds of autumn swept the prairies and flocks of wild ducks and geese flew southward under scattered clouds, small groups of blanket-covered stragglers dotted the dry prairies, their moccasined feet treading softly the parched ground between the Indian camps and the small Episcopal Church. The white residents of the Agency trailed dusty paths to the church to participate in the morning service.

A deep silence filled the church as the frail form of the Rt. Rev. Wm. Hobart Hare followed the young deacon, Mr. Burt, from the vestry to the chancel, while Mr. Wolcott, in his surplice, played the opening hymn. The Bishop's simplicity seemed almost to beg forgiveness for the refinement and culture it was impossible for him to conceal. His hair was thin and prematurely whitened by suffering. Unable to resist what he had considered a divine command, he had left a home of luxury in Philadelphia to fight for the rights of the Indians and to rescue their souls. His sense of justice had been tortured by what he saw as he had braved the roughest journeys across the wild frontier in blizzards or broiling heat. He had slept on bare ground or in filthy hovels infested with cinch bugs, rolled in his blankets or buffalo robe, and had eaten whatever food could be procured at out-of-the-way places or more frequently nothing at all when his stomach refused vilely cooked or greasy victuals. Gold shoulder-straps on a dark blue uniform now looked incongruous beside Indian blankets as Captain Sword stood in a group by the baptismal font and later knelt at the chancel rail for confirmation, the gentle voice of the Bishop unusually subdued with emotion as he laid his slim white hands on the black hair still worn in braids.

In September, Fanny added to her other occupations the instruction of Indian children in the small log schoolhouse, just completed, which stood two hundred yards in front of the Agency enclosure. The work was new to her, but she took it up with much zest and the children learned rapidly. Her desk was covered with whatever autumn flowers the prairies yielded. Fish from the streams were daily brought to her. The deer loped toward her as she went to the school, eager for the greens she picked from the vegetable garden and carried to invite their attention.

Although the demands upon McGillycuddy were numberless, he was supposed to be exempt from sick calls. Yet there were occasions when serving as a doctor seemed almost unavoidable. A young buck came to his office one morning and addressed him as "Wasicu Wakan." It was a long time since he had heard himself called the Holy Medicine Man; the Indians usually called him "Atte." He asked what the Indian wanted. Little Hawk said his wife was ill—he wanted Wasicu Wakan to go to see her. McGillycuddy said he was not the Agency physician. Dr. Grinnell, who had superseded Dr. de Bell, was a good doctor and he would visit his wife. But Little Hawk insisted he wanted the Agent to go with him. McGillycuddy asked where his wife was ill—her stomach, her heart, her head? The Indian said she was sick in her stomach. The Doctor asked if she had had any medicine, if the medicine men had treated her. Little Hawk said she had had only some medicine that Wasicu Wakan had given her at

Fort Robinson. McGillycuddy's curiosity was aroused: medicine he had prescribed two years previously—and for what? He decided to visit the sick squaw.

He found her huddled in a heap, her blanket wrapped tightly about her. She was suffering much pain. Her pulse was rapid. The Doctor told Little Hawk to bring the bottle of medicine with which he had treated her. Little Hawk took down a buckskin bag which hung from one of the lodge poles—a pretty bag, about sixteen inches square, with a design in paint made from baked earth and berries, a typical piece of Indian art. From a conglomeration of knives, tools, bone whistles, and strips of sinew, he drew forth a bottle, which he handed to McGillycuddy. The label bore the date, April 11, 1877, and the directions read: "For sprained ankle. Rub well three times a day." He asked the Indian if he had rubbed the medicine on his wife's stomach. He shook his head—he had given it to her to drink. "Hell," the Doctor exclaimed. "That medicine was not to drink, it was to rub on." Little Hawk looked uncomprehending but responded to McGillycuddy's order for a glass of water. To the latter he added some sulphate of zinc and poured it down the squaw's throat. She was soon belching forth the contents of her stomach; her pulse dropped, and the Doctor departed.

When storms swept the plains and snow lay thick in the valleys the little schoolhouse was closed. McGillycuddy and his wife again visited the Capital, where the Department expressed satisfaction with the Agent's work, convinced that the many complaints which reached the office were inspired by the Indian Ring. The derogatory articles in the press were more than offset by those that upheld his progressive policy, the Commissioner of Indian Affairs had decided.

On his return to the Agency, McGillycuddy felt more than ever optimistic about his policy for the Indians. In the early months of the summer he watched the laying of the foundation for the boarding school. He was certain that nothing would advance the red men as rapidly as a school on their own reservation where they could learn the arts of cooking, sewing, gardening, and housekeeping as well as the subjects taught in books. Though satisfied with what had been accomplished by the end of summer, the Agent was somewhat surprised to receive word from the Indian Bureau that his responsibilities were to be increased by the addition of one thousand of the Sitting Bull Indians, who had belonged in the Oglala bands before their flight with the chief to British America.

Chapter 14

THE LAST GREAT SUN DANCE
OF THE SIOUX

SITTING BULL, after years of persuasion from the government of the United States, surrendered. While herds of buffalo remained in the wilds of British America and the Indians roamed at will, the chief had been deaf to entreaties, continuing a menace to the states with his proffered harbor to discontented Indians at the various agencies. The Indian Office had been aware that, by the inevitable destruction of game in British America also, the Sitting Bull Indians eventually would be forced to return to the United States, and the sooner the better. But not until starvation stared him in the face did Sitting Bull decide to capitulate. He then agreed to accept the immunity promised him on many former occasions, together with the annuities and rations which were due him and his followers as wards of the nation.

Scouts informed the chief of the proposed meeting place for his surrender to General Nelson A. Miles. And the forlorn Indians, trudging woefully over the long stretches of prairie covered with yellow and white primroses and blazing cactus blossoms, reached Fort Buford on the Yellowstone River on July 19, 1881, paupers in the land which was theirs by right of birth, by priority, and by treaties, and surrendered. The old chief was tired, hungry, and shabby as he gave up his arms and said:

"Bear Coat, the white man has killed off our buffalo; we have eaten our horses and our dogs; starvation has forced us to come in. I surrender. But the Great Spirit did not make me to be an agency Indian to eat out of the white man's hand."

The old Sioux prophet had yielded to compulsion; but naturally he felt no affection for the people who had brought

163

destruction upon him and had proved his prophecies false. He was to be sent to Fort Randall, Dakota, while groups of his band were to be returned to the different agencies to which they had previously belonged.

McGillycuddy received instructions to send transportation to the Standing Rock Agency—to which point the returned band had been sent for distribution—a distance of four hundred miles, for the Indians belonging to the Oglala bands. The escort, under Bob Pugh, consisted of one hundred wagons, with supplies for the journey, including a large beef herd.

Weeks passed and the plains were brown when the escort returned with the prodigal band of one thousand bucks, squaws, and children, who sang, in spite of weariness, as they surged down the low ridges north of the Agency, heedless of cactus plants and the huge tumbleweeds which scuttled across the prairie in the high wind. Their troubles were forgotten in the joy of coming home and receiving welcome from old friends, who went out in wagons, on horseback, and on foot to meet the wanderers. They were as happy as the Children of Israel on reaching the Promised Land. There was nothing of the proverbial stoicism of the red man as the shouts poured forth from the returning band and were answered by their old friends.

The Agent and his wife were among those to greet the new-comers, many of whom were old friends, some of them members of Crazy Horse's former band. Little Hawk, a subchief, ran to McGillycuddy's carriage and, shouting his happiness, threw his war shirt, heavy with ermine tails, on the seat. They shook hands warmly, McGillycuddy saying, "So, my friend, you have come back." The Indian looked a trifle shamefaced as though expecting to be reproached for having run away, but answered in his peculiarly deep, rich voice: *"How Atte. Cante waxte."* McGillycuddy told him his heart also was good.

The Brûlé Sioux, who were to proceed to the Rosebud Agency, remained a short time at Pine Ridge, admiring the fine agency and saying they were going to petition to be domiciled there. It was much better than the Rosebud Agency, they said. The returned Oglalas joined the bands to which they had originally belonged, became a part of the life in the camps, and settled down to an existence of comfort and plenty, vastly enjoying their security after the hardships of the North.

McGillycuddy was surprised to find that the additional thousand Indians increased his daily tasks but little. His days since coming to the Agency had been as full as it was possible to crowd them and he was glad that the new members became easily amalgamated with the others. But he felt some astonishment when he received word, shortly after the arrival of the Sitting Bull band, that one thousand Cheyennes from the Indian Territory had been granted leave to return to the hill country and were to be located at Pine Ridge.

Since the Dull Knife flight the Indians who had remained in the Territory had been more than ever dissatisfied. Their agent, Laban Miles, had no control over them and continually suffered indignities from them. Sometimes they locked him in his office and refused to let him out, and at other times they locked him outside and refused to let him in.

The Cheyennes, as a whole, were a more hostile nation than the Sioux; also more intelligent, though individuals among the Sioux—Young Man Afraid, Captain Sword, and Little Wound, for instance—were as fine types as any among the Cheyennes. This band of them had obtained permission to return to Dakota after a delegation had visited Washington and threatened that unless they were allowed to leave the Territory they would burn the agency buildings and strike out as Dull Knife had done. The President had decided to accede to their petition or rather their demand. A letter from Miles now announced that the Indians had departed for Pine Ridge with a cavalry escort. He expressed sympathy for McGillycuddy and remarked that it was a terrible mob that was being transferred to him.

On Sunday morning, a few weeks later, Captain Amiel Adam of the Third Cavalry reported at the Agent's office and greeted him with words of condolence. The Indians he had brought from the Territory were the most independent lot he had ever had to deal with, he said. He was glad to get them off his hands. McGillycuddy asked where his new charges were and was told they were a short distance back with the troops. As he and Adam conversed, the interpreter reported that the Indians were coming in. McGillycuddy walked to the door. He told the interpreter of the camp he had selected for the Cheyennes, saying they were to come directly to the Agency. To his surprise he saw tents being set up in Red Shirt's village. He asked if they were the Cheyennes' tents.

"By God, they are," the interpreter exclaimed.

McGillycuddy told him to go at once and tell Little Chief that the Great Father had sent orders that his band should report directly to him; they must pull down their lodges and come at once to the Agency, men, women, and children; they must bring their horses and wagons, and he would assign them a camp. Until they had done so he would not recognize their arrival and they would get no rations. The interpreter galloped off toward Red Shirt's village.

McGillycuddy then explained to Captain Adam that if the Cheyennes were turned loose among the Oglalas before he got them counted, it would be as impossible to take a census as to count a flock of prairie chickens. Besides Little Chief must understand that some sort of discipline was necessary at an Indian Agency.

A reluctant band, in the course of half an hour, rolled up to the enclosure. At first, Little Chief had refused to come, the interpreter said. They were back in their own country and would camp where they pleased. But the interpreter had told the chief that if he knew what was good for him he would come along. McGillycuddy told the captain of police, who, with a squad, stood in line near the office, to escort the Cheyennes to the camp he had selected and keep them together until they were counted. He would count them the first thing in the morning; it was growing dark then. He told Little Chief that as soon as the census was taken his people were welcome to visit all the villages.

The census taking resembled an attempt to herd a bunch of jack rabbits. The main idea of the Indians was to avoid being counted correctly, for a stuffed census afforded more rations. It was only through the vigilance of the police that, after the lodgers in a tent had been counted, they did not steal into the next tepee to be counted again. But the task at last was accomplished.

The census taking, however, was but the beginning of Mc-Gillycuddy's trouble with Little Chief. Though he had been allowed to choose his own camp, he was dissatisfied when his choice was made. Wolf Creek was too far from Red Cloud's village, he said. He wanted to move nearer to the Oglala chief. McGillycuddy offered two objections: First, it would crowd the camps too closely on White Clay Creek to allow farms to be cultivated. Second, and perhaps more important, in close proximity the two recalcitrant chiefs together would discuss their grievances and plot daily against the progress being made at Pine Ridge to the satisfaction of most of the Indians. McGillycuddy talked often with the disgruntled Cheyenne in an effort to reconcile him to the changes necessary to the welfare of his race; but, unlike Red Cloud, who usually pretended to agree during similar conversations, Little Chief remained stolid and unresponsive.

Another grievance was added to those the two chiefs already endured when McGillycuddy issued a proclamation that the Sun Dance, the great religious ceremony of the Sioux, to take place the following summer, would be the last one permitted at Pine Ridge. He explained to the Indians that although according to the treaty of 1868 they were guaranteed the right to worship in their accustomed manner, that same treaty provided that after proper agencies had been established and schools and churches built the Indians should adopt the customs of civilization in consideration of food and annuities. The subjection of the Sun Dancers to physical torture was contrary to the ideas of civilization and retarded the progress of the red men.

When issuing the proclamation, McGillycuddy stated that those who had made vows to Wakantanka to suffer tortures to appease his wrath or in gratitude for benefactions would be allowed to fulfill their obligations but they must make no more such vows. If they did make them after this last Sun Dance, they must go to some secluded spot in order to execute their promise—it must not be done in public. Punishment would follow a disregard of the order, comprising the withholding of rations from any full-blooded Indian, imprisonment for a half-breed, and removal from the Agency of any white man attending the ceremony. McGillycuddy was determined that the torture practice should cease, and he believed that Red Cloud and Little Chief's threats of rebellion against the edict were but a last bid for authority.

How long the Sun Dance as a religious ceremony had been practiced by the Indians, no one knew. It was a tradition extending beyond the memory of its followers—the supreme festival of worship. It was a celebration at which the accumulated vows of the past year were executed—vows of torture to be endured in gratitude or supplication. They prayed to Wakantanka for aid in battle, for guidance through storms, for healing of wounds and recovery from sickness, with the vow that they would dance the torture dance in his honor the following summer.

The Sun Dance also was a ceremony of initiation into the honored rank of warriors. No Indian who had not danced the torture dance was reckoned a brave.

For generations it had been the custom to perform the Sun Dance rites in some secluded spot removed from the gaze of curious onlookers. Only of late years had it become a spectacle for all who reveled in human torture—and they were legion, McGillycuddy decided, when letters poured in from all parts of the country after his proclamation had been issued, expressing a desire to witness the last great Sun Dance of the Sioux. Some of the letters protested against his mandate in spite of the fact that it was a torture dance as well as a stimulus to war.

Rebellion of the reactionaries against the Agent had not

diminished when in the early spring of 1881 a warrior passed among the villages soliciting candidates for the dance. Here and there an ambitious youth, his period of adolescence ended, signified his intention to become a brave by smoking the pipe carried by the warrior. Weeks were consumed in the selection of grounds for the ceremony. Little Wound on the Medicine Bow, Red Dog in the Wounded Knee Valley, and High Wolf on Porcupine Creek all offered objections to the choice of flats near their villages lest their farms be destroyed. McGillycuddy at length gave permission to hold the dance near White Clay Creek Valley across the Nebraska line.

In the full moon of June, with the valleys and flats green and the ponies sleek and fat, criers passed from camp to camp on the reservation summoning the bands to the designated grounds for the last great Sun Dance of the Sioux. It was required that every man, woman, and child attend the festival.

Captain John Bourke of Crook's staff and Lieutenants White and Goldman of the Third Cavalry represented the government for the occasion, while visitors from far and near, including several ethnologists from Eastern institutions, congregated at the Agency to witness the torture dance. On the opening day ten thousand Indians, the Oglalas augmented by bands of Brûlé Sioux, swarmed on the flats and pitched their tents in the form of an ellipse following the contour of the valley, where to the west cottonwood trees shivered along the banks of the stream and to the east rose the tall, pine-covered ridges.

The single opening in the tent-enclosed space faced the rising sun. Against the white of the tepees were projected vividly the brilliant-colored blankets slung across the lodge poles or worn by the Indians, the eagle-feathered war bonnets, the ermine-trimmed war shirts, the gaily beaded dresses and bags, and the papoose carriers hanging from the backs of squaws or dangling from boughs. One hundred feet from the center of the ellipse stood the medicine lodge, built of canvas and the branches of trees, in which the youthful candidates were sequestered. The privacy of this lodge was carefully guarded; no one but the medicine men who attended the young honor aspirants was allowed admission. None of the young men's faces gave evidence of fear, dread, or even discomfort as they lounged on the white-sage-covered ground in the lodge, where they would fast until after the dance to the Sun God on the third day of the ceremonies. Outside the lodge, charged backward and forward across the great valley enclosure four thousand bucks, each naked except for a breech-clout and paint, shouting and firing guns to clear the area of evil spirits preparatory to the arrival of the sacred pole.

The selection of the pole had been assigned to ten young bucks. After making their choice, these returned at full speed to announce their success with shrill cries. Thousands, led by the medicine men, the head man bearing the sacred pipe above his head, set out to witness the cutting of the pole. A band of drummers and singers accompanied the crowd. All were dressed in their gayest costumes.

On reaching the "mystery tree" the leader of the medicine men set fire to a piece of decayed wood and with it lighted the sacred pipe. After having smoked in honor of the Great Spirit, he delivered a prayer, which was interrupted frequently by shrieks from the assembly. Four chosen young warriors then wielded axes on the tree until it trembled, when the bucks fell back, leaving the honor of the final blows to a maiden, selected for her virtue and beauty, who stepped from the concourse. Two braids, the ends interwoven with strips of red ribbon, hung against her neck, their blackness emphasized by her white-antelope costume ornamented with turquoise beads and porcupine quills. Skillfully she dealt the blows; the tree quivered, swayed, and crashed to the ground, while the shrieks of the crowd mingled with the clatter of drums. The young warriors then stripped it of every branch and charged back to the Sun Dance grounds, dragging the pole and shooting into the air to rid the enclosure of any evil spirits which might have escaped exorcism in their previous efforts.

The pole was set up in the center of the circle, where it rose forty feet above the ground. Banners of scarlet cloth were fastened to it as offerings to the dead. Firmly attached to the top of the pole were twelve rawhide lariats as well as two rawhide figures each eighteen inches long—one that of a buffalo, revered by the Indians as their chief subsistence; the other a mounted Indian, naked, his upright penis proclaiming phallic worship. Blown free from the pole by an occasional breeze, the blackened rawhide figures were silhouetted against the sky.

Visitors to the Agency moved about the grounds, watching the Indians chattering in groups while they ate dog soup from tin cups. A woman from Boston insisted on tasting the soup, but when she saw a hairy paw go into the cup designed for her, she concealed her disgust and passed it to a youth, who took it greedily and picked the bone, unmindful of the hairs.

Omaha dances and squaw dances were then held under the brilliant moon which lit the prairies. Tribal traditions had been passed down through generations by the dances of the warriors, who retold their deeds of bravery, their victories, and the coups they had counted. The "fool women" danced about the pole, each declaring that she had been virtuous for a year and challenging any man to deny her claim. If anyone knew that she lied, it was his duty to proclaim it; for gallantry was not a virtue among the Indians. If none came forward to contest her statement, she regained her status in the band. On this occasion only one woman's word was proved false; whereupon the squaws fell foul of her, batted her about the grounds, and pulled hair from her head. The others were declared eligible for marriage.

The first two days of the celebration having passed, the stage was set for the entrance of the Sun Dancers. Mingled with the babel of strange sounds—the discordant, singsong melody of squaws, the tom-tom of drums, and the shouts of haranguers— were the piercing shrieks issuing from leafy bowers where children were undergoing the ear-splitting ceremony. Two slits were made in a girl's ears and one in a boy's, and iron rings were let into the slits.

As the Agent with his party—including the army officers;
Edgar Beecher Bronson; Miss Fletcher, ethnologist of the Peabody
Institute in Boston; Fanny; George Blanchard; and John Robinson, a black-bearded, militant clergyman—sat in chosen seats in
the circle awaiting the arrival of the dancers, a small boy dashed
screaming from some secluded spot and ran blindly into a pony
herd, blood dripping from hands pressed against his ears. A
squaw rescued him from the herd.

The voice of the official crier now rose above the tumult, urging the necessity of giving to the poor and the obligation to care
for the widows and orphans of the bands. The effect was magical.
Warriors brought ponies into the ring and turned them loose;
bolts of calico and flannel appeared; beads and blankets were piled
at the base of the pole; and many stripped jewelry and finery from
their bodies and added them to the heap, all for distribution at a
later hour.

Acclaimed by thousands of voices and the wild beating of
drums, the twenty young aspirants for warriors' honors, each attended by two medicine men, next emerged from the medicine
lodge, while the crier advanced to the center of the circle and
shouted:

"You are about to witness a great deed. Those who endure the
torture dance are as brave as those who fight for their people."

"Hi-ya, hi-ya!" thousands of voices assented.

Twelve of the young bucks now lay on their backs, while the
medicine men made incisions in both breasts and through them
passed oaken skewers. Not a groan escaped the lips of the candidates. After a buckskin thong two feet long had been laced to
each skewer, the youths rose from the ground and the free ends of
each pair of thongs were fastened to the end of a lariat hanging
free from the sacred pole. Each dancer then stood erect and backed
away until his lariat was taut. A whistle made from the hollow
wing-bone of the eagle was placed in the mouth of each dancer,
who, raising his hands in supplication to the sun and staring
fixedly at it, began to dance, keeping time to the melancholy notes

of the whistles and the hollow tum-tum of the drums and circling to the left. Some of the dancers pulled steadily on the lariats; others alternately slackened on the leashes and dashed violently backward, the blood meanwhile trickling from their lacerated breasts and streaming down their bodies. The sun's rays glared mercilessly down.

After a period of torture the dancers broke loose one by one and they were considered to have passed a test. One initiate failed in his heroic effort to become a brave, and, after a prolonged fainting spell, he was cut loose by a medicine man. Tears were indistinguishable from sweat as he wrapped his blanket around his bleeding body and, with bent head, returned to the medicine lodge.

The last eight aspirants were at length fastened to the lariats hanging from the pole. One by one they tore themselves free, occasionally receiving assistance from a relative or friend in rising, after a fall from heat or pain, to continue the dance. The eyes of a young girl in the watching throng never for a moment left the last figure straining on the lariat, sweat streaming from his backward-bent body, and strips of breast-flesh obtruding at the tug of the leash. She watched in agony her lover's vain efforts to tear himself free. Though the sun's rays were slanting, the heat seemed not to diminish. The medicine men must have cut very deep, she thought, as she saw him run toward the pole and leap backward, his body flexed for the strain, his breasts bulging like a squaw's, but his flesh still holding firm. His young frame tottered; the tom-tom of the drums seemed to mock the feeble wail of his eagle-wing-bone whistle; and the sun shone pitilessly, the boy's eyes never changing their fixed gaze into its light. At last the girl disengaged herself from the spectators and ran forward as she saw the youth waver and the sweat run in rivulets down his satin-shining body. She leaped to the center of the ring, threw her arms about the naked youth, and added her strength to his backward lunge. Now the stubborn strips of flesh yielded and the young lovers fell to the ground, while the shouting of onlookers and the wild beat of drums testified approval of her act.

McGillycuddy, wandering about the grounds, came upon an old man, He Who Comes Back, seated alone except for the medicine man who was cutting bits of flesh the size of a grain of wheat, at intervals of an inch, from his body, starting from his shoulder and making a complete circuit. The Indian sat unmoved and talked with the Agent, apparently unconscious of the blood oozing from each cut.

The hour was late when the crier shouted that the time had come for the shooting of the figures from the pole. Excitement now rose to a higher pitch as hundreds of Indians joined in the contest. A slight breeze cooled the air and wafted the rawhide buffalo and mounted Indian away from the pole. Miss Fletcher's eye, for the first time, caught sight of the figures. She exclaimed that she did not know that the Indians were phallic worshipers: it was most interesting from an ethnological standpoint; she would like to secure the Indian figure for the Peabody Institute.

McGillycuddy explained that the Indians would shoot at the figures until the thongs which held them were cut. There would then be a great scramble to secure them as prizes. He would see what he could do about getting this figure for her. He called the chief of police and told him to try to get the rawhide Indian form when it fell and if he did not succeed to offer a good price to the one who caught it. A lady from the East wanted it, he said.

Oldham was a modest bachelor, and his face wore a troubled look as he walked away. It was still more troubled when, after successfully bargaining with the boy who had secured the prize and being trampled by the milling crowd, he approached the Agent's party, fumbling nervously. McGillycuddy presented the blackened figure to Miss Fletcher, whose exclamation of pleasure turned to a wail as she cried: "Oh, Major, they've mutilated the man." At a glance McGillycuddy noticed the absence of the significant organ. He called the rapidly retreating police chief:

"Where's the rest of this man?"

Oldham's face was scarlet as he drew the missing member from his pocket and handed it to the Doctor, who put it and the rawhide symbol into his own pocket, saying to Miss Fletcher, "I'll fix him so he'll be as good as new."

Before the party left the Sun Dance grounds, Red Cloud joined them. The old warrior enjoyed meeting strangers, especially if he were introduced as chief of the Oglalas. A Methodist minister who stood by took the opportunity to upbraid him for the torture-practice of their religious festival. He compared the benefits of the Christian religion to those of the Indian. Red Cloud listened until the minister had finished speaking, then answered:

"My friend, I am called Red Cloud because in my youth my young men covered the hillsides like a red cloud. As a boy I lived where the sun rises; now I live where it sets. Once I and my people were strong; now we are melting like snow on the mountains, while the whites are growing like spring grass and wherever they pass they leave behind them a trail of blood. They promise us many things but they never keep their promises.

"We do not torture our young men for the love of torture but to harden them to endurance, to test their ability to defend their families in time of war. We have been surrounded by enemies: to the north the Crows and Blackfeet; to the west the Shoshones; to the south the Pawnees; and, pressing on us from the east, the white man. It is necessary we should be warriors. *Henela;* I have spoken."

The sun had set before the chief ceased speaking. Tents were being hastily pulled down, and already wagons filled with camp accoutrement were trailing along the roads in every direction bearing the swarm of sun worshipers and spectators from the grounds of the last great Sun Dance of the Sioux.

Chapter 15

THE DEATH OF SPOTTED TAIL

At midnight of August 5, 1881, a courier, riding swiftly, bore the tidings that Spotted Tail, chief of the Brûlé Sioux, had been murdered by Crow Dog, a subchief. Little Wound's band, living sixty miles east of Pine Ridge, was the first of the Oglala groups to receive the message. At once a cry arose, and it gathered volume as the rider sped on to the west delivering the word at each village, until the night resounded with the voices of the Sioux united in a monstrous wail stretching across the prairies.

It had been well known for some time that there was bad feeling between Spotted Tail and Crow Dog, originating in a quarrel between the chief and Hawk Dog, who, together with Crow Dog, was a member of Hollow Horn's camp. The grudge against the chief lingered in the hearts of Hollow Horn's band, but was most evinced by Crow Dog. This quarrel, however, was not the only cause of his malevolence toward Spotted Tail.

In councils with the Great Father recently held in Washington, Spotted Tail had shown great partiality toward White Thunder, to the exclusion of the other members of the delegation of which Crow Dog was one. He continually deferred to him, sought verification for his statements, and consulted only him as to the desirability of proposals. Crow Dog was jealous; his heart was bad. Still, had these been the only cankers brewing hatred in his heart, the chief might have escaped his vengeance. But his pride had been deeply hurt when, through Spotted Tail's influence, he had been deposed from his position as captain of police, an organization duplicated at Rosebud after the chief's visit to Pine Ridge.

Crow Dog had been proud of his position and of the uniform

betokening his authority. His task had been to ride along the reservation line and collect one dollar a head for cattle belonging to white settlers found straying on reservation lands. One day he had reported in council that a ranchman living on Ponca Creek claimed to have rented some land on the reservation from the chief and to have made payment to him for the lease. Spotted Tail was indignant at this charge, and Crow Dog's dismissal from the force followed. Threats passed between them; but time went on and they were not carried out, and it was a matter concerning the pretty wife of his friend Medicine Bear which finally induced the chief's downfall.

Spotted Tail the statesman, the logician, a man full of wisdom and kindness, was possessed of a human weakness which, in the final analysis, caused his death. He was over fond of women. Not content with the four wives which he had bought with the required number of ponies—unopposed because polygamy was the custom among the Indians—the chief lusted for the pretty wife of crippled Medicine Bear. He took her to his own lodge and refused to listen to the importunities of Medicine Bear's friends that he give her up. The subject was introduced in a council especially called to discuss tribal matters, a council which Crow Dog declined to attend. As on previous occasions the chief refused to relinquish the girl.

While the council was in session, Crow Dog and his wife drove to the Agency with a load of wood and, after disposing of the wood, set out toward camp squatting on the running gear of the wagon, the wagon-box having been removed to accommodate the load. As they drove down the road, four men approached, three walking and one riding. Crow Dog recognized the rider at once. He got down from the wagon, leaving it standing in the middle of the road, while he pretended to search for something in the dust. As the four men reached him he rose from the ground and, without a word, fired at Spotted Tail, who fell from his horse mortally wounded.

Grief and dismay filled the hearts of the Oglalas at word of the Brûlé chief's death. Even Red Cloud, always somewhat jealous of his brother chief, lamented his death. Crow Dog was taken to Deadwood for trial, against the stout protestations of the Indians, who rightly claimed that it was contrary to the terms of the treaty, which provided that all difficulties between full-blooded Indians should be settled among themselves. Though opinion varied as to the justice of the murder, it was generally agreed that Crow Dog should be tried by his own people.

A. J. Plowman, attorney for the defense, visited both the Rosebud and the Pine Ridge agencies in order to obtain information concerning the murder. He found that other than among the Indians of Spotted Tail's personal following the feeling was strongly in favor of Crow Dog. A number of white men also who were familiar with the circumstances unhesitatingly said that he had acted in self-defense, his life having been threatened by Spotted Tail.

After the trial a deputy marshal, passing through Pine Ridge, told McGillycuddy that Crow Dog had been convicted for the killing of the chief and was condemned to be hanged. McGillycuddy said the verdict never would be executed. The crime had been committed on the Indian reservation; the two parties concerned were full-blooded Indians, and each had threatened the other's life. The deputy said an appeal had been made to the Supreme Court but that Crow Dog seemed to have no interest in the matter—seemed not to care whether or not he was executed. McGillycuddy repeated that he would not hang.

McGillycuddy sat alone in his office, the chief clerk and the telegrapher having gone to their quarters, looking over the pile of letters and papers which demanded his attention at the close of a day filled with duties in every department at the Agency. He was deeply occupied when he heard the soft footsteps of moccasined feet in the outer office. The door opened, and Spotted Tail's murderer walked in. McGillycuddy reached for the bell-rope which hung near his desk and pulled it four times while he greeted Crow Dog. The white man and the Indian talked as best they could until the interpreter arrived, which was in only a few minutes. The Agent wanted not to miss anything of what Crow Dog had to say.

When Billy Garnett came in, the Indian explained that he had not been kept in jail. He was allowed to roam about Deadwood, and everybody had been kind to him—the men at the prison and the townspeople. He had been able to get odd jobs—cutting wood, cleaning yards, and doing errands. He was glad to make a little money for his family before he was hanged.

But he was homesick, he said; he was tired of waiting around for someone to hang him. He wanted to see his family. He was going to stay with Red Cloud that night and go on to Rosebud in the morning. He would stop to see McGillycuddy on his way back to Deadwood, but if anyone came looking for him before he got back would the Agent tell him that as soon as he had paid a short visit to his family he would return to Deadwood to be hanged? McGillycuddy promised to do so but assured Crow Dog that he would not hang. However, Crow Dog displayed no interest in the outcome, and the two men shook hands as the Indian left the office.

Late the following day the deputy marshal stopped at Pine Ridge looking for Spotted Tail's murderer and was given Crow Dog's message. He then went on to the Spotted Tail Agency. A week later Crow Dog again appeared at McGillycuddy's office and was told that the deputy had been at Pine Ridge looking for him. Crow Dog said that the deputy had found and arrested him but he was too slow; he had got tired of waiting and was going back alone to be hanged. Again he asked the Agent to tell the deputy where he was if he came looking for him. McGillycuddy took Crow Dog to his home for a meal. Fanny joined the Agent in assuring the Indian of his acquittal; but Crow Dog shook his head, not with incredulity but with complete indifference. When he had finished eating he mounted his pony and turned him to the west. The Agent and Fanny watched him as he rode swiftly into the sunset.

"The honor of the Indian is enigmatical," McGillycuddy remarked.

As expected, the deputy followed the next day and received Crow Dog's message before going on to Deadwood.

In the late afternoon not many days later, as McGillycuddy went into his office he found the now familiar figure squatting on the floor waiting to greet him.

"Me no hang," the Indian said phlegmatically. "Me go back to Rosebud."

For half an hour the Agent and Spotted Tail's murderer talked or visited in silence. Then, "Me go home now," Crow Dog remarked quietly. "Heap long ride." And the Indian followed his shadow as he rode toward the Spotted Tail Agency, this time unpursued by the deputy sheriff.

Chapter 16

BEEF AND WAR DRUMS

McGILLYCUDDY was annoyed. Little Chief, chief of the Cheyennes, was causing him anxiety. With a portion of his band he had moved his camp into Red Cloud's village, contrary to orders. He was openly resisting authority.

The Agent sent for the two chiefs. They came to his office, their faces set and hard. To McGillycuddy's remonstrance against the change of residence Little Chief said he did not want to live on Wolf Creek; according to the treaty he was free to live where he pleased on the reservation. McGillycuddy said that was true so long as he behaved himself. He was not behaving himself—he was inciting the Indians to rebellion—he was stirring up trouble in the camps, and, according to the treaty, under such circumstances the Agent was permitted to withhold rations. The faces of the two old chiefs remained unchanged.

The threat seemed not to trouble Little Chief. He said he wanted to live in White Clay Creek Valley with his brother Red Cloud. The Agent reminded him that there was not enough arable land in the valley to provide for so large a number as the two bands comprised. The two chiefs, ignoring the Agent's remarks, repeated the Cheyenne's first statement—they wanted to live together in the White Clay Valley. McGillycuddy repeated his refusal, saying they were free to visit as often as they liked but unless Little Chief moved back to his own camp his rations would be cut off—sugar the first week; flour the second; and, if he and his band had not then returned to Wolf Creek, beef the third week. Red Cloud assented to the Cheyenne's statement that he would share rations with his band.

The old chiefs then left the office, a dogged look on the face

181

of each. Together they hoped to be able to break the dominance of the young Agent, Little Chief more confident than the Sioux, who had repeatedly measured swords with his "Father" to his own disadvantage. Red Cloud remembered the words of Spotted Tail: "Take my advice, Brother Red Cloud, and don't fight against this boy the Great Father has sent to be your agent. He knows what is best for the Indian. If you don't do as he says, he'll break you up, Brother Red Cloud." But the Oglala chief had refused to listen to his advice, and the coming of his old friend, Little Chief, had renewed hope of triumphing over the white man.

When the first week passed with the Cheyenne band still in Red Cloud's camp, Little Chief's representatives appeared as usual at the commissary where rations were issued weekly. Squaws, the habitual collectors of rations, filed into the commissary through the front door with empty sacks, which bulged with supplies issued by the government as they made their exit at the opposite end of the building. Bacon, tea, coffee, hardtack, sugar, flour—all the foods required for living except fresh meat— were issued to families on ration tickets specifying the names and the number of individuals in the family. But no sugar went into the sacks of the squaws belonging to the rebellious portion of Little Chief's Cheyennes; and supplies ran low in Red Cloud's village before the week ended.

At the next issue these squaws' sacks yawning at the mouths of the flour-chutes remained empty, and the ears of the commissary clerk were deaf to their demands that he give them flour. Murmurs of resentment now arose in Red Cloud's village; the Oglala chief was beginning to regret his offer to share with the rebellious Cheyennes. His band already missed their regular supply of sugar, and now there would be reduction in their bread supply. And in another week, if the Agent carried out his threat, the allowance of beef would be diminished. Red Cloud's people thought gloomily of the days when their bellies had been full.

Little Chief visited the camp on Wolf Creek, to find the unrebellious portion of his band under Spotted Elk living bountifully on full rations. From a green sapling resting on forked stakes over a simmering fire hung sizzling chunks of beef, emitting a fragrant odor. He was thankful that his beef had not been cut off as yet, but was unhappy when he also saw big, brown loaves of bread broken into large chunks and passed prodigally about. He returned to Red Cloud's village determined to prevent the Agent from withholding their cattle. Beef was their mainstay, or had been for many winters when only buffalo meat stood between them and starvation. He would see to it that this calm white man did not deprive them of beef.

On the Sunday night preceding the beef issue, the third week after Little Chief's refusal to return to his camp, Captain Sword and Billy Garnett reported to the Agent that all day the young bucks in Red Cloud's village had danced the scalp dance. Mc-Gillycuddy had heard the drums beating in White Clay Valley. Saturday night they had held a council, Sword said. All of Little Chief's warriors would be at the corrals the following morning prepared to storm the gates and seize the cattle. They even planned to kill the Agent. One of Sword's detectives had sat in the council. McGillycuddy told the captain to have his full police force, armed and mounted, ready to go with him to the corrals at seven o'clock in the morning.

As the Agent and his escort rode across the two miles of broad, open prairie between the Agency and the beef corrals, they met hundreds of squaws and children returning to the camps. "It looks like trouble," the captain said, knowing that only an emergency would prevent the squaws from participating in the beef issue—it was the most thrilling event in the life of agency Indians; it was all that remained to the red men as a reminder of the free life on the plains when they hunted the buffalo with no one to dispute their rights. When the Texas steers, some bellowing and snorting, others silent and wild-eyed with fear, were turned loose from the corrals through a chute leading to the gate on the flat, endless plains, there were always scenes of mad excitement, often threatening danger. The Indians—bucks, squaws, and children—reveled in these scenes. The police captain was right when he said the departure of the squaws and children from the corrals augured trouble.

The sun was two hours high when, as McGillycuddy and his escort rode on, they met Young Man Afraid on his way back from the corrals to warn the Agent that all the Cheyennes were at the issue grounds, heavily armed and resolved, after seizing the cattle and killing him, to strike out for the northwest. They would have to pass through his village, he said, and he would do what he could to stop them. McGillycuddy thanked the chief for his warning and rode on, whistling as he contemplated that that aid would come after he was dead.

Several hundred mounted Cheyenne warriors, grotesquely painted, were strung out in formation from the gate through which the cattle were to be loosed on the prairies. The stocks of their carbines rested perpendicularly on their saddles. On the opposite side of the trail, beaten hard by the hoofs of thousands of steers turned out for slaughter, Sword drew up his men, their carbines resting across the saddle pommels, facing the rebellious Cheyennes. All were red men, the uniformed police and the painted warriors, the two lines typifying the condition existing at Pine Ridge—progress against reaction, civilization against barbarism, development against annihilation. The Cheyennes greatly outnumbered the police, and doubtless would be aided, in case of an outbreak, by the hostile bands of Sioux, who, together with the friendly bands, were crowded at the gates.

McGillycuddy caught sight of Blanchard on his racer, Sam, near the corrals. He rode to him and asked, as a special favor, that he return to the Agency and, in case of an outbreak, look out for Fanny as well as his own family. The trader reluctantly rode away. McGillycuddy then mounted the steps of the platform at the gateway, followed by John Alder, chief clerk, Billy Garnett, and Grass, the haranguer. There was deep silence among the thousands of Indians, who all faced toward the man who stood alone at the front of the platform. His voice showed no emotion as he announced that beef would be issued first to the Sioux and that, as the steers passed through the gate, each consolidation whose name was called must leave immediately, driving the cattle to its village—there must be no shooting on the prairies in the vicinity of the corrals. When the issue to the Sioux was completed, he went on, the friendly Cheyennes under Spotted Elk would receive their cattle and they too must drive them to their camp; the gates would then be closed.

A rumble of disapproval among the hostiles when Billy Garnett stepped beside the Agent and interpreted his words was drowned by the shouts which rose as the haranguer cried "Torn Blanket" and the gates sprang open as if the words were a key which unlocked them. Three Texas steers, wild-eyed and bewildered, dashed through the opening and, seeing nothing to right or left but a solid mass of humanity, tore along the narrow trail ahead in a frantic rush to escape. Out of the throng emerged ninety Indians belonging to Torn Blanket's band, shouting wildly as they followed the fleeing animals and turned them toward their camp, giving no evidence of disappointment at this procedure. This was tame as compared with the accustomed method of killing on the prairies, for then occurred a concentrated scene of mad, fighting, and dying beasts and gay Indians, while the air was thick with frenzied bellowing and the sounds of rifles and guns being emptied into the cattle. Sometimes a crazed steer, his body bristling with arrows, plunged at a rider and threw him as well as his horse into the air. But the advantage of the animal was always short-lived.

Swiftly from the haranguer's lips followed the names of Red Cloud, No Flesh, Red Shirt, and White Bird; and as each was announced the gates disgorged more steers to the waiting crowd. The space near the corrals was cleared of the Sioux when the haranguer began shouting the names of the friendly Cheyenne chiefs. Group after group, following the released cattle, thinned the congregation at the gates, until there remained only the feathered, painted, hostile Cheyennes and, facing them across the trail, the uniformed police force.

"Clear the platform," McGillycuddy said to the three men who had assisted at the issue.

As the employees filed down the narrow steps, McGillycuddy, apparently unperturbed by the possibility of instant death, raised his hand to silence the clamor among the hostile band. For a moment he did not speak as he looked fixedly at Little Chief, who glared angrily back at him. There was no glimmer of fear in the Agent's eye. He was doing his duty, and if a hail of bullets ended the contest—there was nothing to do about it— what-the-hell. After a moment of ominous silence he shouted: *"Tiyopa natakapi! Henela."*

The hostiles sat stolidly, dark glances passing along the line, their half-filled bellies urging attack, but discretion dominating the old chief's mind. Suddenly he made his decision and, accepting the verdict that the issue was ended and they must leave, he lashed his pony into a run and, followed by his feathered band, rode hard toward Red Cloud's village.

Two issues apparently had been concluded: one physical, the other psychological; one of beef, the other of authority.

There were but a few squaws and children who, obdurately, had remained not far from the corrals in anticipation of participating in the slaughter of steers inside the yards. A certain number of Indians, of different tribes, like their more civilized brothers, failed to join any consolidation. Disgruntled, greedy, or contentious, they formed part of no band. Such persons, outlawed by the bands or having withdrawn from them by preference, received their portion of beef from the butcher, who killed the necessary steers in the corral and issued on the block.

Now from a vantage point on the stockade the butcher fired at the animals, while squaws and children watched the trapped creatures, offered no sporting chance, as they milled about the corral bellowing with rage and pain as the bullets pierced their bodies. Sometimes a wounded steer, miscalculating the im-

The beef issue

pregnability of the fence, dashed madly at it and became an easy target for a knife thrust or the blow of an axe.

When the last steer had been felled, the squaws and children —for this part of the revelry was beneath the dignity of the bucks —scurried into the corral and, with hatchets and knives, slashed apart the bodies of the dead or dying animals. It happened sometimes that the slaughterers fell upon a victim too soon and at the first blow of the axe the bullet-riddled beast rallied for a final combat; with feeble bellows he staggered to his hoofs and, with renewed strength, dashed at the mob, who fled for safety to the walls until a bullet or a blow ended his struggles. The squaws assisted in the skinning and cutting of the animals, and were rewarded by the butcher with gifts of livers, hearts, and entrails. With youthful or withered hands they grabbed the choice bits and ate them while the blood oozed from the warm viscera and dribbled down their chins.

The waning moon, unbrushed by a single cloud, looked down on silent prairies. The world seemed quietly asleep. For the time being, at least, McGillycuddy considered he had the situation in hand, though he wondered what Little Chief's next move would be.

He was not unprepared when the Cheyenne came to his office the next morning, accompanied by the Oglala chief, and said that he would return to his camp on Wolf Creek. The Agent took up his order blank and filled in an order for the regulation rations, telling him to go to the butcher for his beef. Little Chief reminded him that he wanted back rations. McGillycuddy smiled and began to whistle. He looked amused as he said, "No, Little Chief; you can't eat backwards." A puzzled look crossed the Cheyenne's face as he gathered his blanket about him and went out in search of the butcher.

Chapter 17

THE OUTBREAK

Though the hostiles had capitulated in their previous encounter with authority, they were far from reconciled to it; and as they smoked their pipes outside the lodges in the evenings they dreamed of past glories, recited tales of bravery, and envisioned a return of freedom on the plains. Red Cloud more than any other regretted the days gone by; more than any other he fretted under the enforcement of life according to the ways of civilization. And it was McGillycuddy who was destroying Indian traditions and inducing the younger generation to live like the white man. It was he who was building schoolhouses, covering the valleys with farms, and making laborers of once mighty warriors. Indian ponies now drew freight wagons instead of carrying braves into battle. Beef rather than buffalo meat and venison hung drying in the sun.

Red Cloud's heart was bad, and with the aid of Little Chief's hostiles he resolved to challenge progress; incited by the worst element among the squawmen and encouraged by Eastern sentimentalists, many of whom were members of the Ring, he determined to make a last stand against the domination of the Agent and the progressives who supported him.

He was encouraged in his hope of victory by numerous articles in the *Council Fire,* a paper published in Washington and edited by Dr. T. A. Bland, whose sympathies for the chief were not wholly unselfish. Bland apparently hoped to secure Red Cloud as a client against the government in a suit for remuneration for the one hundred ponies confiscated after the Sitting Bull campaign. Bland's paper reeked with sympathy for the "broken-spirited chief" and poured anathemas on the head of the "ty-

rannical agent," thus continually provoking the hostility of the
malcontents. It was circulated regularly in the camps and read to
the reactionaries by the disgruntled squawmen whose influence
McGillycuddy was striving to overcome.

McGillycuddy summoned a council, which Red Cloud refused to attend, though the hostile element was well represented
in the assembly. In council the Agent said that they all knew of
the unfriendly spirit in the Red Cloud and Little Chief bands.
For three years Red Cloud had rebelled against the progress
made at Pine Ridge and was now threatening to wipe out the
new system with the hope of returning to the old. But that
could not be done. The chief, he told, had sent a message saying
that his people were tired of him as agent, that he must go away,
that if he and his wife were not gone in three days they would be
killed and their bodies thrown over the Nebraska line. By some
means—what, he did not know—word had reached Fort Robinson that trouble was brewing there. He had just received a telegram from the post saying that troops were being held in readiness to march to Pine Ridge. As yet his orders forbade the troops
to come; he had not forgotten the agreement made with the
Indians that if they would give him fifty of their young men to
act as police he would have no soldiers there. They had given him
the young men. He had kept his promise and had wired Fort
Robinson that he, the friendly chiefs, and the police would handle
the situation. "Was I right?" he asked. A rumbling chorus of
"How, how," filled the council room. The subject would rest
for the present, the Agent then said. They would advise again
the next day.

Over the vast reservation matters were seething. Couriers
passed to and from the Agency and from village to village; groups
of Indians held council at the traders' stores, in camps, and along
the roadways. The air was filled with rumors of coming trouble.

The friendly chiefs assembled the following day to assert their
continued allegiance to the Agent. They had spent the morning
with Red Cloud trying to reason with him, but the old chief had

remained deaf to their arguments. McGillycuddy advised inaction until the following day. Then again the group of friendly chiefs lined the walls of the Agent's office while the long pipe passed from mouth to mouth and the stink of kinnikinnick smoke filled the room.

McGillycuddy told them that word had now reached the Great Father of the trouble at Pine Ridge. Last night in the thunder storm he had tried to speak over the talking-wire. The operator had heard the letters P. R. rapped out on the machine which spoke from great distances. But lightning had flashed and thunder deafened, and the machine had stopped speaking. The operator had done his best. "Repeat, repeat," he had urged, but had heard only great crashes of thunder and sleet rattling against the windowpanes while the lightning opened spaces in the darkness. Again he had heard "P. R.," and then, "Reports have reached," and once more the message was cut off. Hours passed in which he listened intently for the instrument to speak; but it was not until morning, when the storm broke, that the words came clear: "Reports have reached our office today of a hostile move on the part of Red Cloud. You will inform this office at once of existing conditions."

Two messages had followed in quick succession, one from General Sheridan, the other from General Crook, concerning the sending of troops to Pine Ridge. The same answer had been sent to each: "It is true that Red Cloud is hostile. He threatens to kill my wife and me if we are not gone from here in three days. The time is up tomorrow. I do not apprehend immediate danger, but I must have full power and authority to act in the premises." Another wire had come from Colonel E. V. Sumner, commanding Fort Robinson, stating that he had received a telegram from Sheridan that morning to hold troops in readiness to march to Pine Ridge for immediate action. They were not to advance until McGillycuddy called for help.

As Billy Garnett finished interpreting the Agent's words the operator passed McGillycuddy another telegram: "You may arrest Red Cloud and hold him prisoner if necessary to preserve the peace." It was signed by the Commissioner of Indian Affairs. When this telegram also was interpreted to the chiefs, McGillycuddy asked what should be done. For placing responsibility upon them, he felt, increased their co-operation.

Young Man Afraid advised sending a courier to Red Cloud's village with a request that he come to counsel. A sergeant of police accordingly was despatched on the errand.

As he rode to the camp he saw wagons filled with women and children moving with no apparent haste over the low hill-tops.

He returned to the Agency with the chief's answer to the message: "I am Red Cloud, chief of the Oglala Sioux. I am very well. I am on my reservation. I do not wish to hear the message of the Great Father."

McGillycuddy asked the friendly chiefs what they would advise him to do now. White Bird answered that he should send a courier the second time to Red Cloud's village, asking him to counsel. The pipe was passed solemnly from one to another while the assembly awaited a response from Red Cloud. McGillycuddy sent orders to the traders to close their stores; he had already ordered that no ammunition be sold. The chief of police returned and said the stores already were closed. Also two of the traders, with their families, had left the Agency, Mr. Blanchard alone feeling confident that McGillycuddy could handle the situation. McGillycuddy told Sword to go back and ask Mr. Blanchard to bring his family to his home; he must, on no account, change his mind and leave. If trouble came, it would come soon and there would not be time for him to reach Fort Robinson. If an outbreak occurred, the frontier would be ravaged, and they would be overtaken and killed.

The courier sent to Red Cloud's village now returned with a second refusal from the chief. McGillycuddy told his advisers that he was getting tired of this. Little Wound said the chiefs would hold council by themselves and then advise him. As they filed through the office door, Little Wound stopped and spoke to a young Indian who stood holding his pony by the bridle. The boy mounted and rode rapidly away. The chiefs squatted on the ground.

McGillycuddy went to his home and stopped only long enough to assure himself that Fanny was preserving her usual calm. When he saw her busily engaged in some household task, obviously intent upon distracting the mind of her new cook, Anna, from the troubled situation, he went hurriedly to the guard-house and told the captain to summon the entire force and draw them up in line.

To the body of stalwart young bucks the Agent said that he had summoned them to tell them of the possibility of trouble with Red Cloud. He must know exactly where they stood in the matter. They wore the uniforms of the Great Father and were sworn to stand by him. So far they had kept the faith, but they had not yet been greatly tried. Today it might be necessary to arrest Red Cloud, who had been known as their chief. It was possible that war might ensue, in which Red Cloud, himself, and many others might be killed. He would expect them to do their duty as police. If any one in the company felt he could not stand by the Great Father, he should step out of the line.

For a moment the silence was unfathomable. Then Six Feathers stepped forward.

"Red Cloud is my kinsman and my chief," he said. "I cannot fight against him."

McGillycuddy answered that he had spoken honestly—it was all that could be asked of any man. He must go to the guard-house and take off his uniform. Then he could return to his people. No word broke the stillness as Six Feathers walked from the line. Forty-nine apparently wooden soldiers stood unmoved. McGillycuddy told the captain to give the order to break ranks and await further orders.

As McGillycuddy crossed to his office he met the chief of police, who said that Mr. Blanchard was determined to remain at his post and guard his property. His family had refused to leave him. His employees were heavily armed and the log stockade——

A great clattering of hoofs interrupted the message. From all directions came groups of mounted Indians. The chiefs rose from the ground and joined the Agent. "You needn't be troubled, Father," Little Wound said. "These are our young soldiers coming to help us." Red Cloud's behavior had been anticipated. It was Little Wound's son who had stood with his pony beside the door, awaiting orders from his father to summon the warriors.

The council in the office was now resumed. Young Man Afraid said that this message should be sent to Red Cloud: The chiefs are assembled in council. They call on him for the last time to come to hear the words of the Great Father. If he refuses, they will turn over their young warriors to the Agent and ask him to send them and the police to arrest and disarm him. It was the last summons.

As the order was given to the sergeant to bear the message to Red Cloud, Yellow Hair, a renegade Brûlé Sioux who had been exiled from his band and whom the Indians considered crazy, stepped up and asked to be allowed to deliver the summons. When Yellow Hair was gone, McGillycuddy told the chief of police to open up cases of carbines in the storeroom and distribute them among the employees.

On the bluffs overlooking Red Cloud's village could be seen Indians flashing messages to the outlying camps. Throughout the day, young bucks of the hostile bands had passed back and forth from the Agency to Red Cloud's village, keeping him informed of all movements. War was in the air.

As Yellow Hair entered the Indian camp he noticed that the flag flying beside the chief's house hung at half-mast. Though the old reactionary had stoutly opposed the raising of the flag at the Agency, upon learning that it was an insignia of authority he had requested the government to supply one for his own village. And, having learned that a flag at half-mast meant trouble—of just what sort he did not know—he had lowered his to half-mast.

Yellow Hair stepped to the old chief's side, delivered the message, and, laying a hand on his shoulder, said, "Come with me." Red Cloud shrugged the hand from his shoulder and strode toward the flag, determined to tear it down in defiance of the Great Father; but as he fumbled with the knot the rope broke and the flag crumpled at his feet.

"The Great Spirit has deserted me," he cried. "I will come."

At his signal several hundred young bucks, throwing their blankets about their naked, painted bodies, gathered about him. A wagon filled with guns and ammunition fell in behind the crowd as they raced across the valley and stamped into the council room. They filled the benches along the wall, leaving many to squat on the floor, while hundreds who could not gain admittance stood outside. McGillycuddy swung open the upper half of the door between his office, where he and the friendly chiefs were waiting, and the council room. War whoops arose from the mob. "It looks like hell turned loose," he said as he closed the door.

Sword reported that the hostiles were heavily armed and that they intended to kill the Agent. McGillycuddy told him to have the first sergeant report at the office with six privates armed with revolvers. He was to draw up the rest of his men under Sergeant Standing Soldier, in a double line, outside the council room, armed with carbines.

The measured tread of the approaching guard was soon heard. McGillycuddy stepped to the door and gave orders to load the rifles. Again he opened the door into the council room and, followed by Sergeant Pumpkin Seed and the six privates, John Robinson, Billy Garnett, and the friendly chiefs, he went in. The police, according to orders, took up their position in the center of the room.

Little Wound left the group and walked toward the place where Red Cloud sat. He pushed aside a young buck seated by him and appropriated the seat. A strange look crossed Red Cloud's face as his avowed enemy—his hand beneath his blanket—sat

At Pine Ridge Agency

down. McGillycuddy too looked puzzled, wondering if Little Wound had turned traitor.

Iron Hawk, one of the leaders in the Custer Battle, was Red Cloud's haranguer. Leaping to his feet as the Agent came into the council room, throwing aside his blanket and exposing his war-painted body, he bellowed: "Red Cloud is chief of the Oglala Sioux. When he commands, men obey. He has told this white man that he throws him away; that unless he leaves this agency he will be killed." He pointed toward the old warrior, and his voice grew louder as he said: "There sits your chief. Stand by him."

McGillycuddy raised his hand to silence the din that filled the room, then spoke, commanding attention. The meeting was called, he said, that they might hear the words of the Great Father. They would have order in the council. He turned to the sergeant and said, "If any man causes disturbance throw him out; if he resists shoot him."

He had summoned them, he began, to hear the words of the Great Father which he had spoken over the talking wire, Billy Garnett's voice as interpreter trailing his own. Red Cloud had been war chief of the Oglalas for many years; under former agents he had behaved as if he himself were the Agent. Had he been a wise man he would have caused no harm; he would have advised his people to follow the white man's ways. Whether he liked it or not he would have known that they offered the only hope for the Indian. He had told Red Cloud that many times; but he would not listen. He heard only the bad men, the squaw-men who poisoned his brain while they lived off his people. After three summons he had come to hear the Great Father's message. It was this: "You may arrest Red Cloud and hold him prisoner if necessary to preserve the peace."

The old man started from his seat; but Little Wound's hand restrained him. He was no longer fit to be head chief, the Agent continued. Henceforth Red Cloud should be dealt with as a subchief and not even as that if he persisted in stirring up trouble.

His somewhat raised voice was yet controlled as he said, looking directly at the withered, painted warrior: "Never again shall I recognize you as head chief. I depose you!"

With a cry of rage the old chieftain sprang toward the Agent, a knife brandished in his hand. Only a few steps separated the two—the white man, young and slender; the old Sioux, his body, from which the blanket had fallen, painted a livid green, with patches of chrome yellow—when Little Wound stepped between them. With hands uplifted the old warrior cried: "I am Red Cloud, chief of the Oglala Sioux. When Red Cloud speaks, men listen. I have ordered this white man to leave my country. If he dies it is his own fault."

There was tumult in the council room. McGillycuddy again raised his hand. "A word more," he shouted. "The Great Father whose words I speak is to be listened to and not argued with. Clear the council. *Henela.*"

As though hypnotized, the painted, howling mob poured through the doorways, followed by the police, leaving the Agent alone with his friendly counselors.

Little Wound asked McGillycuddy what he thought when he saw him take his seat beside Red Cloud. He wondered if he had turned traitor, the Agent answered. In a quarrel many winters ago, Little Wound said, Red Cloud had killed his brother. He would have taken revenge then, but a messenger from the Great Father had said: "Forget, Little Wound. There has been trouble enough already. War between the bands of a tribe is death to the tribe." He had promised to forget. But today he knew that Red Cloud meant to kill the Agent. He had killed his brother; he should not kill his friend. McGillycuddy shook the red man's hand.

Pine Ridge soon lay under the sun, against the low, rolling hills, as quiet as any New England town on a bright summer day. Indians walked along the hard-baked road on their way to the stores, only one of which they found open. The Agent had sent word to Blanchard that the trouble was over, and the trader had lost no time in unlocking the doors. The clerks stood behind the counter and tore off yards of calico and blue and red cloth and laid out boxes of bright-colored beads from which squaws made their choice. Bucks squatted along the wall as usual smoking the long pipe, smiling occasionally as smoke issued gently from their nostrils.

Sunday remained as peaceable a day as had ever passed at Pine Ridge. Indians flocked into the church in the morning, and later in the day the Agent and his wife drove to some of the outlying camps. Everyone seemed happy. McGillycuddy saw no reason to change his plans made some time earlier to go to Omaha to meet the six women who had been engaged to teach at the new boarding school. He had thought it wise to allay fears of the novitiates in crossing the plains to the Indian country by promising his personal escort. Nothing irked McGillycuddy more than to have his plans upset. He was firm in his purpose, yet he exercised caution.

Consequently when he set out early Monday morning for the railroad he took with him, besides his driver, Wm. A. Foster, his telegrapher, having assigned Donald Brown, the master of transportation, who understood telegraphy, in his place. Autumn was creeping over the Great Plains. The dry grass was ocher- and saffron-colored. The hoofs of the team thudded on the hard road as mile after mile was left behind. Night spread into infinity when camp was made, sixty miles from Pine Ridge. Supper was eaten beside the campfire. Frogs croaked in the stream near by. McGillycuddy's mind was at ease—almost. He felt a sense of elation as he looked at the telegraph wire humming over head in the autumn breeze. Time and space seemed eliminated by the small wire stretched beneath the sky.

"We'll cut it now," he said to the two men who awaited his orders. He liked the feel of power. He enjoyed engaging the power of electricity.

Ott Means stood off a short distance and cast a lariat over the wire. It sagged. McGillycuddy and Foster reached up and drew it lower. The grating sound of a file for a moment united with the croak of the frogs, and the wire was severed.

"Attach your instruments to the end of the wire at the west," McGillycuddy said to Foster.

When the instruments were attached he asked Foster to call Pine Ridge. Donald Brown responded to the call-letters, "P. R." To the inquiry as to conditions at the Agency, Brown answered that almost immediately after his departure Jim Oldham, police chief, Dr. Grinnell, and the trader Cowgill had invited Red Cloud to breakfast and had assured him that they would stand by him and support him in his demands.

From the prairie station flashed back the message: "Get Chief Clerk Alder . . . . have him give orders for Oldham's arrest and confinement in quarters . . . . Brown to act as chief of police . . . . observe movements of Grinnell and Cowgill . . . . wires to be used for official messages only . . . . wire Valentine tomorrow night how matters stand." The plotters now would have to send messages to Fort Robinson if they wished to get in touch with Washington. McGillycuddy then switched his instruments to the east end of the line and advised the Commissioner of Indian Affairs of his actions.

Two telegrams awaited the Agent at Valentine, the terminus of the Fremont, Elkhorn, and Missouri River Railroad at that time. From Pine Ridge came word that all was quiet. The Commissioner wired that it was inadvisable that McGillycuddy should be absent from the Agency in the present state of unrest. To the latter telegram McGillycuddy answered that conditions were satisfactory at Pine Ridge and that he would return as soon as he got his teachers. The telegram was signed as always, "McGillycuddy, Agent."

Valentine was a typical frontier town. Its short streets were punctuated with saloons offering rendezvous to men, many of whom had "left their country for their country's good." Many whose exodus from Pine Ridge had been compulsory were congregated in the new railroad town. McGillycuddy bought a ticket to Omaha and asked the ticket agent to keep his buffalo robe while he went to buy a paper. With Foster and Ott Means he walked to the drugstore, bought the *Omaha Daily Bee,* and, after telling the men the train on which he would return, left his companions and started back to the station.

The town, like most border towns, showed little discrimination between day and night. Cowboys, soldiers, roughnecks, and bleached blondes, frizzed and painted, walked the streets—some steadily, many tipsily. As McGillycuddy drew near a dance hall where a small town orchestra droned out a quadrille, the leader shouting, "Al'la man left; grand right and left," he noticed two men carrying clubs step out of the hall. As he passed he heard the shuffle of their heavy boots falling in behind him. However, they did not come into the station, and he gave them no more thought. The ticket agent invited him into his office to take a nap—there was a comfortable bench there—he would waken the Agent when the train was made up. McGillycuddy, having spent many nights under much less comfortable conditions than a bench afforded, slept easily until he felt a touch on his shoulder. The train would leave in ten minutes.

To men on the frontier there was no stage between sleeping and waking, no somnolent semiconsciousness in which the comfort of a bed or sleeping bag was weighed against the discomfort of a cold room or colder outdoors. Too often had their waking been caused by the hum of bullets, a volley of oaths, or the war whoops of Indians, for them to establish the habit of gliding gently from lethargic slumber into complete consciousness.

McGillycuddy slipped instantly from the hard bench, smoothed his fast-thinning hair, and, rolling up his buffalo robe, asked the ticket agent to keep it for him until his return from Omaha. He felt his hip pocket, where, contrary to his custom on the reservation, he carried a forty-one Colt revolver. Too many of the loiterers owed their temporary residence in border towns to his inhospitality at the Agency. Too many had hurled threats of reprisal at him as they had left the Agency escorted by the police to be put across the reservation line. "You're runnin' this place," the exiled had sometimes shouted; "but wait till we get you on the other side of the line." He had answered that he would carry a coffin with him; but instead he carried the Colt revolver.

He stepped to the station door and looked through the dirty glass at the platform. The smoky-globed kerosene lamps exuded a feeble light. Out on the tracks the cars were being moved about in making up the train. The two men who had followed him to the station swaggered along the otherwise deserted platform, each still carrying a club. A forty-five-caliber revolver bulged in each man's holster. As they passed in the channel of thin light McGillycuddy recognized them both. They had been liberated but lately from the Nebraska State Penitentiary, where they had been incarcerated on his testimony for the stealing of Indian cattle. The Agent shifted his gun to his coatpocket.

The two men walked to the end of the platform, turned, and followed McGillycuddy as he left the station and headed for the train, his right hand clasping the hilt of the gun in his pocket.

The cars jostled, jammed, and lurched, while heavy iron chains rattled, as freight cars bumped together and were hooked on one by one. The noise conflicted with the footsteps of the men, who followed McGillycuddy until, at the door of the day coach, one of the men stepped forward and blocked his way.

"Look here, McGillycuddy," he said. "We've got something to say to you."

The Agent shoved his valise against the man and jumped up the steps of the car, saying this was no time to talk. The men followed him inside, where sat a half-dozen cowboys, a Catholic priest, and a man in town clothes. McGillycuddy took a seat in the middle of the car.

"Damn you, come out and fight," one of the men said, while they both swore loudly. Their eyes were on the muzzle of the gun in the Agent's pocket which pointed toward them.

"I'm not looking for a fight," the Agent answered. "Talk's cheap, but don't make any motions."

The cowboys, the priest, and the man in town clothes looked on, of course interested in the quarrel.

"You're the man who got us sent to jail," the second man shouted. "Damn you." But they only swore; they made no motions.

The conductor shrieked "All aboard."

"Unless you're taking this train you'd better be getting off," McGillycuddy suggested. And a volley of oaths filled the car as the two men lurched with the rocking of the train down the aisle and jumped off.

The man in town clothes said he knew those fellows; they were bad ones. He had wondered what they were hanging around the station for, and he guessed they had heard that McGillycuddy was taking the train and were "laying" for him. Perhaps McGillycuddy would be obliged to shoot one of the bad men some day, and he could rely on him to take his part. He would testify at any time that he had shot in self-defense. His name was Fitz-Warren. It was the Agent's introduction to Judge Fitz-Warren.

Of all the articles published in the press concerning the recent "outbreak" at Pine Ridge which McGillycuddy encountered when he reached Omaha the next morning, none amused him so much as one in the *Laramie Boomerang,* edited by Bill Nye. It read:

McGillycuddy seems to be enjoying one of his periodical troubles with Red Cloud. There appears to be blood on the moon. During the recent uprising of Red Cloud and his followers, word of the disturbance, unknown to the agent and contrary to his wishes, reached the department in Washington. McGillycuddy was notified that troops were in readiness to put in motion.

We notice a dispatch from the gentleman holding down the agency, in the form of an ultimatum to the Indian Office, taking the law in his own hands and refusing to accept troops. The ultimatum was signed tersely, "McGillycuddy—Agent."

Now if that agent up there had the name, Smith, Brown or Jones the affair might pass unnoticed but when the name McGillycuddy looms on the horizon, people pause and ask, "What manner of man is this?" However this autocratic agent has the right-thinking people of the West on his side. Doubtless his course has often prevented a whole-sale massacre on the frontier. He is the type of man who does not wait for the circumlocution of a department three thousand miles [*sic*] away to take action but initiates action himself. In other words he does not wait until he's scalped to have the machinery of the law put in motion.

Had troops arrived at Pine Ridge, contrary to the agreement entered into between the agent and the friendly Indians, it is certain that the latter would have joined forces with the hostiles and killed all the Whites living in the vicinity and scattered out to attack the settlers along the frontier before a sufficient force could have been turned in against them.

McGillycuddy was harassed by reporters, eager for firsthand information concerning the "outbreak" at Pine Ridge. But after a busy day in which he repeated innumerable times that all was quiet on the frontier, he succeeded in getting off on the evening train with the four old maids and the two young women who were to teach the Indian children how to live like the white man.

A violent windstorm swept the country after the Agent, his telegrapher, the driver, and the six women had fallen into quiet sleep on the plains between Valentine and Pine Ridge. It caused the tent poles to crash, the tents to envelop the sleepers, and the women to spring from their ground beds thinking the camp was being attacked by Indians. McGillycuddy assured them of their safety, as he, Foster, and Ott Means released them from the wreck-age. But unprotected by the tents their possessions swept along with the wind and tumbleweeds mingled with the camp accoutre-ments. The women in varicolored robes sought in the darkness strayed articles of clothing, even white undergarments being scarcely visible in the black night. Clouds rode the sky and drops of rain threatened a storm. The wind at length slackened, and by the time rain pelted the prairies the tents were set up again.

But there was no more sleep for the women, though their whisperings did not prevent the men from taking advantage of the few hours before dawn. Then they were roused by a rustling outside their tent. Through the tent flap they saw weird figures,

one with a veil tied over her head, slipping out from the other
tent and heading in different directions, earnestly scanning the
prairies. They saw the women pick up a few wet garments and
continue their search. The men emerged from their tent and,
while Ott Means struggled to start a fire with wet brushwood and
Foster rolled up blankets, the Agent offered assistance to the
women. The search had continued for some time, McGillycuddy
not knowing for what he was looking, when Miss Chaffee, one
of the two younger women, confided to him that a red wig belonging to the woman whose head was enveloped in a veil could
not be found. When the welcome odor of coffee summoned the
searchers to breakfast, McGillycuddy announced that the missing
article had doubtless attached itself to a tumbleweed and was
traveling miles from there by that time. After a breakfast of
bacon, eggs, biscuits, and coffee they resumed their journey over
the muddy roads, the hat of one of the women pulled low over
her brow and tied on with a veil.

Only the lights in the Agent's home and in the boarding
school suggested life at Pine Ridge as the carriage drove up to the
door of the school, where the teachers were greeted by Fanny and
Maggie Stands Looking, a daughter of Chief Stands Looking
and a graduate of the Carlisle School, who was to act as assistant
matron for the new enterprise. A supper awaited the tired women
who disregarded their ruffled appearance and ate heartily.

The following morning McGillycuddy discharged Jim Oldham, the police chief, from the force and advised him to get out
of the country. He took no action against Dr. Grinnell or the
trader, Cowgill; they were government appointees and outside
his jurisdiction. But the police watched their movements.

Newspapers reaped a harvest with the news of the so-called
Indian outbreak. Bishop Hare wrote in the *Philadelphia Inquirer*
after reading attacks on the Agent for the trouble at Pine Ridge:
"I have seen nothing to shake my faith in the excellence of Dr.
McGillycuddy's administration." He expressed a wish that "prac-
tical friends of the Indian cause see the importance of a close

acquaintance with facts and a just discrimination in reference to agents, by which those guilty of actual wrong may be discovered and punished while those who, like Dr. McGillycuddy, have saved the expenditure of large sums to the department and have faithfully labored for the good of the Indian may be maintained in power and encouraged in the performance of duty." A Mr. A. A. Sloan, who wrote that he was at Pine Ridge at the time of the threatened trouble and was advised to get out as soon as possible, didn't think there was any trouble because the Agent dared not oppose Red Cloud and his two hundred warriors with his fifty police; these were Indians and it was doubtful if he could depend on them to oppose the chief. The Agent, he said, had given orders to shoot Red Cloud if he came within one hundred yards of the Agency; but six of the police had taken off their uniforms and thrown them on the ground and left the service. Sloan ended by saying it was thought the troubles would soon be settled.

McGillycuddy wondered who Mr. Sloan was and how he had happened to be at the Agency without his knowledge.

Chapter 18

A STEP FORWARD

McGILLYCUDDY was more elated over the institution of the boarding school at Pine Ridge than over any other single accomplishment since the beginning of his services as agent, barring only his organization of the Indian police. The school was a model of its kind, with large halls, airy schoolrooms, and sleeping apartments, with small, clean beds. The bathrooms were provided with metal bathtubs and with hot and cold water. The living room was comfortably furnished. And the kitchen had a huge range with a capacity of one hundred loaves of bread. Everything was in perfect order when the children, a certain number from each camp, were brought to the school.

On the opening day hundreds of curious Indians—bucks, squaws, and children—hung about the building wondering just what was going to happen to the two hundred youngsters sequestered within it. McGillycuddy advised pulling down the shades at the windows in the large bathroom on the ground floor to exclude the gaze of the inquisitive.

The first step toward civilizing these primitive children was to purge them of various uncleannesses. The several bathrooms as well as the laundry were the scenes of activity, the hair-cutting to be accomplished first, followed by a bath, which would include washing the heads. It was a labor-saving device.

In each bathroom a teacher armed with shears was prepared to begin operations. Curious peepers stood close to the windows on the ground floor, deeply regretful of the drawn shades which barred their observation of the activities carried on behind them. There the matron seated a small boy and, taking a lousy braid in one hand, raised the shears hanging by a chain from her waist. A

205

single clip and the filthy braid would have been severed. But unfortunately at that moment a breeze blew back the shade from the window. The previously baffled effort of a youngster plastered against the casing on the outside of the window was now rewarded by a fleeting glimpse of his playmate seated in the chair and a tall, lean woman with a pair of long shears in her hand prepared to divest the boy of his hair—a Delilah bringing calamity upon an embryo Samson.

Like a war whoop rang out the cry: *"Pahin ḳaḳsa, pahin ḳaḳsa!"* The enclosure rang with the alarm; it invaded every room in the building and floated out on the prairie. No warning of fire or flood or tornado or hurricane, not even the approach of an enemy could have more effectively emptied the building as well as the grounds of the new school as did that ominous cry, "They are cutting the hair." Through doors and windows the children flew; down the steps, through gates and over fences in a mad flight toward the Indian villages, followed by the mob of bucks and squaws as though all were pursued by a bad spirit. They had been suspicious of the school from the beginning; now they knew it was intended to bring disgrace upon them.

McGillycuddy's raised hands, his placating shouts, and his stern commands were less effective than they had been on occasions of threatened outbreak. He was impotent to stem the flight. He calmed the excited teachers, assuring them that the schoolhouse would soon again be filled with children. But their faces expressed disappointment as well as chagrin over the apparent failure of this attempt to civilize the Sioux.

Before returning to the office the Agent and Fanny, who had accompanied him to the school, paid a visit to Blanchard's home, where McGillycuddy gave the family a vivid description of the scenes at the school and remained to tell them of a misadventure in the life of the old chief, Red Cloud. His frame house, with the flag floating gracefully beside it, was not affording the old man complete satisfaction. There was nothing more to wish for in the house itself; but its incomplete household disturbed him. It was too elegant for one wife only, he thought, especially when the one was old, fat, and far from lovely; and he determined to add a younger and more attractive mistress to his menage.

He had viewed the maidens in his village for some time, at length making his choice. She was the daughter of a subchief. One night he had tied three ponies outside her parents' lodge; as he had peered through the grimy glass of the window the next morning he had seen that the ponies were not there—they had been accepted as the price of the girl.

Red Cloud had fetched her to his fine house. The old wife had scanned the intruder; apparently she was not a mere visitor— she carried her belongings wrapped in a piece of red calico; timidly she had laid the bundle on the floor and hidden her face with her shawl. With a cry of rage the old woman had seized a butcher knife and dashed toward the girl, who cowered before her. Holding it over the crouching figure, the woman had showered maledictions on the head of the old warrior. She would kill any girl he brought into the house, she threatened, as well as himself if he persisted in his waywardness. At the first opportunity the girl had fled from the place, and the old warrior, whose passion was long spent by age, having no desire for a row, had lighted his pipe and settled down in his new home with his old wife.

McGillycuddy, having laughed at this recital, returned to his office and sent couriers to the villages to summon the chiefs in council. When they were assembled on the following day he spoke upon the virtues of cleanliness and spared no words in explaining the evil of lice and the comfort the children would experience when divested of vermin. Ten days later the school again was filled, and this time no protestations interrupted the haircutting.

But Red Cloud was not happy. His prestige was not what it had been before the Agent had deposed him; and he asked permission to visit the Great Father in order to talk over his grievances. When his request was granted, he took with him, among other chiefs, American Horse, the straddler. After Red Cloud's departure some of the progressive chiefs visited McGillycuddy to ask that he write the Great Father and ask him to keep Red Cloud in Washington. They wanted to live like the white man, they said; and Red Cloud always would be an Indian.

When the old warrior returned to the Agency, McGilly-cuddy called a council, inviting him to report his visit. He had little to say. He had received no encouragement from the Great Father. He repeated his grievances, and urged that he be re-instated as head chief. McGillycuddy refused, saying that as yet he had not proved his worthiness. American Horse then rose and said that he had spoken well of their Father while in Wash-ington—he had said he was a good man—that they wanted to keep him. McGillycuddy knew he was lying, for already he had heard the contrary. But his smile was friendly, even amused, as he told American Horse he was troubled about him—that he was afflicted with a serious malady in which one leg had grown white while the other remained brown. So far the legs had traveled together harmoniously; but a time would come when the white leg would walk in one direction and the brown in another, and he would be torn into two parts. The Agent shook his head in worried fashion. This occasioned a burst of laughter from the assembly, and American Horse hung his head. There was nothing an Indian disliked more than to be laughed at.

Red Cloud's attention was diverted from his troubles for a time when he was visited by a delegation of chiefs and head men from a Missouri River agency. He received them in war bonnet heavy with eagle feathers. His body was painted. The visitors were dressed in civilian clothes. The delegation was greatly interested in the advanced condition of the Pine Ridge Agency and expressed surprise that the Oglalas were receiving twice as large annuities and rations as the River Indians. They were Christian Indians, they said. They went to church and made no trouble for the Great Father, and yet the Sioux received better treatment.

"My friends from the Missouri River," Red Cloud answered,

"that is your mistake. You are too good. Paint your faces, cut out the seat of your pants, dance and howl, and the Great Father will give you plenty to eat."

The malcontents at the Pine Ridge Agency encouraged him in this belief; and, spurred on by the Ring, he continued to pour complaints into the Indian Office, while the progressives went calmly on their way toward civilization. Except on occasions the attitude of the Agent and the old chief toward each other was apparently friendly. But trouble brewed beneath the surface.

One morning the captain of police reported that the preceding night the chief had held a council at which the young bucks had drawn lots to determine which eight should visit the Agent that day to petition many things. On his anticipated refusal, they planned to kill him. The bucks would be there soon. Should he bring a squad to the office? McGillycuddy said he would handle the situation alone. The captain left reluctantly.

When the petitioners came in, the Agent glanced up from the work on his desk. He invited them to sit down; he would listen to them in a minute—as soon as he had finished his letter. The young bucks squatted on the floor in a semicircle. No one spoke until the Agent put down his pen and asked the reason for the visit. Big Horn, seated at one end of the line, said he wanted some coffee for his sick mother. McGillycuddy wrote an order for the coffee.

The second Indian wanted his wagon mended; and an order to the carpenter was written. The third asked for five pounds of sugar; the fourth asked for a new plow. An order was written for each request, though McGillycuddy resolved to examine the condition of the old plow later.

When all the requests had been granted, Big Horn, seeing their plan dissolve, stammered as he tried to think of something else to demand.

"Don't waste time in asking for more things," the Agent said. "I know of your plan in coming here. It was stupid. I have given you what you asked for. *Henela,* clear out."

The Indians looked surprised as they hunched themselves from the floor, each looking at the other as if hopeful that someone would take the initiative in carrying out their intention.

McGillycuddy then stepped to the glass cage which contained his two pet rattlesnakes. Their diamond-shaped heads lifted as he tapped the glass; their sleek bodies writhed and their fangs darted out. He slid back the door of the cage. The Indians stumbled over each other in their haste to get out of the office. McGillycuddy closed the cage door and went to the window. He saw the group standing in the middle of the road, gesticulating and pointing to each other, obviously each asking why the other had not started something. They were still arguing when they passed out of sight on their way to Red Cloud's camp.

The Agent pondered as he whistled a tune from *Pinafore,* an operetta he had heard on his last trip to Washington: The situation here at Pine Ridge was certainly unique, belligerent, and fantastic. Progress stood at bay against reaction; civilization against barbarism.

He felt a deep sympathy for the old chief, thinking that age did not take kindly to changes—to it the accustomed ways seemed always the best.

Chapter *19*

THE INDIAN RING

THE INDIAN RING—encouraging Red Cloud in his resentment against McGillycuddy, prodding him to rebellion, reporting imaginary ruptures between the factions at Pine Ridge—plotted ever to discover some irregularity in his conduct, something more condemning than the stale accusation of tyranny over the reactionaries. The animosity of an Indian inspector, W. J. Pollack, toward McGillycuddy was well known to Teller, Secretary of the Interior under Garfield, who had succeeded Hayes as president, though his connection with the Ring was unknown. Pollack took advantage of Teller's absence from Washington in order to secure an order to go to Pine Ridge to investigate the charges trumped up against the Agent.

A cold wind and a flurry of snow indicated an early winter, as Pollack, with a half-breed interpreter picked up at Valentine, drove into Pine Ridge in October and became the guest of Dr. Grinnell. An office in the guardhouse was assigned him in which to examine witnesses. It was only after McGillycuddy's violent protest that his own interpreter, Garnett, was finally allowed to be present at the examination of Indians, half-breeds, Mexicans, and whites, the Agent claiming that otherwise his bondsmen would be imperiled and his own reputation jeopardized.

When depositions had been taken from the riffraff about the Agency, the inspector visited the homes of the residents, swore them in, and questioned them. Did they know of any violation of law of which the Agent was guilty? Had he at any time made them presents from Indian supplies? Negations met his prodding. At the Agent's home the inspector requested him to leave the room while he questioned his wife. McGillycuddy refused flatly;

211

it was an indignity he would not tolerate. Fanny knitted her brows when asked if the Agent had given her anything from the Agency supplies. After thinking for a moment she answered that once as she watched the unpacking of huge cases she had asked him if she might have from one a pair of scissors, for hers were very dull. He had answered hurriedly, being busily occupied in checking the goods, that she might have them. Was there anything else, the inspector asked ingratiatingly? There was nothing else. Pollack thanked her and left the house.

At the conclusion of the investigation he wired his charges against the Agent to the department: The accounts were short; the books were not in order; goods belonging to the Indians had been sold to traders with profit to himself; he had made false reports and had feathered his nest with government funds; he had given his wife articles from the annuities. He would suspend McGillycuddy for malfeasance in office and appoint his clerk, John Alder, as acting agent.

The answer came immediately: "You must not interfere with the Pine Ridge agent. He will retain his position until the charges are proven. Inspector Benedict will proceed at once to the agency and his actions in the premises will be awaited." Pollack wired that he knew his duty and authority under the statutes and on Wednesday he would suspend McGillycuddy from duty. Secretary Teller, who by this time was back in Washington, telegraphed that if the inspector continued to disregard orders he would be suspended from office. In spite of the warning, Pollack informed McGillycuddy that he wished to meet him at eight o'clock in the evening.

Presumably McGillycuddy knew nothing of the messages passed over the wires between the inspector and the Department. The telegraph operator, a government employee, could not divulge the communications. But since Donald Brown also was a telegrapher he had understood the messages; and the Agent was quite prepared when he was summoned. He invited all the employees to be present at the ceremony of suspension.

When Pollack appeared at the main office he met the eyes of the large group seated along the walls. He looked apprehensively at them and requested to see the Agent alone. Inside the Agent's private office he remarked he would rather cut off his right hand than perform the unpleasant task before him. McGillycuddy said he should not hesitate to do his duty. Pollack then drew a folded document from his pocket and passed it to the Agent, who read there of his suspension from office. The chief clerk was then summoned and notified that he was to act as Agent until further orders. Alder's protests availed him nothing.

Early the following morning Pollack crossed the plains in a snowstorm to Valentine and the Agent wired the Commissioner of his suspension. Throughout the morning Alder appealed to McGillycuddy for directions in carrying on the affairs of the Agency; but he laughingly refused to give advice, saying he no longer was Agent. These two were excellent friends. The employees repeatedly came to the office and taunted Alder with stealing the Agent's job. The discomfort caused by the jibes of his associates was enhanced when at noon came a wire from the Secretary of the Interior: "McGillycuddy is still agent and you must not interfere with him." Alder swore a muttered oath: "As if I wanted to be agent at this damn agency." The two men laughed.

When Pollack reached his home in Aurora, Illinois, he found a wire informing him of his removal from office and a demand for a refund of his expenses. Benedict soon appeared at Pine Ridge. After a meticulous examination of affairs and a thorough examination of accounts he sent a report as favorable as Pollack's had been adverse. He declared Pine Ridge to be the finest agency in the United States and its books in perfect order. If progress continued as it had in the three years of McGillycuddy's administration, he wrote the Indian Bureau, the Oglalas would soon give the government no more trouble.

Pollack was thus quashed; but the Indian Ring still persisted. Pollack's report of his investigation was published in the *Council*

Fire and circulated in the camps of the reactionaries. This resulted in McGillycuddy being summoned to Washington for a conference.

Winter was on in dead earnest. Through the snowy silence a sleigh bore the Agent and his wife, wrapped in buffalo coats and robes, over the trackless white plains to the railroad. Their cheeks, but barely visible, were smeared with a paste of soot and lard to diminish the glare of the blinding whiteness. The freezing wind thrashed the snow over their coverings and crept inside their ear mufflers. Their voices sounded leaden, as infrequently they exchanged a word from their wrappings. The runners of the sleigh whined dismally. The hungry baying of coyotes was added to the plaint of the runners when night darkened the plains.

But the councils in Washington ended, as had all previous ones, in complete approval of McGillycuddy's methods of handling the Oglalas.

The world beyond the white-robed plains seemed nonexistent, as McGillycuddy, inspecting some work in the carpenter shop, heard the office bell, deep-toned as it pealed through the frozen air, ring once. He listened; there was no second ring. Hurrying to the office, he found an army ambulance outside the door and beside it a sergeant, who saluted and handed him a letter from the commandant at Fort Niobrara. He asked the sergeant to come indoors. The sergeant pointed to an Indian seated in the ambulance. McGillycuddy at once recognized the shackled Brûlé Sioux as Thunder Hawk, who had got into trouble at the Spotted Tail Agency after the death of the chief. McGillycuddy told the sergeant to take the Indian into the office and then read the letter, thus receiving his first intimation of a decision made by the War and the Interior departments consigning the prisoner to his charge.

Thunder Hawk was a close friend of Young Spot, son of the Sioux chieftain, and sympathized with him in his disappointment at not becoming his father's successor. Young Spot had known for some time before Spotted Tail's death that he desired White

Thunder to succeed him, but that did not soften the blow when his wish was carried out; and Young Spot had proceeded to make trouble for his rival. He had gone to White Thunder's lodge and stolen his wife. White Thunder had retaliated by stealing Young Spot's herd.

In company with two friends, Thunder Hawk and Long Pumpkin, Young Spot had concealed himself in some bushes along the trail between his camp and that of White Thunder and, as the latter had passed with his herd, Thunder Hawk had fired, mortally wounding the chief, though a bullet from the latter's gun fired simultaneously had wounded Long Pumpkin. Young Spot and Thunder Hawk had been arrested and taken to Fort Niobrara, charged with murder by Agent Wright. The two Indians had threatened death to the agent when they should be released. Once during their incarceration they had made their escape but had been recaptured on their way to the Spotted Tail Agency. Young Spot had then agreed to abandon evil designs against the agent and had been released; but Thunder Hawk had refused to make any promises and had remained in jail. Months had passed, and the War Department, wearied of the responsibility of the murderer, after consultation with the Department of the Interior, had reached the decision that Thunder Hawk should be entrusted to McGillycuddy's keeping.

McGillycuddy took the prisoner into his private office and, after much persuasion, obtained his promise that if he were allowed to live with some of his relatives on Wounded Knee Creek he would not return to his agency. The Indian thus became a member of the camp, with a sergeant belonging to the band to act as sponsor for him. When for weeks his conduct had been irreproachable, the sergeant grew slack in his espionage. Then, one day, with a hasty word to the sergeant that he was off to kill the agent responsible for his arrest, Thunder Hawk, mounted on a borrowed pony and clutching a borrowed gun, galloped toward the Spotted Tail Agency.

A corporal and six men were immediately despatched in

pursuit of the criminal with orders to report to Agent Wright and request that Thunder Hawk be turned over to them. Wright had not known of Thunder Hawk's arrival until informed by the Pine Ridge police, when he lost no time in ordering out a squad to arrest the unwelcome visitor. These police returned to report that Thunder Hawk was fortified in his cabin and prepared to resist, and that they were unable to arrest him. When the corporal of the Pine Ridge squad requested permission to attempt the arrest with his men, Wright was more than willing to grant the request.

When they reached his cabin, Thunder Hawk opened fire. The police rushed the cabin, broke down the door, and entered. A fight ensued in which both Thunder Hawk and his squaw were wounded, the former in the wrist and his squaw in the thigh. The prisoner was thus recaptured and returned to Pine Ridge, where he was lodged in the guardhouse. When another culprit was brought into the jail, Thunder Hawk looked wisely at him and said, "You'd better do what your Father tells you to do; I disobeyed him and look what happened to me." He pointed to his bandaged wrist.

McGillycuddy wondered if the Indian Bureau was going to add to his responsibilities by making a penal colony of Pine Ridge. However, when Thunder Hawk was given another trial as a member of the band on Wounded Knee Creek, he became exemplary in his behavior and left the village only for occasional excursions to towns near by, from which he often returned with his pocket full of money won at poker.

In making comparison of the situation at the two agencies, Elaine Goodale, a great friend of the Indians, wrote in the *New York Times:*

If the Lower Brule Agency possesses the elements of dramatic interest, Pine Ridge is a fully developed situation. The first represents the blind and chaotic struggle between barbarism and civilization. At the second the forces are played off against each other and accurately weighed and balanced by a cool and powerful hand.

Dr. McGillycuddy, the Red Cloud agent, has been called an autocrat and a tyrant but his is not the mere arbitrary exercise of power. His will is absolute yet he is an agent in the fullest sense of the word, acting under authority of the government, of law and civilization to put down tribal authority. His policy is to use the progressive party as a check upon the other.

There are then at this great agency two fully-organized parties—on the one side this remarkable man, all coolness, nerve and executive force, with a backing of fifty Indian police, well armed and disciplined, under Captain Sword, an almost equally remarkable Indian, and a majority of the chiefs with their bands of followers; on the other the famous old malcontent, Red Cloud, obstinately fighting for his declining influence and surrounded by a little band of dissatisfied, turbulent and non-progressive Indians. . . . .

McGillycuddy, with his superior force, organization and discipline and with the overwhelming weight of law and order on his side, naturally commands the situation. . . . .

There was little excitement at the Agency during the rest of the winter, even the newspapers seeming dull after the cessation of exclamatory articles concerning Pollack's investigation of affairs at Pine Ridge. McGillycuddy said he felt neglected when no one was branding him a thief or a tyrant.

At last the prairies were green with buffalo grass and flecked with bright flowers. Four thousand cattle grazed on the plains—beef for the Pine Ridge Indians, who tilled the soil and planted, rendered content by their full stomachs. Prairie chickens mated and the air was full of the warbling of soaring meadow larks. Robins nested and in the streams not too close to the Indian camps beavers repaired winter damage to their dams, dragging fresh saplings into the water with busy splashings.

Horns were growing on the heads of the deer, encouraging them to take advantage of their freedom to wander farther from the Agency. The buffalo were trim, having shed their shaggy winter coats. Only the eagles showed no pleasure in the spring when they were turned out of the commissary building but hovered near, unfamiliar with the ways of the air monarchs until, after testing their wings, they sped away to the pine bluffs. The nests in the chicken house were full of fresh eggs; green shoots were up in Fanny's garden; and the cat lay on her stomach along the rim of the new fountain in front of the Agent's house, annoyed that the goldfish eluded her claws.

But peace at Pine Ridge was, as usual, of short duration. It was a superimposition, its validity belied by the old animosity which, mole-like, operated beneath the surface. The *Council Fire* continued its diatribes against the Agent; and, while peace reigned in the villages, a group of squawmen and Indians sat about the campfire in Red Cloud's village on a Saturday evening smoking their pipes and discussing the news contained in a copy of the paper received that day.

Youths quitted their games to listen to the scandalous tales of the Agent which they knew invariably followed the perusal of the paper. How was it possible that the Great Father persisted in leaving this wicked, tyrannous man among them in spite of the repeated protests of Red Cloud, Young No Water, an inflammable youth, wondered. This despotic agent whom the chief and the squawmen did not like was breaking up the tribal system, he heard them say. Red Cloud was no longer the potentate he had been before this white man had come to be their agent. The Agent was scattering the bands along the streams and urging them to build more houses and plant more gardens. Soon there would be no semblance of the fighting Sioux in the civilized people living in houses, tilling the soil, and driving their own freight wagons while their children learned the white man's ways in schoolrooms. They would become white men and there would be no Indians left.

"What you want, Red Cloud, is a new agent," Young No Water heard Nick Janiss say, "one who'll do's you tell him to. This here agent's takin' away all yer a'thority."

The youth listened to the talk of the squawmen. All night he tossed on his blanket. On Sunday he sat apart and pondered the subject.

Rain dribbled from gray clouds on Monday morning as

Young No Water bit half-moons from a hunk of black bread and gulped coffee from a tin cup before stealing into the lodge. No one was inside. He slipped his father's gun under his blanket and went past the group squatting about the campfire apparently indifferent to the rain drizzling on them.

After crossing the bridge over the White Clay Creek, Young No Water turned to the north on a road which led past the window of the Agent's private office. He wondered if McGillycuddy would be in his office by that time. He could not tell the hour if the sun was not shining. McGillycuddy was leaning back in his swivel chair reading a paper as Young No Water reached the spot on the road where he could see into the office. It was a paper which John Alder had handed him as he passed through the main office. The article accused him of some irregularities which caused him no concern. But when he read the conclusion: "And beside, he wears corsets," McGillycuddy called to his clerk: "Well I'll be damned if I don't go up to Deadwood and beat up that editor." And he leaned his slim body farther back in the swivel chair. One hundred and thirty-five pounds on a six-foot body did not require corsets to give him a twenty-nine-inch waist.

The Agent wasted no more time in thinking of what others thought of him. A pile of letters on his desk demanded his attention. He was deeply immersed in writing when a bullet whizzed past his head. He hurried to the window to investigate. Another bullet grazed his sleeve. He saw Young No Water quickly conceal a gun beneath his blanket and run toward Red Cloud's village. McGillycuddy went into the main office, where Alder, alarmed by the shot, was pulling the bell-rope. Two peals of the bell startled the white population at the Agency, summoning the captain of police.

Sword lost no time in answering the summons. McGillycuddy told him to take two of the police and go in search of the would-be murderer. Young No Water was taken at a spot nine miles from the Agency. He refused to talk when brought to the office. McGillycuddy's sympathies were stirred—the prisoner was but a boy, barely seventeen. He spoke kindly to the youth in his effort to discover the reason for his action. At last Young No Water said: "The *Council Fire* says you are a bad man—that we should get rid of you—you are making white men of us—so I came to kill you."

"Another Booth," McGillycuddy said to Alder. "He really felt he was called upon to save his people."

A sentence of a month in the guardhouse was pronounced. It would give Young No Water a chance to think things over, the Agent said, as well as protect him from bad influence. The journals made much of the affair, as of each display of dissatisfaction at Pine Ridge. The *Yankton Herald* wrote:

There can be no sort of doubt but that the cantankerous McGillycuddy is utterly unfit for the position of Indian agent as has been frequently demonstrated in the many previous squabbles he has had since holding that position, and the Washington authorities should supersede him with a better man. He is too insufferably arbitrary, pompous and self-willed, if we may use no harsher term, and lacks the necessary judgment to properly administer the affairs of an agency. . . . .

The Detroit *Free Press* quoted the article and commented:

Without fear of contradiction we assert, and with a knowledge of how Indian agencies are conducted . . . . that the Pine Ridge Agency has made greater strides toward civilization than all others combined, and the Indians are better treated, cared for and governed than any others, and it was organized but a few years ago. There is on this agency a perfect discipline . . . . a perfectly friendly disposition existing between the agent and his wards with the exception of Red Cloud and squawmen at stated intervals, when incited by such blatherskites as Dr. Bland . . . . It has been the universal report of every inspector sent out by the government to examine agencies, that the Pine Ridge agency and Dr. McGillycuddy are head and shoulders above all of them.

Thus, with blizzards raging over the plains or with blinding sun on unbroken stretches of snow, another winter passed at Pine Ridge.

Chapter 20

A TROUBLESOME GUEST

IN MIDSUMMER, 1881, McGillycuddy received word that Dr. T. A. Bland, editor of the *Council Fire,* had secured a letter from the Secretary of the Interior authorizing him to visit the Rosebud and Pine Ridge agencies. He wondered what the game was. A more troublesome guest than Bland it would have been difficult to imagine. His unremitting efforts through his paper, as well as through personal communications, to vilify the Agent and create discontent in the camps made his presence in person at Pine Ridge a serious menace.

It was obvious that the report of his coming had been circulating in Red Cloud's village. The great philanthropist, the defender of the rights of the Indians, would restore the chief's tarnished glory, he would settle his right to retain the chieftainship of the Oglalas—so the rumor spread. The hostiles began powwowing, which in itself was incendiary; and trouble at Pine Ridge foreshadowed disaster on the entire frontier.

Not long after Bland's approaching visit had been announced, as McGillycuddy one day crossed the enclosure he saw a spring wagon, surrounded by a shouting mob of Indians, driving down the road in front of the traders' stores. The chief clerk, the telegrapher, and the interpreter, attracted by the noise, were standing in the doorway as he reached the office. McGillycuddy asked what was causing the excitement. Billy Garnett cupped his ear and heard: "Here comes the big white man who will get us a new agent. He is sent by the Great Father."

In the wagon, driven by an Indian, sat a long-whiskered man whom the Agent decided at once was Dr. Bland. Instead of continuing in a straight line to the Agency, the wagon turned a

221

corner and headed for the small log inn. Whoever the man was, McGillycuddy knew he could not have overlooked the many signs posted along the roads announcing that newcomers must report at once to the Agent. He waited a reasonable time before summoning the chief of police, whom he instructed to proceed to the inn, present his compliments to the visitor, and remind him of the requirement.

The long-whiskered gentleman was surrounded by a group of Indians when the police chief walked into the tavern and delivered the message. In reply the newcomer said he would be at the Agency as soon as Chief Red Cloud arrived. He had sent word to him, and only awaited his coming; they would go to the Agency together. Chief Donald Brown said that his orders were that the visitor should report immediately. Bland, recognizing the power of the law, reluctantly accompanied the police chief, and was followed by Tod Randall and H. C. Clifford, two of the worst squawmen at the Agency.

The chief clerk was occupied at his desk and McGillycuddy was standing when Bland came in. Bland extended his hand to the Agent, introducing himself. McGillycuddy said he had guessed who he was—and it was hardly necessary to shake hands. He asked what his business was at Pine Ridge. Bland said he had some business with Chief Red Cloud and carried a letter from the Secretary of the Interior authorizing the visit. He drew an official-looking letter from his pocket and handed it to McGillycuddy. It was addressed to the United States agents at the Rosebud and Pine Ridge agencies: "The bearer hereof, Dr. T. A. Bland, editor of the *Council Fire,* is hereby authorized to visit friends among the Indians in the several agencies, and agents and employes will afford him facilities to do so. It is understood, however, that Dr. Bland is in no way connected with the department and will not interfere in the affairs of the agencies." It was signed by Secretary Teller.

A moment for consideration was necessary. The man was there to stir up trouble. Playing for time, McGillycuddy asked the chief clerk to make a copy of the letter, and while he was doing so McGillycuddy strolled to his desk and apparently sought a paper. When the copy was handed him he returned the letter to Bland, saying, "I cannot permit you to remain at Pine Ridge."

"Can't permit me?" Bland exclaimed. "I'm a citizen of the United States with a letter from the Secretary of the Interior giving me permission to come here. How can you prevent me remaining?"

McGillycuddy explained that he had apparently overlooked the last clause in the letter, which plainly declared that he was not to interfere in the affairs of the agencies. That was exactly what he was there for. He had been inciting Red Cloud and other disgruntled Indians to rebellion for some years. His presence necessarily would interfere with affairs at Pine Ridge, and McGillycuddy could not permit him to remain.

"This is an outrage," Bland spluttered. "I'm a cit——"

McGillycuddy interrupted. They were not talking about the United States, he said. They were talking about the Indian country, where affairs had to be handled according to a code of their own. A sergeant would escort him to the inn, where he could get dinner; the sergeant would then bring him back to the office; and transportation would be waiting to take him to the first stopping place across the Nebraska line. Bland protested, but McGillycuddy was obdurate. He told Sergeant Thunder Bull to escort the philanthropist to the tavern.

Sergeant Cloud Shield, with half a dozen police, stood by the escort wagon when Bland, still protesting violently, returned, followed by Thunder Bull carrying his valise, and a number of Indians and squawmen. McGillycuddy was issuing ammunition to the escort. Bland asked why he was doing that. The Agent answered that he was responsible for the visitor's safety while on the reservation. It seemed almost as if he were conferring a favor on the long-whiskered gentleman.

"Is this final?" Bland asked, hopeful still that the hard-hearted agent might relent.

McGillycuddy advised him to take it so.

A crowd had gathered about the escort wagon, among whom was Frank Stewart, the commissary clerk, who leaned against the office building. Stewart was six feet four inches tall, spindling and sandy-haired. In some adventure of his previous life at sea he had lost an eye. His overalls were splotched with red mineral paint, the result of a job he was doing as a special favor for the Agent—he was always ready to turn his hand to any sort of work for "the Doctor." Bland backed against the same building as the one against which Stewart leaned, and his eye fell on the tall, angular giant.

"I'll not go," he declared and, with a look of appeal toward the paint-spattered man, he asked, "Are you a witness to this outrage?"

Stewart roared—and his voice sounded like waves beating on rocks—"I don't know anything about any outrage, but if you don't get into that wagon, by God, I'll throw you in."

With no alternative in sight Bland climbed into the wagon, saying, "Suppose I come back?"

There was a statute, McGillycuddy answered, which provided that any person returning to an Indian agency after having been duly removed was subject to arrest and imprisonment pending trial before the United States Court. "The guardhouse is there," he added, pointing to the small, barred-windowed building.

As the escort moved off, Bland called back, "My wife said I was a fool to visit your agency."

Stewart's bass voice rolled toward the wagon: "Well, all I've got to say is that your wife has a damn sight more sense than some people."

A notice was posted at Pine Ridge and in the border towns and military posts:

UNITED STATES INDIAN SERVICE.

Pine Ridge Agency, Dakota and Nebraska.

The following-named persons are removed from the reservation in accordance with the law as provided for in Sec. 2417 and 2419, Revised U.S. Statutes:

R. C. Clifford, Squawman, Pine Ridge Agency, Dak.
T. A. Bland, Philanthropist, Washington, D.C.
Tod Randall, Squawman, Pine Ridge Agency, Dak.

———

Residents of either the Dakota or Nebraska portion of the Pine Ridge Reserve, other than Indians of full blood, harboring any of the above named parties, subject themselves to removal also.

McGILLYCUDDY—*Agent.*

Bland subsequently held daily councils at a ranch across the Nebraska line at which Red Cloud and his followers were in continual attendance. Captain Sword, who kept in touch with the councils, reported that Bland offered to get the Oglalas a new agent for the munificent sum of five thousand dollars.

Chapter 21

ANOTHER INVESTIGATION

Aᴄᴛᴇʀ Bland's expulsion from Pine Ridge, Red Cloud again received permission to go to Washington. The charges which he there preferred against McGillycuddy comprised nearly every crime in the calendar, and McGillycuddy was notified that General McNeil, known as the "Palmyra Butcher" owing to an incident in the Civil War and considered the most merciless inspector in the Department, had been ordered to return with Red Cloud to inspect affairs at the Agency.

It happened that as McGillycuddy sat in his office some time after he received notice of the proposed investigation, he heard wild bellowing outside. He knew at once that Billy the goat was again trapped in the new turnstile, a substitute for the gate, which he had been able to open. Billy disapproved of the turnstile. He insisted on poking it about until it stood in a position to admit him; but, once inside, he found the accommodations inadequate and he could not get out. The Agent had assisted him on several occasions, and now hurried out when he heard the goat's screams of rage at his imprisonment. The goat was behaving as on previous incarcerations: he struck forward, and was hit in the buttocks; he kicked, and received a blow on his nose; he then fought front and rear, the gate returning blow for blow. Billy bared his teeth and screamed with rage. McGillycuddy threw off his coat and struggled to free the goat from the turnstile. He had just succeeded—dishevelled, his shirt sleeve torn—when an ambulance drove into the enclosure and stopped in front of the office.

A short, thick-set, gray-moustached man with a dirt-stained valise in his hand stepped out of the ambulance and asked the rumpled man who stood holding the goat by the horns where he could find the agent. McGillycuddy said he was the agent.

"You the agent here?" the newcomer exclaimed incredulously, while his searching eyes for a moment studied the steel-blue eyes of the young man, who was breathing heavily from his work with the goat. McGillycuddy put out his hand, saying this must be Inspector McNeil. The hand was none too warmly accepted.

The spare room at his home was ready for the inspector, the Agent said. McNeil hesitated.

"Perhaps, under the circumstances——"

McGillycuddy interrupted. On the frontier they didn't pay attention to circumstances. The general would fare much better here than at the log inn.

The invitation was accepted rather ungraciously, and the two men set out toward the Agent's house, the inspector expressing surprise when he saw the buffalo stodgily moving about in the adjoining paddock. When they reached the house, Fanny greeted him with her usual courtesy. At dinner there was no mention of the object of the inspector's visit. Other matters were discussed, and the General obviously relished his meal.

After dinner McGillycuddy suggested expediting the investigation by sending criers to the villages to summon the chiefs in council. The circuit, he said, could be made during the night and the council set for the following morning, if that accorded with the wishes of the inspector. McNeil assured him he was anxious to get through with the business as soon as possible.

The stolid faces of the chiefs who sat in silence along the walls of the council room the next morning evinced nothing as to which side they favored—the progressive or the reactionary, approval or disapproval of their agent. McGillycuddy, the inspector, the chief clerk, and the interpreter sat down at the table. McGillycuddy looked about the room. Red Cloud was not present. He wondered—an investigation without the chief complainant?

As he called the council to order, Red Cloud came in. He

stopped at the table and shook hands with the inspector first, then with the chief clerk and the interpreter, and offered his hand last to the Agent. McGillycuddy shook his head and, clasping his hands together, said, "I shake hands with myself, Red Cloud." A murmur of astonishment passed among the onlookers. McNeil pushed the Agent's elbow, bidding him to shake hands with the chief. But again McGillycuddy shook his head. Red Cloud's voice now trembled as he asked why his Father would not shake hands with him. McGillycuddy said he would tell him why: In the first place, it was the custom, no matter who was present, to shake hands first with the Agent. Besides, hand-shaking was a sign of friendship. Was it a token of friendship to lie about a person, to bring false charges against him? He was glad Igamu Tanka* had come to prove or disprove the charges.

The old chief protested he had not brought charges against his Father. McGillycuddy asked the inspector if he were not there to investigate him on charges brought by Red Cloud. McNeil bowed his head.

"It's true, every word I said to the Great Father," the chief said, refuting his previous statement. "You have stolen our supplies and done all the things I told him."

McGillycuddy jumped to his feet. "You lie," he shouted, "and you know it." He turned toward the assembly and said: "My friends, once there lived among you a great warrior; he was the leader of his people, a brave man. His name was Red Cloud. It was he who led the warriors at Fort Phil Kearney where a great battle was fought. That man was daring and fearless. He fought in the open. I respect such a man. But that, my friends, was many winters ago. That great warrior is dead. There stands in his place today a man claiming to be Red Cloud, but it is not so. The one who makes the claim is not even a man—tear off his clothes and you will find only a squaw."

A spasm shook the old man's body. Almost involuntarily he started to raise his hand, in which was a long-handled war club.

* Big Cat, the Indian's name for an inspector, because, they say, he jumps on people.

But the war club fell again to the warrior's side as McGillycuddy continued to speak.

"Never again," continued McGillycuddy, "will I shake hands with the man who calls himself Red Cloud except under one of two conditions—either that Igamu Tanka proves that the charges against me are true or that at some future time in council Red Cloud states that he lied." He told the police captain to report to General McNeil and place the force at his disposal. He then left the council room.

The old warrior turned his wrath on Sword, calling him the white man's slave, the white man's dog; some day his people would rise up against him and kill him. Sword answered quietly: "You are Red Cloud, war chief of the Oglalas. I am only Sword with my fifty young men back of me against eight thousand of my people. I am trying to help them on the road to civilization." He tapped his breast, calling attention to his uniform. "I am only Sword," he repeated, "but I wear the uniform of the Great Father and behind me is the Great Father's army."

McNeil then called the council to order and after an hour of acrimonious wrangling joined McGillycuddy in his office.

"I was never in such a damn council in my life," he said. "Is this the usual thing at Pine Ridge?" McGillycuddy said he was accustomed to such things.

Sword came in to say that the ambulance was ready to take the inspector to the outlying villages. McNeil said he would be absent several days, visiting the camps east of the Agency. McGillycuddy warned him that he would find no comfortable stopping-places and assured him that the spare room at his home would continue to be at his disposal.

The investigation consumed three weeks. The inspector, accompanied by the police, visited all the camps, though he returned to the Agency each evening, saying that McGillycuddy's quarters were the most comfortable he had ever found at an Indian agency. Many subjects were discussed at the dinner table and during the evenings while the music box repeated its repertoire; but the fact that McGillycuddy's honor was being each day weighed and measured was ignored.

On the day of McNeil's departure, as he climbed into the ambulance which was to take him to the railroad, he handed the Agent a copy of the telegram which he said he was sending to the Commissioner of Indian Affairs. When the inspector was gone, McGillycuddy unfolded the paper and read the message: "It is fishing a dry stream to try to verify Red Cloud's charges against the Pine Ridge agent. His enterprise might be advantageously imitated at all other agencies."

At the conclusion of the investigation McGillycuddy left for Rapid City to supervise the shipment of eight hundred thousand pounds of flour from the Gate City Mills to the Agency. He took with him, besides his wife, an escort of twenty-five police and one hundred wagons driven by young bucks. Several squaws and papooses accompanied the party.

The wagons broke an air-line trail to the Black Hills, passing south of the Bad Lands and crossing the Cheyenne River at the mouth of Battle Creek, which they followed to the head of one of its branches where they found the banks of the stream too steep for the wagons to cross. It was necessary to build a corduroy road. The police dismounted and the drivers climbed down from the wagons. As axes were wielded on quaking aspen and box elder trees the sound of a woman's sobs was heard from the thicket. McGillycuddy told the Indians to cease chopping, as he walked toward the spot from which the crying came. A man then appeared from the underbrush, looking from right to left, his face wearing a troubled look. It changed to one of relief when he saw the white man coming toward him. "What kind of a party is this?" he asked.

McGillycuddy told him the Indians were making a corduroy road across the stream and that they were on their way to the Black Hills. The man said his wife was crying because she thought the Indians were preparing an attack and that they had two small children. Fanny said she would go to them. The sobs were still coming from among the trees, but they ceased as she reached the cabin where the white woman huddled with the children in her arms. Fanny soon returned holding the hand of a small boy, while the woman, wiping her eyes with a soiled calico apron, followed, carrying a baby. All sat together by the stream while the Indians resumed their work.

Three days later the Agent's party rolled into camp outside Rapid City. The town looked gay with the two hundred brightly blanketed Indians lending color everywhere. They roamed into the stores and parted easily with their silver dollars. A Chinaman trod softly behind one group and then another, peering into their faces and listening to their conversations, which, though unintelligible to him, sounded more familiar than those he was accustomed to hear in the frontier town. No one seemed to notice his presence as he trailed the Indians along the streets and followed them into the shops. When night came and the blanketed band headed for camp, the Chinaman trailed behind.

McGillycuddy, who had ridden out to see that the Indians were settled for the night, was surprised when the lone Chinaman walked up and asked if he was the boss there. He said he was, and asked what the Oriental wanted. He wanted to go with the Indians, he said; he was Sing Kee; he "washee belly good." McGillycuddy told him to come back in four days and he would take him with them. Sing Kee thanked the Agent and walked off toward the town. Nothing more was seen of the Chinaman at the camp, though he followed the Indians about the town, until the day of departure. The wagons, loaded with flour sacks, were ready to start for the Agency, when Sing Kee arrived carrying a small bundle.

So closely had Fanny allied herself with the frontier that she seemed not incongruous in the motley group riding at the head of the line of wagons in her well-tailored riding habit beside her husband. At the corduroy road Fanny and the Agent went to the settler's cabin and gave presents to the little family who had been so terrified on their previous journey.

Twenty miles from the Agency, Sword rode up to the Agent and asked if the police and the escort wagon could go ahead. McGillycuddy gave his consent, for there was no longer need of an escort; but he was curious as to the reason for the request. However, the police surrounded the escort wagon in which the Chinaman rode and broke into loud singing as they clattered down the trail. McGillycuddy asked the interpreter what they were singing. Billy listened intently and caught the words: "We have found a long-lost brother of the tribe." The rest now touched up their horses and drew near the wagon. As they neared the villages, Indians, attracted by the singing, turned out of the lodges and saw the lone Chinaman seated beside the driver. Some climbed into the wagon exclaiming, *"Hoo-hoo-hay,"* as they peered into the face of the stranger, who resembled themselves though with a slight difference.

At last a squaw caught sight of the single braid hanging down his back and, picking it up, she said, *"Wanjila."* She pointed to the braids of the Indians. *"Nonpa,"* she said. There was but one difference between the Oriental and the Indian—the former had one braid, while the Indians had two. But number of braids was no impediment to friendship, and the Indians welcomed Sing Kee into the bands. McGillycuddy considered him an acquisition when a sign over the door of a shack gave notice that a wash-house was prepared to do business.

Chapter 22

ON TRIAL

A SPIRIT of unrest prevailed at Pine Ridge when in November 1884 the bitter fight between James G. Blaine and Grover Cleveland was settled by the election of the Democratic candidate as President of the United States. No Republican officeholder expected to retain his job. The hopes of the Indian Ring rose high. Surely a Democrat would supersede McGillycuddy as agent at Pine Ridge, and they trusted that it would be a man who would conspire with them to filch from the nation's wards. Red Cloud was encouraged to proffer more charges against him, and the *Council Fire* poured maledictions on his head, while its sheets were wet with the tears it shed over the sufferings of the downtrodden chief.

The *New York Sun* said on August 24:

Agent McGillycuddy, who says that during the five years of his service at that post, he has issued and disbursed between $2,000,000 and $3,000,000 in property and funds, and that he has accounted for every dollar—writes to the *Sun* that charges of fraud and mismanagement again have been brought against him. They have been repeatedly investigated, he says by inspectors, commissions and committees, but he wants them investigated again. He therefore suggests, as "a fair business proposition," that a committee, consisting of one officer of the army, one officer of the Interior Department and one disinterested citizen, proceed to the agency to overhaul his accounts and examine the condition of affairs on the reservation. If the verdict is against him he says he will willingly suffer dishonorable dismissal.

The commission was not appointed, and matters were in abeyance until January, when McGillycuddy's appointment as agent was renewed in spite of the endless charges which continued to pour in against him. Wind whipped the snow into drifts against the buildings within the agency enclosure. White clouds marched over the sky; the sun seemed nonexistent. The buffalo sought shelter beside the commissary building; and the deer, now well-antlered and given to roving in good weather, returned to the Agency in search of food. The sandhill crane temporarily discontinued his walks beside the Agent as he trailed through the snow keeping watch of each department, leaving Buffer his sole companion. McGillycuddy's familiar whistle was heard infrequently, only when he forgot how quickly his breath froze on his long moustache, encasing his mouth with icicles.

While Pine Ridge was still snowbound the Democratic President took his seat; but weeks passed without any major changes in the personnel at the Agency. Spring merged into summer. Though there was trouble in the air, McGillycuddy received no word of a successor.

Red Cloud was now called to Washington, and there his repetition of the story of corrupt practices carried on at Pine Ridge resulted in McGillycuddy being summoned to the capital to answer the charges. He left immediately with his wife and a party consisting of Young Man Afraid, Lieutenant Standing Soldier, and Billy Garnett, who were to act as witnesses in the trial. Donald Brown, chief clerk since Alder's departure the previous year, was left in charge of the Agency.

The Agent and his wife occupied the carriage which followed the escort wagon. At the crossing of a stream twenty-five miles from Pine Ridge, McGillycuddy got out and unfastened the bridles to allow the horses to drink from a hole doubtless made by the driver of the escort wagon. The noisy sucking of water into thirsty throats did not deaden the sound of a rabbit's scurrying from the brush. Startled by it, the team dashed across the stream, felling McGillycuddy, who stood at their heads, and dragging the carriage over him.

On the other side of the stream the vehicle was overturned and Fanny and the luggage were spilled out. The horses broke loose and sped along the road. They were caught by the men in the escort wagon, who hastened back to find Fanny bandaging the Agent's body with towels from one of the spilled valises. She had received no serious injury, but some of the Agent's ribs had been broken.

The wagonbox was now covered with buffalo robes and McGillycuddy was laid on them. The carriage was righted and the scattered luggage collected, and when the team was hitched up the journey to Valentine was resumed.

No one was seen during the day but a Brûlé Sioux riding alone. The party camped that night at a solitary Indian lodge which, for some unknown reason, was staked on the prairie. A short distance from camp the following morning a troop of cavalry was seen riding toward the Agent's party, which came near and halted. They had been sent out from Fort Niobrara, the officer said, on the report of a Brûlé Sioux of an outbreak at Pine Ridge in which the Agent had been wounded. The report was they were bringing him to the post in a wagon. The troop turned about and followed the Agent's party along the fluted road, the jarring increasing the inflammation of his broken ribs. At Fort Niobrara, McGillycuddy was placed under the care of Surgeon Lippincott, who protested violently against his determination to leave that night for Washington after he was properly bandaged.

"I'm going to be tried," the Agent said. "How can I be tried if I'm not there?" He refused to listen to the surgeon's warning and departed on the night train.

Four days later the office of J. D. Atkins, Commissioner of Indian Affairs under President Cleveland, was filled with the heads of departments. Atkins was a one-armed Rebel colonel from Tennessee. Lucius Quintus Cincinattus Lamar, the new Secretary of the Interior, sat by his side. The trial was considered of importance as bearing on the future of the Indian.

Red Cloud sat in an armchair flanked on one side by his attorney, ex-Chief Justice Willard of North Carolina, who had served under the carpetbag governor, Moses, and on the other by T. A.

Bland. Red Cloud wore a new broadcloth suit, white shirt, and polished boots which from time to time he slipped off to ease his aching feet. His long hair, still tied with strips of red flannel, was the only indication of race which the philanthropist and his wife Cora had been unable to persuade him to relinquish. Except for that trifling detail, the reactionary chief resembled a Methodist parson.

McGillycuddy, pale, patched, and bandaged, limped into the room supported by a cane. Beside him walked Young Man Afraid, tall and slim like the Agent, though ten years his senior. His face was clean-cut as a cameo. Behind them came Captain Sword, Sergeant Standing Soldier, and Billy Garnett. The new Democratic officeholders stared at the much-discussed Indian agent, who felt himself *persona non grata* in the assembly.

When he was seated, Atkins asked if he were ready for trial. McGillycuddy said he was ready. The Commissioner asked where his attorney was. The agent answered that he had no attorney— he would conduct his own case—he could not afford to waste money on a farce of this kind. The broken ribs may have made him irritable. Atkins flushed with annoyance. An investigation conducted by the Commissioner of Indian Affairs was by no means a farce, he answered, as McGillycuddy would probably realize before it was finished. The Agent said he had not intended to reflect on the Commissioner or his high office, but he did mean to cast aspersion on a system which forced him to come fifteen hundred miles to answer charges brought by the class of people before him. He looked directly at his accusers. "I will conduct my own case," he repeated, "as soon as I am furnished with a copy of the charges."

Red Cloud's attorney said he had prepared no list of charges; and the case was postponed until the following morning. Then Colonel Manypenny, the first witness, narrated at length the story of Red Cloud's deposition, speaking of treaties broken by the Agent and of Bland's expulsion from the Agency. When asked if he knew anything more than what he had been told—

if he had ever been to Pine Ridge—Manypenny answered in the negative. McGillycuddy said that was all he wished to ask.

Bland now expatiated upon his usual complaints. McGillycuddy promptly answered to the charges against him: The armed police force and the erection of a guardhouse and a flagstaff, both claimed as contrary to treaty, had been authorized by the government. As to the last charge, that he had offered inducements to Young Man Afraid to set himself up a head-chief of the Oglalas, thereby usurping the right of Chief Red Cloud, he suggested that Young Man Afraid speak for himself. Young Man Afraid rose from the floor and drew his blue blanket, embellished with beadwork and porcupine quills, more closely about him. The single eagle feather, signifying his chieftainship, stood upright from his sleek, shining hair. Billy Garnett as interpreter put the question to him. Young Man Afraid looked puzzled. "*Slonya sni,*" he said. Billy explained. This time he understood. His lean body stiffened; and the eagle feather seemed part of a sculptured head. "As far as the memory of the Sioux nation reaches, my father and his father and his father before him have been chiefs of the Oglalas," he said. "I was born a chief; no one can make me one. I am Young Man of Whose Horse They Are Afraid, rightful chief of the Oglala Sioux. Is it not so, Red Cloud?" The old warrior made no answer, and Young Man Afraid resumed his seat on the floor.

McGillycuddy explained the system by which Red Cloud had been appointed war chief during the campaign with the Crows and his refusal to relinquish his dictatorship at the close of the war. He had been a great warrior, perhaps the greatest the Sioux nation had ever had; but he was a plebeian who had risen from the ranks by his superior leadership. It was true, the Agent said, that he had courted the support of the Man Afraid family, who had been steadfastly on the side of civilization and progress. Had it not been for that faction he would have been unable to handle the situation at Pine Ridge for six years without troops. In crucial matters the Man Afraid family had prevailed always.

The trial was concluded, the Commissioner saying that interested parties would be informed of the result. The day following the trial, cards bearing the name Garnett were brought to McGillycuddy's room at his hotel. He sent a request for the gentlemen to come up. Two young men soon came in and said they had read in the papers that Dr. McGillycuddy was accompanied by an interpreter of mixed blood bearing their name. They were interested to know his history. McGillycuddy said he was the son of Colonel Richard Garnett, of the United States Army, by a common-law wife, a woman of the Sioux nation. The Colonel had been in command at Fort Laramie, Wyoming; but at the beginning of the Civil War he had left the United States Army to join the Confederate Army, in which he had become a Brigadier-General of Virginia troops. Billy, his son, had been born after his departure from Fort Laramie. General Garnett, he said, had been killed in Pickett's charge at Gettysburg.

General Garnett, one of the young men said, was their uncle. The General had heard of the boy's birth before he died. They were the sons of his brother. This man must be their cousin. Billy was now summoned and after an introduction to the visitors was invited to their home. They were extremely courteous to him during the time he remained in Washington and urged him to remain with them. But Billy said: "I was born an Indian and raised an Indian. I will go back to my people and die an Indian."

McGillycuddy, with his party, returned to the Agency. The result of the trial was never communicated to the defendant.

Chapter 23

"THE MOST INVESTIGATED MAN"

McGILLYCUDDY's trial had come to nothing; it was as if it had never been held. Red Cloud repeated his petitions for a new agent, saying there was a new Great Father in Washington and he wanted a new Father at Pine Ridge. He was a Democrat, he said, and he wanted a Democratic Father. The old warrior was a politician; he adhered to the party in power.

But how the Department was to extract the thorn in the flesh—a thorn to the Indian Bureau as well as to Red Cloud— was the problem. All charges against McGillycuddy had gone up in smoke. There remained but one man—reputed to be a close friend of Bland's—whose ferreting might disclose some irregularity in the Agent's conduct. The hopes of the malcontents, including members of the Indian Ring scattered over the country, were revived when a commission, consisting of the Honorable W. S. Holman, of Indiana, as chairman, and the Honorables J. G. Cannon of Illinois and Thomas Ryan of Kansas, was appointed to investigate the Pine Ridge agent.

Holman, known as the "Great Objector," had been the candidate of the *New York Sun* for the Democratic nomination for the presidency. He was considered among the best-posted of public men. The committee was to be accompanied on its errand by the Sergeant at Arms of the House, Colonel J. P. Leedom, and clerks.

When it was announced that McGillycuddy was to be investigated again, petitions went in from settlers scattered miles along the borders and the distant Black Hills urging that the farce be discontinued and that the wishes of the homesteaders and of nine-tenths of the Indians should prevail against the falsehoods of Red Cloud and his supporters. These petitions were ignored.

When the time came for its visit, according to custom, Mc-Gillycuddy drove out with the police escort to meet the commission. The mid-July sun on the parched plains showed no more mercy to the commissioners than to the natives. Judge Holman was surprised to be greeted by the man whom he had come more than halfway across the continent to investigate on charges of corruption. It was a trifle embarrassing, and the Judge showed no inclination to be friendly.

When the Agency was reached, the police escort forming in double line beside the gates as the vehicles bearing the distinguished guests drove into the enclosure, the "Great Objector" offered his first objection by refusing the Agent's invitation to dinner. The other guests accepted with pleasure. Judge Holman was driven to the boarding school, where rooms had been prepared for the party. There was no hint of unrest in the group gathered around the Agent's well-spread dinner table, where fish, game, and wine called forth exclamations of surprise from the visitors. Fanny felt no apprehension concerning the investigation; she was thoroughly accustomed to them, and felt certain it would end as all the others had done. She wore a thin white summer frock and the diamond earrings the Agent had bought her on their last trip to Washington.

It was Wednesday when Judge Holman arranged his plans for the investigation while McGillycuddy summoned a council for the following day. An air of excitement pervaded the Agency, and on Wednesday afternoon the chief of police reported the presence of several squawmen who had been ordered off the reservation but were now boasting of the part they would play in the council. Holman had sent for them, they claimed.

The Judge was standing in front of the post office when, following orders, the chief of police presented the Agent's compliments and asked if he had authorized the presence of the renegades at the Agency. The Judge seemed annoyed at the question. If they were not there with his permission, the police chief said, his orders were to arrest them. Holman, his face red with anger, said he would see the Agent. And a messenger arrived at McGillycuddy's office soon after, with a request that he appear before the commission.

"I don't like the attitude of your chief of police," the Judge spluttered, when McGillycuddy went to his office in the boarding school. "His manner is not respectful. Are you responsible for that?"

The Agent replied there was no discourtesy intended in sending to inquire as to the presence of the squawmen at the Agency, but, with all due respect to the commission he could not allow anyone to interfere with the management of Pine Ridge and unless the outlaws were there under his authorization they would be placed in the guardhouse. The chief of police and all employees were taught to obey the orders of the Agent. Pine Ridge was remote from courts of justice, and in emergencies it became necessary to take seemingly arbitrary action looking toward the protection of life and property. In fact, so apparently arbitrary was the authority of the Agent and so absolute was the respect for that authority that if he were to order the arrest of every member of the commission the police would not hesitate to obey the order.

A grunt of anger issued from Judge Holman's lips. McGillycuddy continued, saying there was no question of the Judge's authority to call for persons and papers necessary for the success of the investigation and he would assist the commission in the matter by ordering the chief of police, who was also deputy marshal, to report to him with fifty mounted police. The chief would summon anyone this side of hell whose presence the commission desired; but he, McGillycuddy, must be informed of the names of those persons. "I see no necessity for friction, Judge Holman," McGillycuddy added, "but so long as I am agent I shall attend to the details of management at Pine Ridge. Do you sponsor the presence of the renegades at the Agency?" Judge Holman refused to accept the responsibility. So rapidly did news of this spread that by the time the police went in search of the conspirators they were well on their way across the Nebraska-Dakota line.

At one o'clock the following day, crowds assembled for the great council. Red Cloud was convinced that this imposing commission was set on giving him a new agent, as Holman had held frequent interviews with the reactionaries. But Young Man Afraid's feelings were hurt by the Judge's refusal to see him when he had called upon him.

The council was held on the grounds of the enclosure, with the opposing factions clearly aligned against each other. Red Cloud sat with his followers, numbering about one hundred and fifty; and, across a fifty-foot unoccupied strip, sat Young Man Afraid with one thousand or more progressives. Ugly words were bandied across the open space before the council opened. The commission, the Agent, and the Agent's interpreter took their places at the end of the dividing area. Captain Sword said in an aside to McGillycuddy that it would be wise to have a squad of police patrol the open space between the two factions; and the order to do this was given.

The Agent then opened the council, saying that the commission consisted of wise men who had come to hear their complaints. "Tell them your troubles," he said; "but one thing I advise—speak the truth." And he asked Judge Holman to conduct the council.

Holman called on "Chief Red Cloud" to speak. Before rising, Red Cloud motioned his haranguer, No Water, father of the youth who had attempted the Agent's murder, to announce him. The agitator rose and cried, "Red Cloud, chief of the Oglala Sioux, will speak. Hear him."

The old man hunched himself from the ground and, without preamble, said: "Our Father is a bad man; he is cruel; he treats us badly and does not give us the food the Great Father sends us. I have seen the new Great Father and the new Secretary and the new Commissioner, and they all speak kind to me. They make my heart good. We want an agent who will not put good men like my friend, Dr. Bland, off the reservation when he comes to pay me a visit. If you don't take this agent away with you, I will no longer be responsible for his life nor for peace here. He doesn't like us and we don't like him. He has taken our money and put it in his own pocket."

Until the last charge McGillycuddy sat unmoved. Then, like a flash he rushed at the old man and, shaking his fist in his face, he shouted: *"Niya owakonka. Iotaka!"* Though he did not understand that McGillycuddy had called Red Cloud a liar and told him to sit down, the Judge was startled by his action and looked pale as he laid a restraining hand on the Agent's arm. An ominous silence pervaded the crowd, on which the sun beat hot. The police stood at attention. Red Cloud looked about: not a member of his band stirred. The old man gathered the folds of his blanket about him and slunk to his seat on the ground.

Young Man Afraid now rose and said that Red Cloud spoke for only a few. He raised the fingers of one hand. He himself spoke for many. He lifted his arms above his head and opened and closed his uplifted hands many times. They had all they could eat, he said, plenty of reapers and mowers, plenty of seed. They had their council of leading men who settled disputes. They liked their Father and wanted to keep him.

After listening to a number of other and inconsequential speeches Holman said he had heard their stories and would speak to the Great Father. To the Agent's proposal that the Indians give an Omaha dance that evening in honor of the commission, Judge Holman agreed, though with no evidence of pleasure.

Toward sundown early comers squatted on the rock-hard ground outside the enclosure. The crowd swelled rapidly until hundreds of bucks, squaws, and children formed a great circle, weird in the fading light. Youngsters romped in the dusty road, indifferent to the heat which lingered in the evening hours. Budding warriors raced their ponies across the hot prairie. Occasionally a whimpering papoose was dragged from a beaded bag slung on the back of a squaw and suckled at huge, flabby paps made accessible through loose sleeves of from one to six greasy calico dresses.

At length the Agent and his party arrived and took the seats placed for them. From the distance came faint ululations of male voices. The sky was alight with the brilliant sunset's afterglow. As the howling voices drew near, the colors on the horizon paled; and only the flames from the huge bonfire lighted the scene when, like painted demons, the dancers issued, yelling, from the darkness into the luminous, sweating circle and the drums beat madly.

"*Hi-ya, hi-ya,*" shrieked the dancers, as they wound their way around the fire, their greased, painted bodies glistening in the flame light while the eagle feathers in their war bonnets swayed to their movements. Out from the group came a single dancer, who related his deeds of bravery—three Blackfeet massacred eight winters ago—and three thumps of the drumsticks emphasized the daring deed. Another danced forward and announced four killed in the Custer Battle, and from the hollow drums came four echoes of his achievement. Others narrated the number of coups they had counted, the number of scalps they wore; and the more loudly the writhing, chanting dancer proclaimed his victories, the more madly the drums beat out their untuneful acclamation.

The excitement had reached its height when Sword came to the Agent to tell him that many of Red Cloud's young warriors were carrying carbines under their blankets and were planning mischief. As he spoke, the butt of a shining gun glinted below the blanket of a passing buck. McGillycuddy ordered a distribution of police among the crowd, with instructions to keep close watch on the movements of the reactionaries. He advised his wife to make some excuse to get the women to go with her to her home. A few of these visitors, too polite to protest, cast backward glances at the gorgeous bronze figures rhythmically circling in the fire light, as they reluctantly followed their hostess.

They had just entered the Agent's house when there came a tap at the door. Young Man Afraid asked if his Mother had a gun. "Mine in tepee," he explained. "Me sit here on steps."

Colonel Leedom, noticing that the women had departed immediately after the Agent had spoken to them, asked the reason. McGillycuddy made some excuse, while his eyes scanned the mob, watching for any hostile movement. Leedom insisted that something was wrong, and the Agent acknowledged that Judge Holman had stirred up a devilish feeling among the hostiles. Many were armed, and there was a possibility of trouble. He would be the first target, most likely, he said; Leedom replied that he was not going to wait for his turn and, gathering up the members of the commission, he hurriedly returned to the boarding school.

When Red Cloud observed the vigilance with which the police watched his band, he decided that his plans had been discovered; and, responding to some calming signal, his warriors all settled down to enjoy the feast which followed the dance. When it was finished, the painted dancers and the onlookers melted into the night on their ways to their various camps. McGillycuddy went alone to his office, set a few papers straight on his desk, and turned out the kerosene lamp. The moon shone in the window, lighting the glass cage in which his pet rattlesnakes coiled. He tapped the glass, and the rattlers roused and stared stonily at him. It was past midnight. He turned the key in the door as he stepped outside. Instantly he was surrounded by a band of warriors. "*Taku wacin?*" he asked; but scarcely had he spoken the words when he recognized the friendly faces of his most ardent supporters among the younger generation. "Where you go?" one of the young warriors asked. McGillycuddy said he was going to the boarding school to say good night to the commissioners. "We go with you," another of the youths said; and, surrounded by the painted horde of his trusted friends, the Agent went his way to the school, while clouds drifted across the moon, leaving the prairies in darkness. At the gate of the school grounds he thanked the young Indians for their kindness and bade them good night. He found the commissioners assembled in the Judge's room, looking troubled. He ignored their appearance and said he hoped they felt satisfied with the day's proceedings.

"This is the damndest place I ever got into," the Judge said. "Do you think there will be an outbreak before morning? Are the police with you?"

McGillycuddy laughed and assured him that the trouble was over by that time, though it had looked squally for a while. The Indians were much like children, he said. They got excited about something and were liable to get into mischief unless one got the upper hand immediately. When that was accomplished they usually were docile until something else occurred to put ideas into their heads. He had no police with him; they were on regular schedule—most of them asleep, while the usual number were on duty at the guardhouse.

"Did you come here alone?" the Judge roared.

McGillycuddy told him of the band of young warriors who had accompanied him to the school. Thomas Ryan asked if he thought it safe for them to go to bed—they had intended to sit up all night and leave, if they were alive, at the crack of dawn. McGillycuddy assured them they were as safe as they would be sleeping in their own beds in Washington. But they still looked uneasy when the Agent left the group, though he reiterated his assurance that no trouble impended.

He was surprised when he found the young bucks waiting for him outside in the darkness, which was intense except when flashes of lightning lighted the prairie. Again they surrounded the Agent as they traversed the distance to his house while the rain beat down.

On the Agent's doorstep sat Young Man Afraid, with the borrowed gun across his knees, keeping vigil over "Ena," Fanny. The Agent expressed his gratitude for their friendliness and stood for a moment watching the group as they set out in the rain for their villages. Fanny lay asleep, undisturbed by the storm. The Agent undressed and went to bed. The thirsty earth sucked up the welcome rain. His door stood open throughout the night.

At an early hour the "Great Objector" and his party set out for Rushville, a new railroad town about twenty miles from the

Agency, accompanied by an escort of police, the interpreter, and the old chief, Red Cloud, who occupied the time in making requests of Judge Holman. To his insistence upon having a new Agent, the Judge said that all he could do was to report his wish to the Great Father. As the train pulled out, Billy Garnett saw the Judge shake his fist toward Red Cloud; his lips moved, but what he said could not be heard.

McGillycuddy was not informed of the result of the investigation. Like its predecessors, it had died a-borning. One paper wrote that Holman was "a crony of Cranky Bland and was stuffed to the brim with Bland's animosity to McGillycuddy" but that he was so badly scared at Pine Ridge that he promised to give Red Cloud all the land between the Platte River and the British possessions—he promised everything but a new Agent.

Another paper wrote:

An investigation ought to investigate. At some stage in the proceedings there ought to be a rest . . . .

The agent at Pine Ridge has been the most investigated man of the age. Special agents have investigated him; religious societies have investigated him; Congress has investigated him and the great and good Dr. Bland has investigated him and, with the exception of the last whose exit was in no sense a triumphal march, McGillycuddy has been pronounced a good and faithful servant of the government and the most capable manager of the Indians known to the department. In spite of this the farce of investigation has to be played. Years of service; proven honesty and worth; charges disproven again and again all go for nothing when a few enemies conspire to send up an echo of the old complaints to Washington.

Bland wrote in the *Council Fire* that he had hoped to be able to announce in that issue that Agent McGillycuddy would be dismissed and a new and much better man put in his place. The indications were that McGillycuddy was to be closely watched during the remainder of his official life, he wrote. He had held off the issue of his paper for a week, hoping to be able to make the announcement of McGillycuddy's dismissal. The article was headed, "Disappointed But Not Discouraged."

Another paper wrote that the Agent was a man of great courage or he would not dare to eat, drink, or sleep within pistol shot of the terrible vengeance of old Red Cloud, who would, if he dared, murder the Agent in cold blood and devastate the green pastures and grazing herds of northern Nebraska. The editor said he was compelled to say that nothing but the iron rule of this agent had kept the bloodthirsty old chieftain from the warpath and made the settlement of the White River country, Old Red's hunting grounds, among the grand successes of the day.

So tyrannical had McGillycuddy been painted by his detractors that a visitor to Pine Ridge wrote later that he looked in surprise when he met the Agent—"for this was the terrible McGillycuddy who is charged by his enemies with every crime in the calendar and who is certainly the terror of all 'bad' Indians and the hero of all 'good' and younger Indians. It seemed impossible this mild-mannered and pleasant appearing gentleman could be the tyrant he had been so frequently represented to us, but a few minutes' observation was sufficient to convince us that anyone who sought to dispute his authority would soon feel the weight of his iron rule."

Though no charges resulted from the Holman investigation, the feeling of insecurity among the officeholders at Pine Ridge increased. The prominence which the Agency had gained throughout the country complicated the situation for the new administration, office seekers besieging the Indian Bureau for the potentially lucrative job of agent at the largest agency in the United States. The position if handled in conjunction with the Indian Ring would be a bonanza.

Another winter passed while the brains in the offices of the Department of the Interior worked to conjure an excuse for ridding the Indian Bureau of the Pine Ridge agent. New appointees arrived at the Agency, superseding the Republican traders, while still the Indian Bureau labored to establish accusations of fraud against McGillycuddy. At last an idea was conceived: McGillycuddy should be ordered to accept a private clerk appointed by the department. His Irish temper was well known in Washington, and unquestionably he would refuse to displace his faithful clerk, Donald Brown. Upon his refusal it could be made to appear to the public that he dared not accept a government-appointed clerk who would disclose his irregularities.

The prophecy was correct. McGillycuddy did refuse in advance to accept any chief clerk other than one of his own choosing. He wrote Commissioner Atkins that he was a bonded officer in the sum of sixty thousand dollars. He was responsible to the government for the issue of supplies amounting to half a million dollars yearly. In his absence his chief clerk became automatically the agent in charge and handled the issues and funds; it was contrary to custom to appoint clerks for bonded officers; he would accept no government appointee.

The matter was held in abeyance for some time before McGillycuddy received notice that a new clerk was on his way to Pine Ridge. He wired his refusal to accept him.

For a time business at Pine Ridge continued according to custom. The Agent whistled as he hurried from office to commissary, to stables, carpenter shop, and guardhouse. Then one day as he and Fanny were riding among the camps while he inspected crops and farm implements, a messenger rode out to tell him that an inspector had arrived at the Agency. They turned their horses and rode homeward.

"This is the end," he said to Fanny as they got off their horses.

The inspector was waiting in the office. He asked if McGillycuddy had changed his mind about accepting the new clerk. Though his Irish blood was up, McGillycuddy answered suavely that his mind was unchanged—he would not give up a good man who had served the government faithfully.

"In that case," the inspector said, "I am under orders to relieve you. Captain Bell of the Seventh Cavalry will act as agent."

It was the last trick in the game which had run for seven years—a game played by various players to eliminate McGillycuddy. And on this trick McGillycuddy's opponents played the ace of trumps. His obstinacy, his sense of justice, and his loyalty to his efficient clerk allowed no possibility of another course for him.

Some weeks were consumed in taking inventory. Captain James Bell, finding Donald Brown invaluable in the unfamiliar work, protested violently against accepting the new clerk and asked to be relieved unless Brown was retained. He was ordered to accept the government appointee or stand court-martial. Dolefully he saw Brown depart.

Ox teams and a police escort were furnished the ex-agent when he and Fanny set out across the road he himself had helped to build, on their way to their new home in Rapid City, the two buffalo lumbering along in the train.

NEW FIELDS FOR McGILLYCUDDY

Chapter 24

CALLING A BLUFF

Though the government had rid itself of McGillycuddy, it was still greatly troubled. A howl had gone up over the Northwest at his removal and it seemed necessary to make some show of a case against him in order to justify the arbitrary act of the Secretary of the Interior in removing him from office against the protests of the people on the frontier as well as those of Senator Dawes, Herbert Welch, Bishop Hare, and many others. The pretext was accordingly raised that had he and his clerk not been in collusion in stealing from the government he would not have objected to having a clerk assigned him.

To accomplish this purpose the vast machinery of the Department of the Interior—so wrote the *Pioneer Free Press*—was set in motion to ferret out some flaw in McGillycuddy's accounts that would serve to raise a doubt in the minds of the people as to the integrity of his administration of the affairs at Pine Ridge. To this end, the *Press* contended, Indian inspectors and special agents without number were ordered to Pine Ridge to examine the Agent's accounts, in the hope of trumping up some charge of fraud that would hold water long enough for the Secretary of the Interior and the Commissioner of Indian Affairs to crawl out of their uncomfortable dilemma. But, the *Press* predicted, the result would be a sad disappointment to a few disgruntled and sycophantic nonentities who seconded the efforts of the Department.

The *Press,* however, lacked the gift of prophecy. They were astonished when the announcement came forth that McGillycuddy had defrauded the government in the sum of twenty-eight thousand dollars—a herd of cattle, a wagon train, and other items were not accounted for. The news was heralded from coast to coast: "The famous ex-Indian agent is a defaulter . . . ."

McGillycuddy now wired the Commissioner: "I court full investigation and am under bond in connection with all supplies handled at Pine Ridge." He sent copies of the telegram to the press, which headed articles: "McGillycuddy Courts Investigation." "The Noted Ex-Agent Wants to Be Prosecuted." A correspondent for the *St. Paul Pioneer Press* called on the Commissioner to ask what action was being taken to collect the sum which McGillycuddy was accused of appropriating. Atkins replied that the office had the matter under advisement but as yet was uncertain what action to take regarding the fraud.

McGillycuddy's wrath was boundless when he read in the papers of this interview. He wrote the Commissioner saying that, in his opinion this was not a matter of discretion on his part. If he had any reason to believe that any official in his Department had been guilty of fraud, it was his sworn duty to prosecute the case. He demanded that without delay these charges be brought before the United States Grand Jury for investigation and proper action taken or that the Commissioner come out in a point-blank statement of charges and he would promise him abundant opportunity to prove the truth of the charges under a libel suit of fifty thousand dollars. He had retained Hon. Wayne McVeigh of Philadelphia as his counsel. He suggested that the Commissioner drop the tactics of the politician and come out as a man—in Western parlance—put up or shut up.

More headlines appeared. In due time the Treasury Department communicated to McGillycuddy that "On a re-examination of your accounts you are found indebted to the government for the sum of one hundred and twenty-eight dollars, a traveling expense item disallowed by the department for the reason that the Secretary of the Interior exceeded his authority in ordering you to make a certain trip to Washington." The missing wagon-train, the Indian stock, and other items which he had been accused of stealing evidently had been located.

The degree of authority possessed by the Secretary of the Interior, whose Department invariably had paid his traveling expenses on his trips to Washington, was no concern of McGillycuddy's—he wrote a check for one hundred and twenty-eight dollars and sent it to the Comptroller of the Treasury.

The investigations of the "most investigated man of the age" were thus concluded.

The Doctor's time since going to Rapid City had not been occupied entirely in fighting for his honor. He had been considering the many opportunities offered him. Eventually he accepted the presidency of the Lakota Banking and Investment Company and the vice-presidency of the Black Hills National Bank. He was also appointed Surgeon-General on the Governor's staff.

The editor of the *Omaha Bee* commented on the fact that the Pine Ridge agent evidently had become rich on fifteen hundred a year, while the *Herald* retorted that, though it knew nothing of McGillycuddy's wealth, his salary had been raised to twenty-five hundred because of his efficiency and, being a frugal man living where his expenses amounted to little, it had been possible for him to save practically all he had made. McGillycuddy laughed at both articles. He was free from government service, and he was happy. He was but thirty-seven years old, and still lean, though his hair was sparse. He was as much a human dynamo as in his youth.

But banking alone did not satisfy him—he needed outdoor life—more active work. He began organizing a hydroelectric and power company and undertook the construction of its plant. His single buggy might be seen at any hour of the day on its way to the reservoir where he supervised the building operations. He was a master of details. As the machinery was installed, his inquisitive mind led him into many narrow escapes. Static electricity is one of the important factors to deal with in a mountain country, and in handling the dynamos he sometimes encountered an unexpected short circuit which sent him flying against the wall in an unconscious heap. These experiences rendered him a trifle more cautious but did not hinder his experiments.

The residents of the town watched with interest as the white sandstone foundation of a house for McGillycuddy was laid on the slope of the hill north of town. They looked surprised as the walls of red sandstone went up. They were astounded when the frame walls of the second story were painted olive green. The local paper wrote that Dr. McGillycuddy was building a house the like of which had never been seen before—it would be looked upon as an innovation, but one of the Doctor's very peculiar characteristics was to be odd and it was not likely that he could be prevailed upon to change his mind in regard to the outlandish architecture of his very costly residence. But the Doctor said he liked color; he was accustomed to painted Indians; besides, it harmonized with the landscape; the red Jurassic sandstone matched that which bordered the valley which the Indians called the race course.

When winter came the Doctor and Fanny sat cosily beside their fireplace and talked of the many happy days on the plains without regret. They were still young enough to enjoy new experiences and old enough to be glad to be settled in a home of their own. Many Indians visited the Hills and hung about the Doctor's home, receiving cups of coffee, slices of bread, and fresh-baked cookies and doughnuts. They wanted their Father and Mother to come back; it was lonely at Pine Ridge without them; they inquired for the buffalo, the bull and cow. There was a calf also, the Doctor told them. He had turned them loose in the valley near town. They often attached themselves to a passing ox-train, worrying the oxen for a time and then returning to the valley. They also fretted the school children as they played outside the country school. But no one interfered with the Doctor's buffalo.

But one thing troubled McGillycuddy: Fanny was gaining weight alarmingly. She had frequent headaches; her color was high. She herself was not worried; the headaches did not last long and when one was gone she occupied herself as usual working in the flower beds and driving about with the Doctor. But one Sunday morning after she was dressed for church, since the Doctor was not quite ready to start, she walked down the steps of the front porch and out on the lawn to see if there were fresh blossoms on her plants. There the Doctor found her fallen among the flowers: she had had a stroke.

She lay in bed for many weeks, the nurse who had been engaged to attend her sometimes fretting the patient because of inability to understand her hesitating speech. Only the Doctor never failed to know what she so earnestly struggled to communicate. He had the advantage over others—he understood the Indian signs which she gave with her left hand. Many times he interrupted his business to go up the hill to see if she was comfortable and contented. Late one afternoon during a meeting of bank directors, the rain beating hard on the windows, the telephone rang. The nurse was in despair—she could not understand what Mrs. McGillycuddy wanted. The Doctor left the meeting and hurried through the rain to his home. Fanny's face lighted up with relief when he came into the room. Her left arm fluttered up and down; then she made a beckoning movement. Her bird was out on the porch, the Doctor explained; she wanted it brought inside. When the bird-cage hung in the window near her bed, Fanny fell asleep.

After many months she was well enough to walk about the house with assistance. She went driving, with a companion who had taken the place of the nurse, in a low phaeton with a fringed top. She returned with a smile the greetings which met her on every side as they drove through the town.

As the Doctor's income increased he invested in other enterprises. The banks loaned heavily to farmers. Rapid City was the most promising town of the Hills country, the Doctor often remarked. The years brought increasing prosperity and their life followed a normal course.

Chapter 25

SITTING BULL'S LAST BATTLE

In the autumn of 1890 obvious restlessness prevailed among the Indians over the West from British America to Texas owing to the prediction of the "second coming of the Messiah." The belief arose that there would be a restoration of the good old hunting days, and a return of the buffalo and the deer when the Messiah came.

The agitation was entirely religious in character at its inception. But the Messiah craze, McGillycuddy said to Governor Millett in one of the many talks they held on the subject, was affording the Sioux an opportunity to demonstrate their resentment of conditions which had grown more intolerable to them as the years passed. Their discontent was due, not to any one cause, but to a combination of conditions, cumulative in their effect and dating back many years—in fact to the inauguration of a now obviously faulty policy in dealing with the Indians. There had been a succession of broken treaties and agreements. The agreement made recently involving their relinquishment of half their remaining lands had barely won the assent of the Sioux nation and had been bitterly opposed at the Pine Ridge and the Rosebud agencies.

And it was at these agencies that the present trouble was fulminating. A reduction of the annual issue of beef afforded the principal cause of rebellion, the staple article of subsistence having been cut from 6,250,000 to 4,000,000 pounds. The contract on that beef, moreover, was violated in that, whereas it called for northern ranch beef, beef from Texas with an unparalleled shrinkage in winter was substituted. And drought on the plains in '89, causing a failure of crops, had added to the sufferings of the red men.

By the fortunes of political war, weak agents had been placed in charge at some of the agencies at the very time that trouble was brewing. This was noticeably true at Pine Ridge, where a notoriously weak and unfit man had been appointed agent. Mc-Gillycuddy remarked to the Governor that, as for the Ghost Dance, too much attention was being paid to it. It was but the symptom or surface indication of deep-rooted, long-existing trouble; as well treat the eruption of smallpox and ignore the constitutional disease.

By the time Pine Ridge definitely became the center of agitation the Governor ordered McGillycuddy, as Assistant Adjutant General, to go to Pine Ridge, whither troops had already been sent, to ascertain the probability of danger to the settlers in Dakota. The bands of hostiles had gone into camp in spots remote from the Agency before McGillycuddy's arrival. Red Cloud, though a sympathizer in the Ghost Dance movement, was taking no active part in it, as he was an old man whose fighting days were over. He had remained at the Agency and had been frightened by the coming of troops for which Agent Royer, terrified at the situation, had wired. General J. R. Brooke, commanding the Department of the Platte, had arrived at Pine Ridge a few days before McGillycuddy, with an expedition of one thousand men, after a forced march from the railroad, and was evidently preparing for battle.

News of McGillycuddy's arrival spread rapidly over the reservation. The leading Indians, including Red Cloud, called a council and requested that Wasicu Wakan come and explain the reason for the coming of troops. McGillycuddy received permission from Brooke to attend the council.

Red Cloud spoke: "These soldiers have stolen here in the night; it looks as though they were here to fight; we do not want to fight. We ask you to take these soldiers away and we promise that in one sleep after they are gone everything will be quiet. We will give you twenty-five of our young men as hostages until all is settled."

McGillycuddy said that he could not make promises as he had done when he was the agent; he had no power now at Pine Ridge; but he would take the message to the soldier-chief. He would ask him also to meet the chiefs in council the following day.

Brooke consented to attend a council. In the assembly Red Cloud rose and, pointing to McGillycuddy, said: "That is Wasicu Wakan. Seven winters he was our agent; I did not want him then; he came from the army; he was only a boy. There was bad feeling between us; but when he went away four winters ago, he said: 'Some day you will say that my way was best for the Indian.' I will tell him now that he spoke the truth. If we had listened to him, we would not now be having this trouble. We did much worse things when he was our Father, but he never sent for soldiers. We settled our troubles among ourselves. We want you to take the soldiers away. We will give no trouble to anyone."

"Are you a Ghost Dancer?" Brooke asked Little Wound, who had risen to speak.

The old chief, who had saved McGillycuddy's life in a former council, answered: "My friend, over sixty winters have passed over my head. I am too old for dancing. But now that you have asked me that question I will tell you what I have heard of the Messiah and the Ghost Dance.

"There came to my people a few sleeps ago, a young Indian from the North; his name is Porcupine. He told us this story. 'I was commanded in a dream to go a great many days' journey to the west where I should come to the great fresh water [Walker's Lake, Nevada]. I went as I was told, and in the lodge of Wavoka, the Paiute dreamer, I met a tall white man with golden hair and whiskers and blue eyes. He was a well-spoken man. He spoke to me in these words: "Porcupine, I am the Messiah. Many winters ago I visited this place to try to save the people who had become wicked, whose brains whirled. They had lost their ears; they could not hear, and they could no longer see straight. They had lost the road to the happy hunting ground.

" ' "I lived among those people more than thirty winters and tried to put them on the right road, but they would not listen. They tortured me and hung me on a great wooden cross. The Great Spirit was sorry for me and took me back to my home. But it was spoken that some day I should come again. I am the Messiah. I have come again to try to put the people on the right road.

" ' "The winter is coming and snow will soon cover the ground. When the spring comes I will go to visit the tribes, but because of the way I was treated when I was here before, I have arranged signs and dances by which, if I am so received, I shall know that I am among friends. I will then remain with them for a while. If I am not so treated, I shall pass them by. So I would ask you to go ahead of me with these signs and dances and tell the tribes that I will visit my friends when the grass is green in the spring." '

"Porcupine has come to us with this story," Little Wound continued. "Whether it is true or not I do not know, but it is the same story the white missionaries have told us—that the Messiah will come again. I gathered my people together and told them, 'If it is a good thing we should have it. If it is not a good thing it will fall to the earth of itself. Therefore learn the signs and the dances, that if the Messiah comes in the spring he will not pass us by'."

Little Wound turned to McGillycuddy: "If the Messiah is not coming, and by his coming will not make us a great people again, to give us back the land which the Great Spirit gave us for our home, why have the white soldiers come here to stop our dancing?"

McGillycuddy did not reply. At the close of the council he told the general that Little Wound's remarks gave the key to the whole situation. The Indians would dance through the winter; and when the spring came and the Messiah did not appear, matters would adjust themselves. "Were I still agent here," he added, "I should let the dance continue. The coming of the troops has frightened the Indians. Winter is here—a time when they do not go on the warpath if it is possible to avoid it. If the Seventh-Day

Adventists prepare their ascension robes for the second coming of the Saviour, the United States Army is not put in motion to prevent them. Why should not the Indians have the same privilege? If the troops remain, trouble is sure to come—not through the old warriors, but through the men too young to have felt the power of the white man in the Sitting Bull campaign."

"Do you think you could settle this matter?" Brooke asked, with a touch of sarcasm.

"I might be warranted in the belief," McGillycuddy answered, "since more serious troubles were settled here when I was agent, without the aid of troops."

Pine Ridge as a focusing point was increasing in importance. The agitated bands of Sioux in camp outside the Agency were augmented daily by bands of Brûlé Sioux from the Spotted Tail Agency. On Saturday evening Red Cloud called on General Brooke to request that McGillycuddy be sent to the hostile camp to advise with the leaders. Brooke refused, saying he would send an emissary of his own.

Two twelve-pound howitzers were located at the Agency—one on a knoll before the enclosure, pointing north up White Clay Valley; the other at the back of the Agency buildings, pointing toward Blue Horse's camp. Blue Horse went to see McGillycuddy to ask him to use his influence to have the gun pointed some other way. "There is no trouble in my camp," he said, "and it might go off and hurt someone." McGillycuddy made the request, but the howitzer remained where it was.

Herbert Welch, head of the Indian Rights Association, wired the President from Philadelphia, urging that the experiment of McGillycuddy's mediation be tried; but to no avail. On Sunday the Doctor was in Ed Asay's store when Frank Merrivale, an interpreter, came in and told him that the hostiles were continually asking that he come out to them. McGillycuddy said he had asked the general's permission to go to the hostile camp but that Brooke refused to allow him to do so.

That evening, Ed Asay entertained the officers, McGillycuddy, and Agent Royer at dinner. Wine flowed freely. The bottles, sent from Fort Robinson, were marked, "Compliments of the Messiah." There was much gaiety among the guests. Toward the end of the evening there was a knock at the door—someone to speak to the agent. Scraps of excited remarks were caught by the guests in the dining room after Royer answered the summons: "Wouldn't listen!" "Gone away!" "Bad Lands!" "Mc——!"

"It's come!" Royer shouted, returning to the dining room. "War's come! The hostiles would not listen to Merrivale . . . . they shot bullets over his head . . . . they've killed a lot of cattle and struck out for the Bad Lands!"

The following morning McGillycuddy met Merrivale again. Merrivale told him—what Royer had not repeated—that while shots had been fired over his head, the Indians in the hostile camp had cried: "Send McGillycuddy to us! We will counsel with Wasicu Wakan!"

While these things were happening at Pine Ridge, the old Hunkpapa chief, Sitting Bull, in his retreat forty miles south of the Standing Rock Agency, also awaited the second coming of the Messiah. Still hostile in spirit, he repeated, "I was not born to eat out of the white man's hand." Though his pride had stooped to accept food from the government, he refused to kiss the hand that bestowed it. The nine years which had passed since his surrender had not modified his resentment and, at the proclamation of the return of the Messiah, an almost extinguished hope awakened in the old chief's heart. Once more he lighted the prophet-fires and, reading in the spiral smoke-columns the promise of a restored freedom for the red man, he joined, or at any rate sponsored, the Ghost Dance, led by Kicking Bear, a medicine man.

Shortly before the issue of the government order to stop the dancing, Short Bull had visited Sitting Bull's camp bearing the message that the dance must continue even though troops surrounded the villages. Clothed in the ghost-shirt they would be invulnerable to the white man's bullets, he said. And grasping at hope, the old warrior had united with the hundreds who trusted in the promise. For some time the question of Sitting Bull's arrest had been under advisement by the government, the troops, and Agent McLaughlin at the Standing Rock Agency. McLaughlin advised against the arrest while the weather remained pleasant; but all felt that the chief was planning mischief.

At last the days shortened, ice covered the streams, and the roads were snow-covered. The dance continued fitfully. Winter would now be sapping the enthusiasm of Sitting Bull and his followers for resistance.

On December 12 the military order for the arrest of the old prophet was received at the Standing Rock Agency. Combined plans were laid to accomplish the project on the twentieth of the month. A week before the date set for the arrest, Sitting Bull, having received an invitation to come at once to Pine Ridge to meet the Messiah who was about to appear at that agency, asked permission to make the journey. Though he had asked the privilege of going, the police—Indian police—who kept vigil over his camp felt sure that if the request was not granted the chief would go without permission. They urged his immediate arrest.

The order of arrest was given, and at dawn on December 15 a cordon of police under Lieutenant Bullhead surrounded Sitting Bull's home. Ten police entered, while the remainder, standing guard outside, were immediately surrounded by one hundred and fifty excited members of the band, who pressed them against the wall. The old prophet was asleep when the police went in. Awakened, and given an explanation of their mission, he said, "I will go with you." It was not until he reached the door and saw the guard pressed against the wall by his band that he became excited and called on his followers to rescue him.

Lieutenant Bullhead was on one side of the chief, Sergeant Shavehead on the other, and Sergeant Tomahawk behind him. The guard was endeavoring to make a passageway through Sitting Bull's band which confronted them. As the old chief struggled in the doorway to free himself from his captors, pandemonium was let loose. Firing began on both sides. Catch the Bear fired first, wounding Bullhead, whose gun sent a shot into Sitting Bull's back. Simultaneously Bullhead received a shot from Red Tomahawk's gun. A desperate hand-to-hand battle followed—forty-three against one hundred and fifty—divided, as at Pine Ridge, by a chasm of opinion, progressives against reactionaries, each equally staunch in conviction and courageous in action. But the trained forty-three soon got the upper hand of the untrained mob and drove them into the timber near by.

The police now mounted guard over Sitting Bull's cabin, into which they carried the dead and wounded, as well as over the corral, which was filled with ponies in preparation for Sitting Bull's anticipated journey to Pine Ridge to meet the Messiah. The Messiah had met the old prophet in his own camp.

By a rapid night march two troops of the Eighth Cavalry under Captain Fechet arrived, two hours after the killing of Sitting Bull, to see a white flag hoisted in the camp. Notwithstanding, two shells were fired into the village. Tomahawk now rode out alone, carrying the flag, to meet the troops.

Those of Sitting Bull's people who had fled into the timber followed up the Grand River. In the valley were deep drifts of snow. There had been no time for the fleeing crowd to add garments to those in which they had been sleeping: Their feet were bare. The squaws carried wailing babies whose frost-bitten hands, noses, and ears were rubbed with snow as they sped along. They carried no food.

Captain Fechet wisely sent a courier after the fleeing band, instead of pursuing them with troops, to tell them that no punishment would be inflicted on them if they returned to their homes. They would be held in no way responsible for the trouble which had occurred in the camp. Most of the poor, frightened creatures were only too thankful to regain the shelter of their tepees.

The body of Sitting Bull was taken, with those of the other dead and wounded, from the camp. With the exception of the old chief's, the bodies were taken to the Standing Rock Agency.

Sitting Bull's body was taken to Fort Yates, where it was put into a drygoods box and given unhallowed burial secretly in quicklime. The great medicine man, Ta-ton-ka-i-yo-ton-ka—who had remarked once in a passionate outburst, "Indians! There are no Indians left but me!"—had attained the wish expressed three months previous to his arrest when, breaking the peace pipe, he had exclaimed, "Now I wish to die." And with his downfall the great Sioux confederation was overthrown.

The Bad Lands was the obvious objective for the remnant of Sitting Bull's band which fled after the murder of the chief. This country, which God forgot after it had served its purpose as the habitat of prehistoric creatures, was furnishing sanctuary already for the Pine Ridge Indians who had been driven from their agency by fear of the troops.

A world of legend lay beneath this parched area. Bones of the creatures of bygone centuries, since unearthed from the bowels of this forsaken land, had revealed mysteries unshared by the *genus homo*. No fossils wrenched from its stolid depths indicated the presence of man throughout the procession of time. "This hell with the fires extinguished" was a fiery furnace in which the devils had had no human kind on whom to practice their tortures. Its caverns yawned farewells to ammonites, bacculites, oreodons, dinosaurs, mastodons, and hippocampi which had inhabited these regions in centuries past and had lain in silent tombs for generations until prying man subsequently ripped them from their graves and placed them in museums to be gaped at by idle passersby. Recollections of giant snails, cane-fish, wolves, reptiles stretching twenty-foot necks, reptiles with leathery wings spreading twenty feet, gigantic toothed birds, elephants, and three-toed horses were graven in the unconsolidated rocks. "La Terre Mauvaise" the French trappers had called this ravaged land; "Macoce Sica" was the name by which the Indians expressed its desolation.

The White River on one side and the Cheyenne on the other to all appearances had contrived to forget the Bad Lands lying crumpled between. In the chaos of blackened valleys, cliffs, and gorges, here and there, as though a note of pity had touched the heart of the designer, a tiny spring bubbled from a crevice and formed a pool in the tragic graveyard.

It was this desolation itself that qualified the Bad Lands as the asylum for the redskins, terrified at the interruption to their preparations for the coming of the Messiah by the arrival of the troops. With the certainty that the Sitting Bull refugees would endeavor to reach this cloister, requiring a passage through the open country east of the Black Hills, General Miles, who had gone to Rapid City and established headquarters there, ordered troops from Fort Meade and Fort Robinson to patrol that part of the country.

A few days after the start of the patrol Colonel E. V. Sumner encountered a large body of Indians with their families pushing south. It was the remnant of Sitting Bull's band under Big Foot on their way to the Bad Lands. Sumner placed them under arrest, the Indians making no protest and agreeing to come into camp at a designated spot in the evening. Thereupon Sumner withdrew his troops, happy to avoid an encounter. When evening came, however, Big Foot did not appear. By rapid movement he had pushed on toward the Bad Lands. A battalion of the Seventh Cavalry under Major Whiteside set out in pursuit of the wily fugitives, who were overtaken and who then unresistingly proceeded with the troops to a point in Wounded Knee Valley. Whiteside, fearing his force was insufficient to control the band, though they showed no sign of hostility, sent a courier to Pine Ridge for more troops.

Colonel J. W. Forsythe, with the remainder of the Seventh Cavalry, advanced at daybreak the following morning to the Wounded Knee camp and assumed command. During the night, a messenger had arrived with advice from Red Cloud that Big Foot's band should not surrender their arms. "If you give them up," he sent word, "they will kill you as they did Sitting Bull." However, they had already relinquished a large portion of their guns to Whiteside the previous day. Red Cloud's advice had come too late.

Forsythe, now suspecting that not all the arms had been surrendered, ordered a rigid inspection. All of Big Foot's band were drawn up in line. In front of the line, on a slight rise, four Hotchkiss machine guns were trained directly on the Indian camp, where hung a white flag, a sign of peace and a supposed guarantee of safety. Troops of cavalry were stationed paralleling front and rear of the line as well as on the flanks. Captain G. D. Wallace, with a sergeant, was ordered to search the bucks for concealed weapons.

Halfway down the line of one hundred and forty redskins stood the priest of the Ghost Dance, Yellow Bird, making signs and haranguing his people. "My children," he cried, "don't be frightened—the Great Spirit is with you—your ghost shirts will protect you from the white man's bullets!"

The blankets of three bucks were thrown open by the sergeant and no weapon discovered. As the blanket of the fourth Indian was thrust open, the sergeant exclaimed, "This damn cuss has a rifle under his armpit!" At once Yellow Bird stooped to the ground and, gathering a handful of earth, threw it into the air.

A shot echoed in Wounded Knee Valley. A volley followed, a veteran of the Seventh Cavalry crying, "Remember Custer and the Little Big Horn!" Guns, revolvers, knives, and war clubs for a few minutes battled against the volley-firing. Wallace fell, riddled with bullets. Soldiers stationed front and rear of the Indians were of course in line with bullets intended for the red men. As soon as a soldier fell, his gun was seized by an Indian.

A half-breed interpreter, Phillip Wells, standing beside General Forsythe, tripped the General in order to save him from the knife thrust of a warrior, and to save himself leveled his rifle before him. At this the maddened warrior slashed across the weapon at the interpreter's face, and Wells' nose was left hanging by two small wings.

McGillycuddy, who had just returned from Rapid City, where

he had gone to consult with General Miles, hearing that troops had gone out to meet Big Foot's band at Wounded Knee, rode out to the camp. The sound of firing penetrated the frozen air as he approached the camp. The battle was over when he reached the place, where hundreds of dead and wounded strewed the ground. Three hundred redskins, men, women, and children, had paid the price for their preparations to welcome the Messiah.

McGillycuddy rode back to the Agency. At an intersecting road he encountered a wagon load of blanketed Indians, who stopped him: "Don't you know me, Wasicu Wakan?" one of the bucks greeted him. McGillycuddy hesitated. "When you were our agent you made an agreement with us that if we would give you fifty of our young men to act as police the soldiers would not come to our agency." He threw open his blanket and showed a fresh wound from which the blood poured. "Look at that, Father!" he said. "I was one of your police. How about the promise?"

"A promise, Thunder Cloud, is of no value," the Doctor said, "when one ceases to have the power to fulfill it." He rode beside the wagon to the Agency, took Thunder Cloud to his room, and dressed his wound.

Snow fell the night after the battle, blanketing the hacked, bullet-ridden, frozen bodies which covered the field. At length the dead Indians were laid in trenches, like sardines in tins, and the unthawed earth was shoveled over them. Those of the wounded redskins, thirty-three in number, who were willing to accept the services of the doctors were installed in the small Episcopal Church, which had been equipped with cots.

McGillycuddy went there in search of disabled friends. At the door of the church he met American Horse, who asked him to go in and see Hunts the Enemy by Night. They went to the wounded Indian's cot, and American Horse explained that his friend was Wasicu Wakan, once their medicine man, for seven years their Father. He was wise, American Horse said, and Hunts the Enemy must listen to him. The Indian was badly wounded.

A rifle ball had passed through his cheeks, breaking out the teeth on both sides and shattering the roof of his mouth. His left knee too was wounded, but the incessant worrying of splintered bone on his lacerated tongue troubled him more than the knee wound, which the Doctor explained was the more serious. Amputation of the leg was imperative, McGillycuddy told him.

"But if I lose a leg," the warrior said, "I shall not be able to ride a horse."

"If it is not amputated you will not need a horse," the Doctor replied. "In three sleeps you will die."

"In three sleeps, then," the Indian responded, "I'll be in the happy hunting grounds and I'll have both legs and can ride after the buffalo and the deer."

The Indian, a member of Big Foot's band, was buried two days later.

A young girl, part white, who also refused surgery smiled at the Doctor as daily he stopped beside her cot. She too passed to the other side, her body mangled by a shell.

As the Doctor left the improvised hospital one evening at twilight, he met in the churchyard an Indian woman whose blanket held a papoose against her back. She was unkempt; utter hopelessness was in her eyes. She spoke perfect English, saying, "Don't you know me, Doctor?" McGillycuddy's eyes questioned. "I'm Maggie Stands Looking."

"Maggie!" the Doctor exclaimed. "You, a blanket Indian after your training at Carlisle and your service at the boarding school!"

"Oh, don't remind me, Doctor," Maggie pleaded. "I lost my place at the school after you left. I couldn't get another job. I was no longer one of my own people. I married an Indian, so I might have a place among them. This is my baby," she said, nodding backward to the smutty-nosed papoose. "I'm tired of this life, Doctor. Could you find me a job in the Hills?"

The Doctor promised to try.

A wagon surrounded by a crowd stood near the sawmill, and

the Doctor, led by curiosity, joined the group. In the wagon lay the body of a cavalryman, an Italian named Francischette, who had been missing since an engagement subsequent to the Wounded Knee battle. A reward for his recovery—alive or dead —had been offered.

The body had been stripped; scalp, goatee, mustaches, and eyebrows had been cut off; arms and legs had been severed, except for tendons which held them to the body. In the slashed belly coiled the frozen entrails, while arrows stood fixed in the naked breast.

McGillycuddy expressed consternation at the sight. "I thought you had given up this barbaric practice!" he exclaimed.

"Six days ago, Wasicu Wakan," a bystander explained, "one of our Indians was scalped on the battlefield at Wounded Knee. For a scalped Indian there shall be a scalped white man."

McGillycuddy learned later that a young lady in the East had requested an officer to bring her an Indian scalp as a memento. The mutilation of the white man's corpse was the price she had paid for the souvenir.

After the engagement of the hostiles with some troops of the Seventh Cavalry under Colonel Forsythe, McGillycuddy met Young Man Afraid at three o'clock in the afternoon. The chief inquired: "Who was the officer killed a half hour ago near General Brooke's camp, twenty-five miles down the valley?"

He had heard of no such incident, McGillycuddy said, and asked how Young Man Afraid could have got word from such a distance in so short a time.

"It's true," Young Man Afraid insisted.

McGillycuddy went to Miles' quarters and told him what the chief had said. Miles attached no importance to the matter, which McGillycuddy half believed, knowing the subtle methods of communication of the Indians.

Three hours later a courier reported that Lieutenant Casey's body had been taken to Brooke's camp by Johnny Richard, a half-breed interpreter, and three Indians. The courier explained that the lieutenant had been scouting alone across the country when the Indians had met him in White Clay Valley a few miles from the hostile village. Johnny had asked him where he was going and he had said he was on his way to confer with the hostiles. Johnny had told him he would be killed if he went there alone, but Lieutenant Casey had refused to turn back. While they had sat on their horses, talking, Plenty Horses, a Carlisle boy, had ridden up but had taken no part in the conversation—had just listened to what the others were saying. It had been several minutes before the lieutenant had consented to abandon his plan to go to the hostile village. As he had set off toward General Brooke's camp accompanied by Johnny and the three Indians, who had wished to see him safely out of that district, Plenty Horses had turned in the opposite direction. The others had gone but a short distance when Plenty Horses had turned and fired. Casey's horse had lunged and the officer had fallen to the ground, dead. Johnny had yelled at Plenty Horses, but he had gone off down the road. Plenty Horses was arrested subsequently at the Spotted Tail Agency and taken to Sioux Falls for trial.

McGillycuddy later was foreman of the Grand Jury on the trial of Plenty Horses for the killing of Lieutenant Casey.

Plenty Horses frankly admitted the killing of the officer and said: "I am an Indian. Five years I attended Carlisle and was educated in the ways of the white man. When I returned to my people I was an outcast among them. I was no longer an Indian. I was not a white man. I was lonely. I shot the lieutenant so I might make a place for myself among my people. Now I am one of them. I shall be hung and the Indians will bury me as a warrior. They will be proud of me. I am satisfied."

But the judge charged the jury that they could not find the prisoner guilty of murder. A condition of war existed; the officer who was killed occupied the position of a spy and suffered death in consequence.

Plenty Horses was acquitted and returned to his people—a hero.

The councils between the officers and the leaders of the hostiles continued. It was bitter weather in the middle of January when the Indians surrendered their antiquated weapons—as usual, withholding some of their modern Winchesters. Snow covered the hillsides and lay thick in the valleys as the war-weary Indians trekked into camp in White Clay Valley. Over the ridges came long lines of mounted Indians; on trails halfway down the slope walked Indians afoot, while farther down in the valley wagons and travois crawled dispiritedly along the road bearing women and children, the sick, and the wounded.

As red men gathered about McGillycuddy to bid him good bye before his return to the Hills, Young Man Afraid, shaking his hand, asked: "Is there nothing that can be done, Wasicu Wakan, to prevent the whites from having another outbreak and bringing so much trouble to the Indians?" McGillycuddy felt sore at heart as he parted with his old friends.

On his return to Rapid City he was asked repeatedly whom he considered responsible for the Wounded Knee Battle. His answer was: "Whoever fired the first shot. After that, nothing short of the Almighty could have stopped the killing."

Life resumed its normal course in the gateway city. Business prospered in the Hills country. The banks loaned more and more generously. The Doctor remarked occasionally that certainly he had wasted many years of his life on small government pay. But when, in 1893, the crash came and banks went under, he reversed his judgment and declared that a salary paid by the government, though small, was an excellent thing.

A year later McGillycuddy accepted the position of President of the School of Mines in Rapid City. Besides conducting classes he engaged in the examination of mines, frequently sleeping on samples of ore to forestall the possibility of their being salted. Fanny enjoyed life until she had a second stroke, and it was only by the Doctor's ceaseless care that she lived until 1897.

Her death left the Doctor stricken. His home offered no further attraction without the companion who had shared it as well as the many hardships of the frontier with him. And when he received an offer of a position as medical inspector for the Mutual Life Insurance Company of New York covering the western half of the United States, with headquarters in San Francisco, he accepted without hesitation.

The pet buffalos were now presented to the Smithsonian Institution in Washington, D.C., and the Doctor locked his doors and left the country he had helped to establish.

Chapter 26

A NEW LIFE, AND OLD FRIENDS

McGILLYCUDDY's new life was so unlike the one in which for a quarter of a century he had served in the Middle West that, to himself, he seemed another person. It was as if an amputation had severed him from the man who marched with columns of troops in blistering heat and bitter cold, who had feasted on venison and fish from sparkling streams, and who knew the pangs of hunger inducing men to eat the flesh of the horses they loved. Some other man, not himself, it must have been who had stood in constant danger of death from Indians rebelling against the methods of civilization he had imposed upon them which they did not believe offered the only hope of their survival. More than ever he understood their distaste for the dull life of sowing and reaping as a substitute for hunting buffalo and deer on the Great Plains and fishing in mountain lakes. He dwelt on regrets that it had been necessary to break the spirit of the old Sioux warrior or abandon the effort to save his people from the cruel injustices practiced upon them.

The Doctor was then but forty-eight years of age—too young to forsake a life of expansion, too old to enjoy a severance from the past. As he traveled in Pullman cars or in steamers along the West Coast from strange city to strange city, he wondered if he had made a mistake in leaving the country where he had spent the happiest years of his life, where lived friends with mutual interests, where prevailed a warmth of feeling unknown in metropolitan life—friends who had known his wife, his work. With fanatic ardor he had wooed his former life; scarcely with resignation he accepted the new one.

However, his territory included the Great Plains, and after

thousands of miles of West Coast inspections he welcomed the hush of the prairies, vibrant with memories. Once again in the Black Hills the Doctor felt at home. Friends greeted him on every side. As he passed a saloon in Deadwood a heavy-set woman came through the slatted door. She was drunk. She stumbled toward the Doctor and threw her arms around his neck. McGillycuddy drew back a trifle, not recognizing the fat woman. In half-sobbing tones she said: "Don' ye know me, Doc? Don' y' know y'r ol' fren' Calamity?" The Doctor patted her shoulder and even submitted to a slimy kiss from the liquor-stenched mouth, as he said, "Well, well, Calamity. You needn't be surprised I didn't know you. I haven't seen you since—let me see, I don't remember the year—you'd make two of the girl I knew then."

"It seems jes a li'l while back that we wus cumin' up here frum Laramie a-lookin' fer gold," Calamity remarked, scarcely coherent.

The two walked up the street together arm in arm while they recalled events of bygone years. Calamity sobered enough to tell him of her child, a little girl; she was going to put her in a convent; she didn't want her to have the rough life she herself had had; but she didn't know where her money went; people gave her money but it disappeared; she wondered where it went. McGillycuddy supposed the goldpiece he gave her would go as the rest had gone—for liquor—but he hoped it would make her happy for a time. She was dead before he visited the Hills again.

But the years touched McGillycuddy lightly. He was lean as a rail; though quick, he never seemed hurried. Apparently he was adjusted to his changed life, although if led to talk of his experiences on the frontier a wistful look filled his eyes as he remarked, "Those days can never return; there are no more frontiers to invade."

Recollections of the past were renewed when Buffalo Bill paid his visits to the Coast with his Wild West Show. On the first of these visits, when the Doctor went to the Indian camp he was greeted with something other than the traditional Indian stoicism.

"*Hoo-hoo-hay!*" the red men exclaimed. "*Atte.*"

After the first greetings a squaw asked, "*Ena tukten?*"

McGillycuddy laid his head on his hand as he answered, "*Ena istima.*" On hearing that their Mother was dead the mourning cry passed through the camp. A squaw pointed to a young woman and child standing beside him and asked who they were. The Doctor explained they were his wife and daughter. His wife, he told them, was the little blonde daughter of the trader Blanchard.

"*Hoo-hoo-hay!*" the Indians exclaimed, repeating the familiar ejaculation uttered often when they had seen the small child with the long fair hair.

Great excitement was caused at the Fairmont Hotel where the Doctor lived, when the warriors, dressed in their native costumes, with eagle feathers trailing from head to foot, paid him a visit. They urged him to come back to Pine Ridge. All was changed since he had left—they had not so much to eat—they were not so happy as in the days when he was their Father. McGillycuddy told them that he too wished for the old days; but they would never come back, any more than the buffalo would return to the plains.

A gleam of hope for renewed excitement was raised in the Doctor's heart when the United States entered the World War. He wrote the War Office asking to be sent overseas as a surgeon or a reconnaissance officer. He asked an appointment as surgeon with the Red Cross. The answer to each request was the same: "Too old."

He didn't feel old. He was certain he could stand any hardship, and he longed to be in the thick of the fight.

But when in 1918 the influenza epidemic which was taking heavy toll in foreign lands trailed its venomous path across the Atlantic and struck American shores, the Doctor prepared for service. Fear gripped the nation as the disease spread rapidly in every direction and, withstanding all efforts to stem its tide, the death-dealing enemy stalked toward the Pacific Coast leaving wrecked homes and graveyards filled with dead. Sporadic cases sprang up around San Francisco Bay. Schools, churches, theaters, and cinema houses were closed; but the number of cases increased daily, and soon the epidemic had gripped the West Coast.

McGillycuddy visited the Chief Surgeon of the Public Health Service of the Pacific Coast in San Francisco to offer his services. Dr. W. C. Billings said he had heard of the Doctor's field work and that he would call on him when the situation required more than medical skill. It probably would be in some remote district. Would McGillycuddy be able to leave at a moment's notice? The Doctor answered that he could leave at any time and go anywhere.

Three days later he was summoned to the Public Health Office. Influenza was raging at the New Idria Mines in San Benito County, a strategic point, Billings said. The mines furnished about one-half of the quicksilver supplied to the United States government as fulminate for caps of cartridges. There was an aggravated condition at the mines. The I.W.W.'s and other Socialists who were working there were trying to force the mines to close down in order to cut off the supply of quicksilver. Some troops from the Presidio had been sent there to head off interference—the situation was peculiar. McGillycuddy was to have a free hand in managing the situation; the government was back of him; many lives were involved; and he should do whatever he thought best. Four Red Cross nurses would accompany him to the mines.

McGillycuddy fingered his small goatee. He was not troubled about I.W.W.'s or Communists, he said; but one thing did bother him—he didn't know a damn thing about influenza. Would Dr. Billings give him some advice as to how to treat it?

"I can't advise you," the chief surgeon said. "Not one of us knows a damn thing about it, either. Just use your own judgment."

McGillycuddy said he would just treat symptoms, then.

It was all anyone could do, Dr. Billings answered.

McGillycuddy went to the hotel, packed his bags, and, with his black medicine case, marked with a large red cross, in his hand, took the first southbound train.

The condition at the mines was chaotic. The superintendent, Mocine, said that he had heard through Dr. Billings that McGillycuddy was an engineer as well as a doctor. He advised that McGillycuddy take over the entire management of things until the epidemic was under control. Mocine said he would take the Doctor to the military camp and introduce him to Lieutenant Murray. Murray was prepared to render any assistance in his power toward getting the situation organized. The disease had spread among the troops as well as the miners.

Four cars with soldiers as drivers were supplied for the Doctor's use. There was no hospital at the mines until at the end of two days an emergency tent hospital with floors had been constructed. Forty cots were set up, and all were immediately filled. A nurse was located in the valley to care for the sick who could not be accommodated in the hospital.

After organizing the medical situation, McGillycuddy attacked the three saloons, which were selling poor liquor. They must be closed. After some demur and a threat to bring a sergeant and men to close them if they had to tear them down to do so, the saloons closed. Also any interfering I.W.W. was ordered from the mines.

McGillycuddy noticed a strange condition at the mines—none of the furnace men had influenza. He studied the problem and decided that in separating the mercury from the ore in the furnaces the air became permeated with volatilized mercury, causing salivation in the furnace men and rendering them immune to the disease. Even dogs which hung about the furnaces were salivated.

The idea was worth using. If mercury acted as an antiseptic, he would ask the superintendent to switch the miners back and forth to the furnaces during the epidemic. Mocine readily agreed.

Two soldiers were carrying out a man named Quien, a Slavonian, from the hospital as the Doctor returned to the tent. He raised the sheet which covered the body. It was as black as any Negro's. One of the soldiers asked why the dead man grinned: "He looks as if he were tickled to death." *"Risus sardonicus,"* the

Doctor said, and paid no attention to the puzzled look on the soldier's face.

A nurse beckoned him to a cot toward the back of the tent as he went inside. She said that the patient's arms had been making a circular movement for the last two hours. He was worn out. The Doctor said no ordinary drug would control *paralysis agitans,* as he gave the miner three drops of *cannabis indica.* In half an hour the patient slept quietly.

McGillycuddy himself had a touch of the "flu." He did not sleep well. Night sweats bothered him. He took some of the medicine which he had compounded—aconite, belladonna, and tincture of gelsemium—and kept on with his work.

For two weeks every bed in the emergency hospital was full. As soon as a patient was discharged or carried out, dead, another took his place. The third week the cases were of a milder form, and soon the epidemic was under control.

McGillycuddy now received a wire to proceed to the oil fields farther south. The disease was of a less virulent character in the oil fields. The Doctor slept in a bare, cold schoolroom, coughing badly and with a temperature of one hundred and two. He made no mention of it, and was sent to other unorganized districts until, toward the end of November, he was called back to San Francisco.

On November 10 the Doctor reached San Francisco and reported at headquarters. Dr. Billings noticed his cough and said he must take a rest; it was hard service he had given him; and he anticipated no more such difficult jobs. McGillycuddy merely said he was glad to be still in the running.

The telephone rang before the Doctor was dressed the following morning. Dr. Billings said he was sorry to ask him to engage in another task so soon, but a wire had come from Washington requesting him to send one of his best physicians to Utah, where the epidemic was at its height. Would the Doctor go? When McGillycuddy consented, he asked him to come to his office that day and prepare to leave for Salt Lake on the first train.

McGillycuddy opened a cedar chest, sniffed the strong odor of moth balls, and took out his buffalo coat, his sealskin cap and gloves. The coat seemed very heavy; he felt less strong than in the days when he had worn it on the Great Plains. It seemed incredible that there should be such cold anywhere as in the country where he had worn it. In California he never wore a coat, not even when young men snuggled their necks into turned-up collars. He laid the clumsy garment back in the cedar chest. Someone would provide him with suitable wraps if the work called for drives into the country, he thought.

The streets of San Francisco rang with joy on November 11, 1918, as the Doctor went to headquarters before setting out for Utah. People hugged each other—strangers passing on the streets. They shouted and danced, while bells pealed forth the glorious news that the armistice was signed, the great World War over.

After receiving instructions from Billings the Doctor made his way through the crowds to the ferry building. The Bay was smooth; gulls, spotless white or touched with gray, perched on the ferry rails and dashed, squawking, into the water to grab the refuse poured out from the galley. The valleys and hills were green, the gardens filled with flowers. Up in the mountains the scene changed, and on the plains it was winter.

The surgeon-in-charge met the Doctor at the Salt Lake station. He looked disappointed. He had asked, he said, for a physician who could go into the mountains—one who could stand high altitudes and zero weather. No local physicians could be spared from the towns, and nurses were lacking even in the cities. McGillycuddy said he was accustomed to cold and high altitudes. He wished he had brought his buffalo coat, but he would borrow a heavy one from somebody. While lunching with the surgeon-in-charge the Doctor was told that it would be necessary for him to organize the work, engage what help he could get at the mines, and send out for needed supplies and medicines.

In the car waiting outside the hotel to take him to the mines, the Doctor found a heavy coat and some blankets which had been provided for him. A blizzard raged on the mountains some eight thousand feet high when the car pulled up at the office of the superintendent of the coal mines, who greeted the Doctor enthusiastically though he too looked apprehensive as he noted his age and his frail form.

A campaign to wipe out the epidemic from the camp was immediately begun. The superintendent was eager to assist, and the miners who were not already laid low by the disease rallied to the call for help. The volunteers were grouped in three details—the first to make a daily round of the camps and report new cases; the second to carry food to the patients and to keep fires burning in the cabins; the third to serve as nurses. There were no women among the volunteers. The rest of the population had taken to their cabins, and those not already stricken were prepared to barricade their doors against even the volunteers lest some specter of contagion lurked about them.

The Doctor visited wherever an appearance of the malady occurred. With the black medicine case in his hand he climbed the beaten, snowy paths up the mountainsides and poured drops from the small phials. When he returned to headquarters in the superintendent's office he sank easily into any unused chair and almost instantly fell asleep. Any chair—straight-backed and flagrantly uneasy—his swivel chair before his desk—always served his purpose as well as a rocking chair. His position varied according to the seat in which for the time he rested his slim body. In a comfortable chair his head reclined against its back while the foot which dangled from his crossed knees swayed gently to and fro. And invariably his long, slender fingers were interlaced on his lap, their leanness suggestive of fine instruments employed to alleviate pain. He wakened easily at the faintest footfall.

Connelly, the head nurse, was not aware that the Doctor had been asleep when he came to the office to report some trouble in a cabin where a woman lived alone. Each day he had tapped at her door to ask how she was, and each time she had called out, "Go away; I'm all right." But that afternoon there was no answer to his inquiry, though he could hear a low muttering inside. He wasn't usually scary, he said; but somehow he didn't like to go into that cabin alone—he wasn't used to women, and that one was sort of different from the others.

The Doctor buckled on the galoshes with which he had been equipped for the mountain trails. Light on the forested mountains was growing dim. The occasional wail of a wildcat from a tree-top mingled with the crunching sound of footsteps as the two men ascended the trails, the wind shifting a fine mist of snow into their faces. The cap lanterns worn by the men cast weird shadows on the trails.

The door of the cabin on the mountainside was locked. There was no sound inside, no light. The Doctor and Connelly crawled through a window in the lean-to. The room stank.

The light of the cap lanterns fell on the face of the woman tossing deliriously on the wretched bed. The Doctor felt her pulse, while Connelly lighted a half-filled kerosene lamp. The uneven wick slithered a coil of smoke up one side of its dirty chimney. The Doctor extracted a bottle from the black medicine case, rinsed a sticky glass, and dropped ten drops of medicine into it, adding some water. The woman's head lurched protestingly against his arm as he held the tumbler to her lips.

The bed was in a horrible condition. The Doctor said they must clean it up. Connelly repeated that he wasn't used to women; he didn't like messin' round them. But the Doctor urged him on. In a box under the bed he found some clean sheets and a calico wrapper which would serve as a nightgown. Water was soon heated on the rusty stove and operations were begun.

When the work was completed and the woman lay still in the clean bed, the Doctor and Connelly sat down beside the stove. The wind blew a gale on the mountain and a wildcat's distressed wail carried into the cabin where the Doctor watched his patient between fitful naps. The sick woman muttered at last—stirred. Her head rolled from side to side. She opened her eyes, looked bewilderedly at the clean sheets and the calico wrapper, then saw the men seated beside the stove. Her bewildered look changed to one of wild anger as she raised herself on her elbow and shrieked: "Get outta here you bald-headed old scoundrels! How dare you take advantage of a poor, sick woman? Get out; get out!"

Connelly hastily lunged through the door. But the Doctor spoke to her: She had been ill; no one had harmed her; she would be all right now, and he would see her in the morning. The woman looked at him suspiciously, showing no sign of being pleased with his promised call. The Doctor took up his lanterned cap and went out. It was desolate on the mountain.

With the epidemic under control in the mountains McGillycuddy was sent to different points in the state. Every facility was afforded him by local physicians, overburdened with work, as he organized the field. Frequently he was summoned back to a town on a recurrence of the mysterious disease.

Christmas and New Years passed before the Doctor returned to San Francisco. The epidemic then seemed to have been exterminated, and McGillycuddy severed his connection with the Public Health Service and resumed his usual work.

Chapter 27

FIGHTING NEW ENEMIES

The influenza epidemic, which previously had seemed to speed on wings, migrated only slowly to Alaska. And it was on an April afternoon that Dr. Billings called to ask McGillycuddy if he would take charge of the Public Health contingent being sent to the North where the disease was reported to be devastating the villages. The United States cruiser "Marblehead" would leave the dock at six o'clock. Could he be ready to go in four hours?

McGillycuddy, now seventy years of age, packed his bags and was at the dock at six o'clock. Dr. Billings met him and introduced him to the ship's surgeon, the four naval reserve surgeons, and the twelve nurses. The ship set sail and after stopping at Seattle to take on food, medical supplies, and fuel proceeded directly to Unalaska, the southernmost point of the Aleutian Islands.

The Aleuts were a friendly people, ready to tell McGillycuddy of the misfortunes they had suffered from the disease. It had killed hundreds of the inhabitants but was then under control, the local medical service reported, though it was still raging along the coast in the fishing and packing stations. They turned over to him a forty-foot gas launch, the "Attoo," and a coast guard steamer, the "Unalga," and McGillycuddy set out for Cape Constantine, taking with him four naval apprentices and some nurses.

As the ship reached port, the Doctor stood on the deck of the launch and scanned the coast. No habitation was in sight. A gentle breeze blew offshore bringing with it a cadaveric odor. There was something wrong, the Doctor said, not far inland. The apprentices hesitated a moment before going into the water to launch the yawl.

Near a small grove of low trees stood a rude dwelling which

seemed uninhabited. A stench oozed from the windowless cabin, and the foul air filled the Doctor's nostrils as he opened the door and looked in. A human form, scarcely visible in the dim light, lay stretched on a couch covered with skins. The body appeared inanimate except for facial contortions indicating life. The doctor advanced, almost stifled with the odor of decomposition—maggots writhing over the face of the dead man made it appear that his features moved. The body was dragged with ropes to a newly made grave.

Beside a corpse on a trail near by, down which a solitary man trod, lay a dog which growled viciously but did not stir as Mc-Gillycuddy passed on the opposite side of the body, on his way to meet the lone traveler. The Aleut had walked fifty miles, he said, from Igarochauk on Wood Lake, where word of the Doctor's arrival had raised hope that the epidemic which was killing off the inhabitants might be checked if he would visit them.

There was nothing to detain the Doctor at the port after he had searched the district and found no villages and only an occasional body lying in the brush, which was buried immediately. Accordingly he pushed on in the "Attoo," taking the lone messenger with him, and reached the mouth of the Wood River to find the coast guard steamer waiting in the fog-dimmed sea. After a meal on board the steamer McGillycuddy returned to his launch and went up the river to the little village of Igarochauk, arriving there in the arctic twilight. There was no sign of human life on shore, though the party was savagely greeted by a pack of Malamute dogs gone mad with hunger. The passengers beat off the dogs, having to shoot some of them before they could land. They fought their way among the starving creatures to reach the village, which lay in silence except for the baying of the animals. There the barabaras appeared deserted. But in cabin after cabin, reeking with the stench of rotten flesh, lay the dead, which were dragged out and buried.

A room which the Doctor entered alone was empty, but beyond a door at the back of the hut was the sound of nibbling, gnawing, and chewing. He opened the door and discovered, on the floor, the body of a man, his head in the paws of a huge Malamute dog. Disturbed in its feast, the animal sprang at the intruder and set his teeth in McGillycuddy's left hand. With his right the Doctor grabbed the infuriated beast by the throat and shouted for help. The coastguardsmen standing outside rushed in. A shot sprawled the snarling animal on the floor. His bloody jaws relaxed their hold on the Doctor's hand.

In many of the cabins were bones stripped clean of flesh by the teeth of starving dogs. Carcasses of animals were among those of human beings.

The remnant of that night at Igarochauk was spent on the launch; and after the short period of purple darkness the "Attoo" pushed up the Wood River.

At the next landing, where were only scattered cabins, the Doctor and his men were joyfully greeted by a large white collie dog which stood alone on the bank of the river. He leapt at the Doctor, who was the first to land and, with huge paws resting on his shoulders, licked his face lovingly. He did not leave McGillycuddy's side during his inspection of the village, which had not been so seriously affected by the epidemic as places visited previously. It was learned from one of the Aleuts that the dog had been found on a lonely trail, obviously lost. His welcome to the white men seemed to prove that his lost owner had been white. McGillycuddy's urgent request that he might purchase the dog was refused and, as the boat pulled away from the landing, the wails of the great white animal trailed after it, growing fainter in the distance.

The launch now proceeded down the Bay to Port Haiden, where a heavy outbreak of the epidemic had been reported. In the shallow water the men landed in the yawl. Around a group of a dozen cabins one hundred feet up a narrow trail, buzzed swarms of blue-bottle flies in air fetid with the smell of cod, halibut, and decayed flesh. From one hut only issued a sound. McGillycuddy opened the door. A boy of four or five years, munching a bit of dried flesh, rocked a woman's bloated head held tightly in his small hands as he sat beside her dead body on the earthen floor. From side to side the swollen head was jostled, while the child muttered words in a tongue strange to the Doctor, who presumed he pleaded with his mother to speak to him. Thirty-eight decomposed bodies were dragged out of these barabaras with ropes and burned in trenches. The small boy—the only person alive in the district—sat stolidly in the boat while it pushed on to the "Marblehead," still cruising along the coast. Other orphans were picked up en route and taken to Dillingham, a village near Cape Constantine.

When news spread that a group of orphans had been landed at the Cape, a request for the children was made by the Eskimos with the promise of caring for them. But on learning that children thus taken were used as slaves, the officials denied the request and the orphans were placed in an orphans' home near the fishing station.

The "Marblehead" now sailed up the coast, stopping at ports to inquire concerning conditions at inland villages. But the epidemic was dying out in Alaska, and, after two months in the North, the ship steamed out of the Bering Sea in the early morning for San Francisco, with a huge white albatross perched on its prow. All day the great bird remained on its perch except for occasional dippings into the sea for food. At long intervals a whale was sighted rolling in the waves of the Pacific.

Chapter 28

"THE ONLY ONE LEFT"

As the span of threescore years and ten allotted to human life was rounded out, the Doctor determined, after again severing his connection with the Public Health Service, to take the examinations for registration as a practicing physician in the state of California. He had never done so. Occasionally during his early years in the state he had been called by the President of the Medical Board and asked to take them, but he had answered that he had no intention of practicing in California. Possibly the Board president had heard he had served on occasions—it was true, emergencies only. He had not forgotten the Hippocratic oath he had taken—let me see, yes, more than half a century before, to help humanity when called upon, of course without fees.

But now when he decided to take the examination he discovered that the first requisite was his certificate from the state in which he had practiced last. He had none. The attorney for the State Medical Board wrote to Michigan as well as to Dakota, and received word that McGillycuddy had practiced in both states before the issuance of certificates had been required. Dakota was vexed—it was up in arms. Their doctor hindered from becoming a member of the California Medical Association for lack of a certificate! It would pass a bill before the legislature issuing a special certificate to their "old doctor." In the meantime the attorney discovered that, since McGillycuddy had been in practice before the California law requiring certificates had been passed, he would on that basis be eligible for examination.

The President of the Medical Board knew McGillycuddy. He said he had no intention of putting a list of questions before the Doctor. He knew of his work as a field surgeon and in the death-dealing influenza epidemic. Would the Doctor choose a subject and speak to them? McGillycuddy thanked him and asked if it would be agreeable for him to talk on influenza. It would please the Board, the President answered.

McGillycuddy then told of the effect of the absorption of volatilized mercury from the furnaces of the quicksilver mines on influenza germs; of the hopeless cases of black death, the corpses turning nigger black and the mouths set in a ghastly grin; of the fatal effect of cheap liquor on influenza patients; and of the benefit of good whisky when the heart was wearing out. He told of the successful treatment of *paralysis agitans* with *cannabis indica* and of his original compound of belladonna, aconite, and extract of gelsemium for the treatment of the disease—one drop for a year-old child, two drops for a two-year-old child, and the dose increased according to age.

The Doctor sat down.

The President of the Examining Board said: "When Dr. McGillycuddy investigated the policies for the Mutual Life Insurance Company of New York in Reno, Nevada, where I was examiner for the company, he turned down a case, favorably reported by me, for a heart weakness. Without a stethoscope he discovered a flaw which I had not noticed.

"Dr. McGillycuddy shall not be kept waiting the usual six weeks before receiving notification of the result of the examination. Whatever the state of California has to give in the privilege of practicing medicine and surgery is his from this time."

McGillycuddy continued his accustomed life. He had not intended to engage in the regular practice of medicine; but he felt a satisfaction in being a member of the California Medical Society.

With declining years the Doctor's stories were heard less often. He regretted that in his labor of practical idealism among the Sioux it had been necessary to deal so arbitrarily with the recalcitrant old chief Red Cloud, and maintained that they would have been friends in former days as in later years but for the influence of squawmen, the Indian Ring, and Eastern sentimentalists. Often

he looked at faded photographs of Fanny, of old army friends—
Sheridan, Sherman, Terry, Crook, and Custer and of Buffalo Bill,
Wild Bill Hickok, California Joe, and Calamity Jane. And as he
recalled the close associations of bygone days he invariably remarked: "I'm the only one of the old crowd left."

After the passage of fourscore years and ten, the Doctor's physical strength declined, but not his courage. Daily he walked outside, in winter as in summer without overcoat or hat. One summer
evening McGillycuddy drifted into unconsciousness, and a few
days later followed the trail across the Great Divide.

On the following day, June 7, 1939, the flag at Pine Ridge hung
at half-mast. It hung from the staff erected sixty years previously
by McGillycuddy, where had floated the first flag raised at an
Indian agency in the United States—an act for which he was
tried by the Commissioner of Indian Affairs. Indians congregated, and from mouth to mouth the word was passed, *"Tasunka
Witko kola estima."* A low murmur of sadness pervaded the air
when they learned that Crazy Horse's friend slept.

His ashes have now been carried to the top of Harney's Peak,
South Dakota, and placed in a crypt prepared for them by the
Department of Forestry of the United States Government.